The Isle of Man & the Jacobite Network

Frances Wilkins

Books by Frances Wilkins
all published by Wyre Forest Press

Scottish Books
Scottish Customs & Excise Records [1992]
Strathclyde's Smuggling Story [1992]
Dumfries & Galloway's Smuggling Story [1993]
Family Histories in Scottish Customs Records [1993]
The Smuggling Story of Two Firths [1993]
The Smuggling Story of the Northern Shores [1995]

Manx Books
In print
George Moore & Friends [1994]
Manx Slave Traders [1999]
2,000 Manx Mariners [2000]
In preparation
The Running Trade [November 2004]
Out of print
The Isle of Man in Smuggling History [1992]

Dalemain Series
In preparation
Hasell & Co. 1736-1794 [May 2003]
Future Titles
Hasell & Son 1794 -1865 [May 2006]

The Isle of Man
&
the Jacobite Network

Frances Wilkins BA

Wyre Forest Press

ISBN 1 897725 15 9

Printed by:
Bookcraft
First Avenue, Westfield Trading Estae, Midsomer Norton, Radstock BA3 4BS
Tel: 01761 419167

Published by:
Wyre Forest Press
8 Mill Close, Blakedown, Kidderminster, Worcs DY10 3NQ
Tel: 01562 700615 email: frances@franscript.freeserve.co

CONTENTS

TABLES

FIGURES

Acknowledgements and sources:

Reproduced by kind permission of
Manx National Heritage paintings etc.   (23), (28) and (32)
    Documents   MS 10071 Petition File 1716 f7 (19 & 34)
    MS 09707 AP44B-28 (29)
National Portrait Gallery, London paintings by   Michael Dahl (20) & Alexis Simon Belle (24)
National Archives for Scotland   NAS 508 2/1/12 (11)
The National Trust for Scotland painting by   Alan Herriot (6)
Nelson Thornes   Figure 23: The English Marches towards Scotland in the 15th and 16th Centuries from A E Smailes *North England* Thomas Nelson 1960 (7)

The Duke of Buccleuch painting by   Sir Godfrey Kneller (5)
Ian Craik photograph of   painting by unknown artist (27)
William Wallace old photograph of   Fingland (10)
The owner maps by   Mortier 1693 (2), République Francais de marine (8), Peter Fannin 1789 (18)

Private collection of engravings from originals by   Sir Godfrey Kneller (1), unknown artist (4), Kneller (14), Vandyke (15), Sir Peter Lely (16), Paul Vansomer (22), Walker (25)
Camden's Britannica (3), Hibbert Ware (17) *The History of Henry Esmond* by William Makepeace Thackeray 1852 (9)

Photographs by the writer   9, 12, 21, 26, 30, 31,33

ACKNOWLEDGEMENTS

Several people have contributed to the research for this book from staff in record offices and libraries to members of societies to private individuals. It would be invidious to select any for special mention. As a result, everyone is listed according to his, or her, location.

On the Isle of Man: the Manx National Heritage Library, Tynwald Library, Sandra Bolton, Frank Cowin, Priscilla Lewthwaite, John Martin, Maisie Martin, Martin Moore, Chris Pickard, Tricia Power, Angela Rogers and Celia Salisbury Jones.

In Scotland: Ayrshire Archives, Broughton House, Kirkcudbright, Carnegie Library, Ayr, Dumfries Archive Centre, Ewart Library, Dumfries, National Archives of Scotland, both General Register House and West Search Room, Stewartry Museum, Kirkcudbright, Stranraer Library, National Trust for Scotland, Royal Highland and Agricultural Society of Scotland, Scottish Genealogical Society, Scottish Portrait Gallery, Sheena Andrew, Josie Beattie, Beauchamp Blackett, the Duke of Buccleuch, Ian Craik, David Devereux, Brian and Graeme Geddes, Eric Graham, Barbara Hargreaves, Charles Hunter, Willie Johnston, Robin and Ann Kirkland, Michael Moss, Ben Notley, Robert Paton and family (Gate Slack), Marion Stewart and William Wallace and family (Fingland).

In England: Cheshire Record Office, Cumbria Record Office, Herefordshire Record Office, Lancashire Record Office, Public Record Office, Tyne & Wear Archives Service, Francis Aglionby, Susan Aglionby, Anne Baker, Edward Corp, Alan Grigg, Robert Hasell McCosh, Brett Langston, Roger Nixon, John Oliphant and Margaret Thornton.

The Manx Heritage Foundation funded part of the research at the Manx National Heritage library.

This book is dedicated to the staff of the Manx National Heritage library.

INTRODUCTION

It was inevitable, because of its location in the middle of the Irish Sea, that the Isle of Man would not remain immune to the dramatic events that were taking place in England, Scotland and Ireland during the Jacobite rebellions. This book does not give a detailed description of the Island and the Jacobite cause, however, as that story does not exist. In 1715 there was no proclamation on the Isle of Man of James III (the Old Pretender) as the rightful king of Great Britain. Although the majority of the House of Keys were described as Tories, there was no clearly defined Jacobite faction on the Island. Yet, despite the tireless efforts of Governor Horne, there was no wholehearted indication of allegiance to George I.

The more obvious impact came from those individuals who lurked on the Island 'out of harm's way'. They mixed socially with the local inhabitants, inspiring some of them to join in their 'disaffected healths' – toasts to the Jacobite cause – so introducing an alarming undercurrent of rebellion against the Lord of Man's authority, the Manx church and the crown of England. An equally significant impact came through the Island's lifeblood – trade. It was inappropriate to enquire into the political leanings of one's partners yet more than one partnership was brought to an abrupt end by the defeat of the rebels at the battle of Preston in November 1715, and the subsequent reprisals. Several of the 'principal merchants and traders' on the Island appealing to the Duke of Atholl in the early 1760s for protection against interference in their business by the English crown, were in fact 'banished' Scots. This did not mean that they were all Jacobites – divided family loyalties resulted in people leaving home for pastures new.

As a result, this book is a series of stories with a common theme: links between the Isle of Man and the Jacobite network. What makes these stories of particular interest is that, with one possible exception, they are not about the famous figures of the day – the kings, dukes, lords and earls – but about the ordinary people, whose lives were changed irrevocably by the Jacobite rebellions.

The research necessary to produce these stories has included studying the late seventeenth and early eighteenth century archives held at the Manx National Heritage library and several weeks spent following leads at archive centres, record offices and libraries in England, Scotland and Ireland.

The Manx archives contain intimate details of supposedly private seditious conversations talking place in houses all round the Isle of Man. There could be several reasons why these conversations were reported to the governor, including revenge, so that their significance in attempting to piece together what was happening on the Island at this time might be questionable. It is possible, however, to confirm a high proportion of the topics supposedly discussed in these seditious conversations. The best example of this is Mary Hendrick's exposure of the plans made by the Northumbrian Jacobites before the battle of Preston. It has been possible to confirm the information detailed in other accusations from both contemporary documents and modern secondary sources. Several of the 'strangers' who took part in these conversations have been found off the Island - and in some cases their political leanings identified.

A parallel line of enquiry involved all the merchants who were involved in trade with and on the Island from 1689 onwards. The 'hit rate' in terms of their other activities was higher than expected. According to the Manx archives Robert Douglas, the second son of the Laird of Flugland and the former collector of customs at Glasgow, was deeply involved in the running trade. Research at Stranraer library into the murder of another Douglas, the 4th Duke of Hamilton (see John Murray's visit to the Island in December 1713) identified Robert as the son of the Laird of Fingland, and the leader of a troop of horse at the battle of Preston.[i] Therefore, the links between the Isle of Man and the Jacobite network continued to expand.

There were some red herrings. According to a supposedly reliable description of Castletown, 'there was formerly a house in Malew Street called the 'Big Tree' house ... for one period occupied by Thomas Harley, brother of Robert Harley 1ˢᵗ Earl of Oxford, who is believed to have been sent over here because of his Jacobean tendencies. Harley spared no money on the building and it possessed much elaborate panelling. Harley was buried at Kirk Malew ... Among his interests was the "South Sea Bubble" in which he lost money'.[ii]

The Earl of Oxford did not have a brother called Thomas but a cousin, who was one of the directors of the South Sea Company and who played a significant role in the Jacobite cause. He was excluded from the Act of Grace in 1717, so making him, in theory, a fugitive. There is a memorial to this Thomas Harley in Kinsham church, Herefordshire. The memorial states:

> *To the Memory of Thomas Harley of Kinsham Esq. The second son of Thomas Harley Esq., who was the third son of Sir Robert Harley of Brampton Castle. During the reigns of King William and Queen Anne, he served in Parliament for the County of Radnor. In this and every other station he made the true interest of his country his chief study and his constant aim. Disinterested loyalty, unprejudiced judgement and steady resolution distinguished all his public actions. In his private life a sincere and friendly heart, a liberal and charitable hand, vivacity of wit, variety of knowledge, and polightness [sic] of conversation made him highly valued and lamented by the best and greatest men of his time.*

He died January 8 1738, aged 71. Thomas Harley of Big Tree house was in fact the third son of William Harley and grandson of another William Harley, who was born at Malew in 1634. He clearly spent some time off the Island, amassing a fortune, before returning to act as collector for Poole & McGwire, the farmers of the customs on the Island in the 1720s. He died in 1741, aged 65, and was buried in Malew church.

Some of the Herefordshire Harley manuscripts are held at the University of Nottingham, where there is correspondence from Nicholas Harley of Castletown, who was not directly related to either of the Thomas Harleys, and from John Rowe and William Seddon, the deputy governors, with the Earl of Oxford. This correspondence might not have been located without the misinformation about Thomas Harley of Big Tree house.

Several people have helped along the route of the Isle of Man – Jacobite network, from the staff of the Manx National Heritage library to farmers in the remoter parts of Dumfries and Galloway, and Northumbria. I hope no one is omitted from the list of acknowledgements.

There is no attempt to describe either the Manx or British history and politics of this period in detail. This information can be found in a wide range of other publications, several of which are listed in the Recommended Reading section. When necessary, background information has been provided in several of the other sections, to help in understanding the significance of some of the stories. The history of the Manx legal system, which was so crucial to those accused of drinking 'disaffected healths' on the Island, has been considered only in the context of the relevant the cases. Once more information is available elsewhere.

The approach has been chronological, as far as possible. The time periods covered in some of the sections do not necessarily correspond to the dates discussed in the standard histories of the period. They relate more closely to the impact of the Jacobite rebellions on the Isle of Man. For example, December 1713 was significant because of John Murray of Dumfries's visit and its subsequent repercussions.

Each of the rebellions covered a relatively short time – on one occasion only a few days. Yet the people involved lived their lives before and afterwards. Events affecting John Hunter and Robert

Douglas before the battle of Preston in 1715 and John Aglionby and John Bignall after that defeat of the rebels have been included to complete the picture.

There are some brief insertions linking three or more time periods. The Englishman, Captain Thomas Harley, fought in Ireland for King Charles I and his son Nicolas, who was on the Isle of Man from the late seventeenth century, applied to the Jacobite Robert Harley, Earl of Oxford, for a position in the customs service. The grandson of Colonel Robert Duckenfield, who secured the Isle of Man for the Parliamentarians, died on the Island in the 1740s, deeply in debt (see Who was Who).

At the end of each story, there is a Postscript, describing subsequent events. The 'Who was Who' section provides further details of the individuals involved in events on the Island. Sometimes there is a plethora of detail, including a will held at the Manx National Heritage library and information off the Island. On other occasions, it has been impossible to identify the person with any real certainty. The Notes include not only sources but also a few explanatory comments, where necessary, and suggestions for further reading.

Various rules have been applied in an attempt to clarify the story. Where there are several spellings of the same surname one version has been used throughout the text. In some cases the version used by the individual has been adopted. For example, Richard Maguire is referred to as McGwire in his will, held on the Island. General McCartney has been chosen in preference to Macartney, because of the number of official documents using that spelling.

The New Style calendar has been adopted for all dates: 31 January 1713/14 has been written as 31 January 1714. All references to values of money over £10 have been rounded down to the nearest pound: £17 15s 6d appears as £17. Unless otherwise indicated these values are in pounds sterling. Any quotations have been modified to take account of modern spelling and punctuation. In particular, 'And' has been omitted from the beginning of a sentence.

The English term 'rebellion' has been applied throughout in preference to the Scottish 'rising' because of the Isle of Man's connections with the English crown. James Francis Edward Stuart has been called James III in any English context, James VIII in a Scottish context and, where appropriate, as the (Old) Pretender.

No claim is made that all the links between the Isle of Man and the Jacobite network have been identified, or included in this book. The research continues, however, so that any new, reliable, information would be gratefully received.

The writer has made every attempt to remain an observer – no personal comments have been made about the appropriateness or otherwise of the Jacobite cause.

---

[i] Robert Douglas was identified as the son of the Laird of Fingland and a Jacobite in Robert Edgar: *The Records of the Western Marches Volume I An Introduction to the History of Dumfries* 1915
[ii] The information about Thomas Harley and Big Tree house was obtained from an article by George Callister in Manx Notebook. He commented 'these notes by Sir J. D. Qualtrough were kindly loaned to me by his son Ian. They were obviously used for a talk which he gave to a church audience ...'

Figure 1: James II (1685-1688)

THE JACOBITES

Jacobite: from Jacobus, Latin for James

<u>Note</u>: The book in general, and this section in particular, is supported by Appendix I, which provides a list of the English monarchs and the Lords of Man between 1405 and 1766.

The term Jacobite was applied to a follower of James II of England and VII of Scotland. When his nephew, William of Orange, landed at Torbay in 1688, the King fled to France with his Catholic wife and their son, James Francis Edward. In order to escape from St James's Palace, the Queen dressed herself as a laundress and disguised the baby by wrapping him in a bundle of washing.

Several peers, representing the majority of the English people, had invited William III to England. They heralded his arrival as the Glorious Revolution. James had also been king of Scotland, however, and the support for William there was not universal, particularly amongst those who had been opposed to the union of the crowns in 1603. The initial unrest in both Scotland and Ireland led to the Williamite Wars, which will be described briefly in a later section.

When James II died in 1701, France and Spain proclaimed his son as King James III of England and VIII of Scotland. In Great Britain he was known as the Pretender to the throne. With both French and Spanish assistance, the Jacobites schemed to restore the Stuarts as the rightful monarchs.

1708   A French fleet with the Pretender on board tried to land at Burntisland on the Firth of Forth.

1715   <u>The First Rebellion</u>
        Starting in September with risings in both Scotland and England, proclaiming the Pretender as king of Great Britain, this was defeated by the capture of a mixed group of English and Scottish Jacobites at the battle of Preston on 13 November and by the indecisive outcome of the battle of Sheriffmuir fought in Scotland the same day. When the Pretender landed at Peterhead a week later, the rebellion was virtually over. He returned to France in February 1716.

1719   <u>The Little Rebellion</u>
        Backed by the King of Spain, this was to have been a simultaneous invasion of England and Scotland. Two ships arrived in the Outer Hebrides but the main Spanish fleet, headed for England, was wrecked in the Bay of Biscay. Having moved to Loch Alsh, the Jacobites and Spaniards captured Eilean Donan castle. This was bombarded from the sea and the large powder supply ignited, destroying part of their base. The land force was defeated at the battle of Glen Shiel.

1745   <u>The Second Rebellion</u>
        This was lead by Bonnie Prince Charlie on behalf of his father. They were now distinguished as the 'Old' and the 'Young' Pretender. Having received a lukewarm welcome in Scotland, the Prince decided to march into England and reached Derby. On his return to Scotland, he was defeated at the battle of Culloden in April 1746.

1766   The Jacobite rebellions of the eighteenth century ended with the death of the Old Pretender at Rome on 2 January 1766.

        This virtually coincides with the Act of Revestment in 1765, which ended a period in Manx history.

The Jacobite Rebellions

The Jacobite supporters were not a united group but included several different factions, each tending towards their own agenda. The Scottish Presbyterians were nationalists, wanting to re-establish a Scottish king on the throne of Scotland. Their detailed manifesto, which was read out in Kelso church on Sunday, 23 October 1715, is summarised in Appendix III. The Scotland-orientated aims must have confused their English companions. The Highlanders were unwilling to cross the Border into England not only because they believed that they would be either hacked to pieces or sold as slaves to the plantations[1] but also because their fight was in Scotland.

During the reign of Charles II, England had divided into two political parties: the Whigs and the Tories. The Whigs supported a government by monarchy, according to 'the ancient foundation', but they believed that parliament and the people should have sufficient power to control events. The extreme Tories believed in the hereditary right of the House of Stuart and even their more moderate members would not 'suffer the King to lose any of his prerogatives'.[2] The extreme Tories were known as the High Church party.

There was a tendency for these political parties to be distributed geographically with a concentration of the High Church Tories in the north. A Northumbrian led the English Jacobites in 1715 and they marched into Lancashire because they believed that thousands of High Church Tories would join them there. The failure of this promised support led to recriminations, the Tories who had joined the First Rebellion complaining about those who had stayed at home:

> *That party, who are never right hearty for the cause till they are mellow, as they call it, over a bottle or two, began now to show us their blind side; and that is just their character, that they do not care for venturing their concerns any farther than the tavern. There, indeed, with their High Church and Ormonde, they would make men believe, who do not know them, that they would encounter the greatest opposition in the world; but, after having consulted their pillows, and the fume a little evaporated, it is to be observed of them, that they generally become mighty tame, and are apt to look before they leap, and, with the snail, if you touch their houses, they hide their heads, shrink back, and pull in their horns.*[3]

In other words, these people were Jacobites when drunk and Hanoverians when sober. Certainly, the majority of instances of disaffection to the English crown on the Isle of Man were words spoken during drinking sessions, when toast after toast had been proposed. The Duke of Ormonde is discussed in the section on the Act of Grace.

The Catholics wanted a Catholic king on the throne once more. Surprisingly some of the Quakers joined them. In April 1687 James II had issued the Declaration of Indulgence, which allowed both Catholics and Protestants to serve God 'in their own way'. This meant that the Quakers were now free from persecution and produced in them a loyalty towards the Jacobite cause. Jacob Turner from near Lurgan in Ireland county Armagh was a Quaker. In 1708 he was in partnership with another Irish merchant, John Bignall, who now lived in Douglas, and the English Jacobite Captain John Hunter. Bignall also claimed to be a Quaker, insisting on affirming rather than swearing on the bible when he was asked to give evidence in the Manx courts. He was often in company with Jacobite sympathisers. In 1717 the Quaker, William Deale, was accused of proposing a toast to the Irish Jacobite, the Duke of Ormonde.[4]

This was in 1715. The situation was very different by 1745. The Presbyterian William Craik, surveyor of customs at Dumfries and an ardent Jacobite, wrote to his friend and neighbour, the Catholic Earl of Nithsdale, trying to dissuade him from joining Bonnie Prince Charlie in Edinburgh. His arguments are reproduced in Appendix IV.

Postscript

In September 1730 John Bignall was charged with owing his Dublin partners, Michael Sampson and William Thwaites, nearly £300. The case was transferred to the Admiralty Court and the water bailiff, John Cort, attempted to swear in a jury of six merchants to consider the company's accounts. Bignall intervened, however, taking some of the intended jury's hands off the bible and 'so went out of the room and did not stay to see them sworn'. He was fined 1s 4d for this act of contempt.[5]

NETWORKS

From the beginning, there was a major question: where did Moore's customers come from? How did he manage to develop such an intricate network of contacts over such a wide area? Were they each recommended to him by word of mouth or was there some strong link, which Moore tapped into and used for his own means? The first possible solution was that all Moore's customers might be Jacobites. However, apart from the odd individual in one place or another, this does not seem to have been so – and there is a suggestion that, based on his personal feelings, Moore would not have been involved with these people anyway. Therefore, the question remains unanswered. [George Moore & Friends: Letters from a Manx Merchant (1750 to 1760) Frances Wilkins 1994 Introduction]

Networks can be described in simple terms:

> A knows B, C and D
> B knows A, C and D but also E
> C knows A and B and E but also F, G and H
> D knows A and B and H but also I, J and K

The running trade required an intricate network of contacts. Charles Dalrymple was a merchant in Glasgow, who used the Isle of Man as a storehouse for his goods. He was in partnership with John Hunter and had close links with Robert Douglas, who also used the Island. Both Hunter and Douglas were Jacobites. This does not mean that Dalrymple was necessarily a Jacobite. Hunter was in partnership with Isaac Turner and John Bignall (see p. 2).

Thomas Coates was a merchant in Whitehaven. He had links with the Hunter, Turner, Bignall partnership, with Bignall independently and with several other Isle of Man-related merchants, including the Manxmen John Murray and Philip Moore, John Aglionby and Edward Nash. Aglionby was a Cumbrian Jacobite now living in Douglas. Murray and Moore often spent their evenings drinking with Jacobite sympathisers either at his house or at the house of John Hale, the king's officer in the port. There is no evidence that Thomas Coates was a Jacobite.

Walter Lutwidge was another Whitehaven merchant. It appears that he was not a Jacobite. He was in partnership with Jacobites in Kirkcudbright. He supplied Aglionby and Nash on the Island with tobacco sent from south-west Scotland.

John Bignall's customers included the Jacobite Maxwells from near Dumfries. Shortly before his death, Bignall frequently visited the house of Lancelot Dawes, who had fought on the government side at the battle of Preston in 1715. George Moore supplied the Jacobite Kennedys of Culzean in 1750 and 1752 with rum, brandy, wine, claret and tea. In 1745 he had sent four hogsheads of wine to Major General John Campbell, who commanded the government troops in Argyll.

Trade was clearly a more powerful factor than political principles. As a result, the running trade is a dominant theme throughout this book.

Various cross-country routes had been established through the Borders, first by the reivers and then by the smugglers. In 1715 Robert Douglas, an eighteenth century reiver as well as a smuggling merchant, carried letters and instructions from the Earl of Mar at Perth to the Northumbrian Jacobites, who were marching through the Borders collecting supporters. The Jacobites did not forge the initial network. They used the pre-existing reiving/smuggling routes as a means of communication.

Because of the Island's deep involvement in the running trade throughout the Jacobite period, it was inevitable that people there would be in constant contact with Jacobite sympathisers, so forging links between the Isle of Man and the Jacobite network.

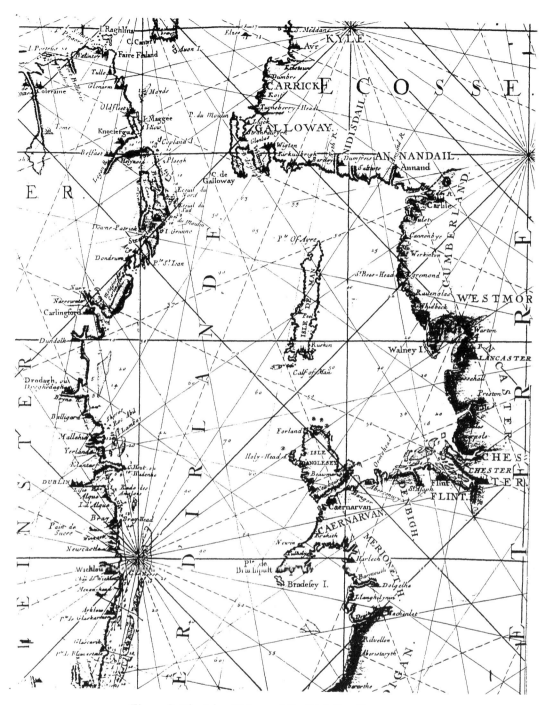

Figure 2: The Isle of Man and the Irish Sea Coasts

The Isle of Man was perfectly located as a supply base for the Irish Sea coasts. In May 1724 the collector at Dumfries received information from William Henderson, the king's officer at Ramsey, that nine boats were ready laden there with brandy and tobacco, all bound for the Galloway Firth. The collector of customs at Whitehaven wrote to the Board of Customs in London on 27 July 1750 reporting that on the 25th. he and his staff had seen 'from the hills a fleet of their boats of 10 or 11 sails, all laden, passing this harbour at about three leagues distance, steering for the Borders. Yesterday we perceived three or four more following them'.[6]

THE ISLE OF MAN AND THE RUNNING TRADE

It is well known that the Isle of Man is the great storehouse wherein the French and other nations deposit prodigious quantities of wine, brandy, coffee, tea, silks and other India goods, which are there admitted upon only low duties and afterwards smuggled upon the coasts of Great Britain and Ireland in small boats or wherries built for that purpose. [The memorial of the merchants and owners of ships in the port of Whitehaven, humbly addressed to the Right Honourable the Lords Commissioners of His Majesty's Treasury in 1754].[7]

In the context of the Jacobite rebellions, any suggestion that the Isle of Man was used as a storehouse of French goods must have alarmed the people living round the Irish Sea, and the government in London. In fact, several of the merchants who signed the Whitehaven memorial traded regularly with the Island, either warehousing their own goods there or purchasing cargoes from Manx merchants. The real story was far more complex, and interesting, than that suggested by the memorialists.

Henry IV granted the Isle of Man to the Stanleys in 1405. Although it was emphasised that the Island was held 'of the king', the Lords of Man had complete rule over the Island's people, merely owing allegiance to the English crown as a superior feudal monarch. This independence meant that different laws applied on the Island. The effect of this was considerable. As there was no law against treason on the Isle of Man, no structure existed there for charging people who were disaffected to the English crown. The Manx people were entitled to certain privileges in debt cases, to the detriment of the other merchants who had settled there and whose only means of ensuring equality was to apply for naturalisation. Both these issues are discussed later.

Possibly most important of all, lower customs duties were paid on the importation of goods from overseas and, in theory, the British revenue cruisers could not sail within the headlands of the Island, or board any ships within the harbours. An excellent haven had been created for the running trade – the hub of a smuggling network.

A proclamation dated 9 August 1661 referred to 'a sort of lewd people called Smuckellors, never heard of before the late disordered times, who make it their trade ... to steal and defraud His Majesty and His Customs'.[8] This is the first known reference to 'smugglers' in the English language. The running trade had been in existence for centuries. The main difference was that now it had become a more organised operation, involving a wide range of people from wealthy merchants with their large houses and estates to boatmen and carriers, who supplemented their meagre incomes with a few extra shillings per day. There were several stages in this running trade:

> purchasing the cargoes of contraband and high duty goods in Europe or the Americas;
> transporting the goods to the Isle of Man;
> storing the goods in warehouses until it was time to repackage them into smaller containers;
> loading these containers onto small boats and wherries;
> sailing from the Island to the various coasts round the Irish Sea, preferably during the dark of the moon;
> landing the goods on shore and transporting them to temporary hiding places or directly to the customers;
> collecting the money that was due from these customers.

Four aspects of the running trade are of particular significance to the Jacobite network story. Although a wide range of goods was smuggled into Great Britain, the tobacco trade occupied several of the merchants with Jacobite connections. An explanation of that somewhat complex trade has been included here. The goods were run onto all the coasts round the Irish Sea but in several cases this was only part of their journey. Customs officers in Ayrshire seized casks landed in Galloway and packs of tobacco were moved from the Solway shore to warehouses in Newcastle-upon-Tyne. Merchants who later joined some of their customers at the battle of Preston used this Borders route.

There were Manx customs officers on the Isle of Man but the king's officers at Douglas and Ramsey appear more frequently in the Jacobite context. An explanation is given of the supposed role of these people on the Island. Finally, Nicholas Harley's attempt to persuade the Lord Chancellor that he alone could stop the smuggling trade is described here, not because Nicolas was a Jacobite but because his relation, Robert Harley, the Earl of Oxford, was one (see Introduction).

The Tobacco Trade
Ships sailed to the tobacco plantations in Virginia and Maryland from the south-west Scottish ports of Kirkcudbright, Dumfries and Annan and the north-west ports English ports of Whitehaven and Liverpool. Their cargoes were imported legally into Britain and the duties paid at the custom house. The tobacco was stored in the merchant's warehouse and often shipped off again in smaller amounts to Europe. The reason for this was the Plantation Act, according to which tobacco could only be exported from the British Plantations in British vessels and only landed in Britain. Part of the market for this tobacco was in Europe, particularly France. Agents for the French tobacco merchants lived in Glasgow and Liverpool, and on the Isle of Man. They negotiated the prices with the tobacco importers, often before their vessels had left the Americas. Once it could be proved that the tobacco had been exported legally, the merchant could reclaim his duties – this was known as drawback.

Because of these high duties, the price of tobacco for the home market was excessive. As a result, merchants would send their tobacco to Europe – Dunkirk, Rotterdam, Bergen and Christiansand were common destinations. They would claim the drawback. In the meantime, the tobacco had been collected by smaller vessels and landed on the Isle of Man, where it was warehoused until it could be run into Britain again. The profit margins were comparatively small, yet apparently worthwhile, considering the size of the trade in illegal tobacco. Inevitably, several of the merchants took short cuts, pretending that their tobacco had gone to Europe when in fact it had been landed directly on the Island. The time covered by this book (1688 - 1766) includes various changes in the laws. At some stages, it was possible to land tobacco from Great Britain on the Island legally, although it was never legal to send it back there again.

The collectors of customs at Dumfries became obsessed by the tobacco movements of Walter Lutwidge and his uncle, Thomas, merchants at Whitehaven, who landed their Virginia and Maryland cargoes in south-west Scotland because at first the customs officers were 'nicer' to them there. The letter book for the Dumfries custom house from 1721 to 1728 includes nearly 40 letters from the collectors to the Board of Customs in Edinburgh, indicating their determination to catch the Lutwidges, despite the apparent lack of support from their English counterparts or the king's officers on the Isle of Man.[9]

The main problem related to the cargo of the *Queen Anne* of Whitehaven, Alexander Arbuthnott master, which arrived in Scotland from Virginia in September 1723 with 233 hogsheads on board, containing 207,000 lbs of tobacco. She landed 50 hogsheads at Kirkcudbright and 183 at Annan.

By October 1724 the situation was this:

No. of Hogsheads	Containing 000 lbs	Exported on board
45	36	*Lachmere* 'to Isle of Man'
121	116	*Moyan* of Carlisle to Dublin
42	33	*Mary & Betty*, Luke Hughes, to Isle of Man
16	11	*Mary* of Parkgate from Carlisle to Isle of Man
224	**196**	

In theory, there were nine hogsheads containing 11,000 lbs of tobacco still stored in Lutwidge's warehouse at Gratney, near Annan, waiting for a permit to be transferred to England. In the meantime, the collector at Dumfries became highly suspicious of the activities of the sloop *Lachmere*, William Ramsey master, which was wrecked in south-west Scotland during November 1723:

14 October 1723	Given a coastal cocket (permit) from Whitehaven to the Isle of Man with 9 hogsheads & 1 barrel tobacco and 8 chalders coals
15 October 1723	Arrived at Annan
28 October 1723	45 hogsheads of *Queen Anne*'s cargo shipped for the Isle of Man
31 October 1723	11 o'clock in the morning sailed: wind east-north-east steered a course for Silloth in Cumberland
1 November 1723	Arrived at Neston near Dumfries with 9 hogsheads & 1 barrel tobacco and 8 chalders ot coals
20 November 1723	Stranded at Orroland west of Barlocco Bay between Kirkcudbright and Dalbeattie 9 hogsheads & 1 barrel staved and the tobacco washed ashore

The collector was convinced that the *Lachmere* had run the 45 hogsheads on shore in England or Scotland between 31 October and 1 November 1723. As he wanted to confirm that these had not been landed in the Isle of Man, the collector sent one of his officers, Mr Tomlinson, to see William Henderson, the king's officer at Ramsey (see below). Henderson stated that the *Lachmere* had been to the Island, some time between the 1st and 20th November, and landed tobacco there. The Dumfries collector now wanted to know exactly how much tobacco was involved. He suspected that it could not be the original 45 hogsheads but some other tobacco that Lutwidge needed on the Island rather than in Scotland or Cumberland, possibly for some customers there. He believed that this tobacco had been shipped on board the *Lachmere* either at sea, from one of Lutwidge's incoming Virginia ships, or from one of his warehouses along the Solway shores.

John Sanforth, the collector on the Isle of Man, would not sign a certificate detailing the amounts of tobacco landed there, so that there was no official information to be used as evidence. Tomlinson had contacted the Manx customs officer in Ramsey, who 'could do him no service for he is an officer for the Earl of Derby and it seems as it's contrary to the laws of that Island to grant any certificates anent the landing of any goods from Britain'. Tomlinson needed a payment from the Board of Customs in Edinburgh of 'what sum you think fit for his charge and trouble in going to the Island'.

The Dumfries collector persevered and in March 1724 he received a note, possibly from Joshua Robinson, Sanforth's clerk, of all the tobacco imported into the Island from 24 June to 25 December 1723. This showed that since his initial enquiries <u>50</u> hogsheads had been 'stuffed' into the collector's books. Someone had attempted to confirm that the 45 hogsheads had been landed there after all.

This was not a single occurrence. Now that communications had been established between them, Henderson reported to the Dumfries collector that, at the end of December 1723, 'there came a small barque into Ramsey Burn from Kirkcudbright with about 22 hogsheads of tobacco on board. She stayed there till the 14th February, when she took on board a boat load of brandy, which was sailed from Douglas to her, and then sailed for some place on this [the Scottish] coast, without putting one hogshead of her tobacco on shore in that Island'.[10]

The Dumfries collector suffered from other frustrations in his attempt to catch the Lutwidges. In February 1724 he forwarded to the Board in Edinburgh a letter from England about 'what vile practices Mr Lutwidge is using by intercepting my letters, taking them out of the office at Whitehaven and breaking them open. I am confident it will convince the Honourable Board more and more of his guile and I humbly beg that you will please to represent this to the General Post Master at London and advise me whether or not Mr Lutwidge and the post master at Whitehaven can be prosecuted on this affair. For, if it be winked at, it will be impossible for me to maintain any longer a correspondence with the officers at Whitehaven'.[11] The Lutwidges took their trade back to their home port.

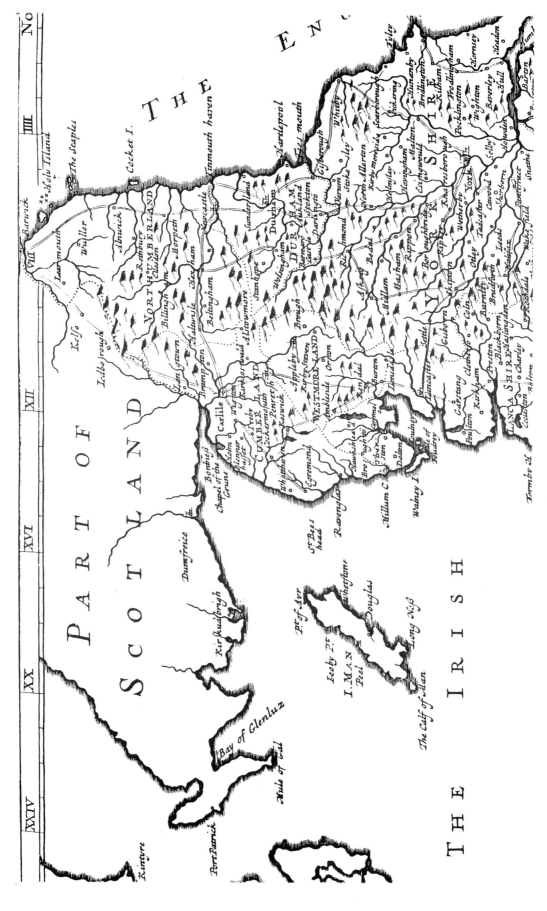

Figure 3: The Borders

The Borders Route
Both the Lutwidges and the Hunter, Turner, Bignall partnership, which is described in the section on Two Borderers, used the Border route to transfer their tobacco and other goods from the Solway to the extensive markets in the north-east of England.

In November 1724 the Dumfries collector reported to the Board that the Lutwidges were supplying customers on both sides of the Border and that 'the countries which are furnished from Annan do certainly consume great quantities of tobacco'.[12]

The impression often given by the custom house letters is that the smugglers themselves carried the goods through the Border country. In 1783 Mr Armstrong, the supervisor of riding officers at Newcastle-upon-Tyne, complained to the Board of Customs in Edinburgh about the lack of success of the Dumfries customs officers in halting the flow of smuggled goods along the Solway. He described the smugglers as having 'associated themselves with formidable bodies to carry and convey these goods through the country into Cumberland, Northumberland, Newcastle and the Southern Counties with firearms, threatening the riding officers with murder whenever they meet them'.[13] In fact, during the Jacobite period the transport system was well organised and involved a series of agents and warehouses with local carriers moving the goods between them.

In November 1739 Lutwidge's agent at Darlington, Leonard Ward, had sold tobacco to his customers without having any supplies on hand. Lutwidge wrote to him, 'the season of the year is such that there is no sending any tobacco from Scotland by carriers so that I must drop the matter until the spring ... However, I do design, God willing, to send some as soon as the roads are passable'. The Northumbrian and Scottish Jacobites were in the Borders during October and November of 1715.

Lutwidge was concerned about Ward's customers because 'I find that when goods are not on the spot the buyers cries stinking fish'. As a result, 'that you may not be worse than your contract, I'll send five packs from hence [Whitehaven] by the Penrith carrier and order my friend there to forward them by the Newcastle or Barny [Barnard] Castle carrier'. This was not only inconvenient but also 'they go through so many people's hands that there is no knowing who to charge with loss of weight or damages, if it should happen'. Ward's contract had been for tobacco at 7¾d per lb. ready money. There had been a recent increase in the price of tobacco and Lutwidge could not well afford to sell at less than 8d per lb. In this instance, however, he was prepared to make an exception for Ward.

King's/Queen's Officers on the Isle of Man
From the 1680s there were two English customs officers on the Isle of Man, one based at Ramsey and the other at Douglas. They were in the invidious position of being able to observe what was happening but, in theory, take no action. On 21 October 1723 William Henderson at Ramsey wrote to the Board of Customs in London, drawing their attention to the large quantities of rum landed on the Island. They reminded him that he did not have 'any power to seize goods in the Island, but only to make observations on the trade there and to represent the same from time to time to this Board'.[14]

In November 1724 Henderson sent a letter to the collector at Wigtown, which was forwarded by express to Dumfries. This contained information about a wherry due to sail from the Island, which had already arrived on the Scottish coast and run her cargo. It also described

> *some abominable villainous practices, which a certain officer at the port of Kirkcudbright hath for some time been guilty of ... not only trading with the smugglers and conniving at their practices but also of disaffection to his Majesty's person and government, a crime which I am heartily sorry to hear any officer accused of. I have written to Henderson, requesting him to condescend upon the person and to get as full proof as possible of the facts he alleges against him.*[15]

There is no evidence that Henderson provided any further information about the Kirkcudbright customs officer whom he accused of disaffection. His attempt to incriminate Richard McGwire, one of the farmers of the customs on the Isle of Man is described in the section on the Pretender's Birthday.

Figure 4: Charles I (1625-1649)

Nicholas Harley and the Earl of Oxford

This section describes a link between an army captain under Charles I, a trader on the Isle of Man and the Jacobite Earl of Oxford, who was imprisoned in the Tower of London for his views.

The Ulster civil war started on St Ignatius day, 23 October 1641. It was triggered by the fear that the Catholics were conspiring to expel the English and massacre the Protestant settlers in Ulster. Charles I sent English troops to Ireland, where Thomas Harley served as captain of foot and chief engineer under the Marquis of Ormonde. Harley was owed 'for his service and materials of war' over £3,000, which could be confirmed by the authorities in Ireland.

Because of the king's subsequent problems, Harley was not able to claim his money until 'the happy Restoration of King Charles II'. Instead of cash, he was offered a position as master gunner, in Ireland. Harley died before he could take up this post and his family, who lived in Wexford, never received any recompense.

Harley's son, Nicholas, went to live on the Isle of Man. He appears regularly in the customs ingates and outgates from the 1670s onwards, as both a master and a merchant. Most of his voyages involved local trade between Castletown and Liverpool or Dublin. In 1698 Richard Cowle of Castletown sold Harley a town house, garden and backside and a miln.[16]

It is probable that Harley suffered financially because of his honesty, at a time when large sums of money were to be made through the running trade. James White of Wicklow was at Liverpool during May 1693, when Harley had told him that Henry Cottier 'did truck or exchange his timber and poles, which he brought to this Isle, for brandy'. This was reported to the Admiralty Court on the Isle of Man, believing that it might be 'a means to discover that brandy was brought over' from the Island. No action was taken.[17]

On 9 May 1705 Harley, 'in the presence and hearing of the deputy governor', verbally attacked William Seddon, who was then the deputy comptroller, 'maliciously and falsely' stating that 'he knew some foul things by him … and in a short time he would make them known'. Seddon claimed that these scandalous words had 'greatly damnified his good name, fame and reputation and the trust reposed in him … within this Isle'. Harley was arrested and had to provide security that he would not leave the Island until the matter could be tried in court. There is no evidence about the outcome.[18]

It is probable that Nicholas was related to the Herefordshire Harleys (see Introduction). When legal shipping did not provide him with a sufficient income, he applied to the Lord Chancellor of England, Robert Harley, the Earl of Oxford, for a post in the customs service. He wanted to be appointed as a tidesurveyor on the Isle of Man with 'the command of a yacht or some small cruiser' that could sail between Dublin and Chester, or at Whitehaven, where there was currently a vacancy, or to any other post that would help to support his family.

Harley enclosed a report, giving information about the running trade from the Island. Ships from Liverpool and other ports that were headed for North Britain would call there, 'pretending to be wind bound', and take on board as much tobacco and brandy as they could carry. These goods would be 'covered' by the cargo already listed on their cocket, permitting them to transport items coastwise. As a result their cargoes were 'not mistrusted and [they] lands them with safety and are not suspected'. The same method was used by Irish ships calling at the Island for timber or other goods.

He was convinced that none of the Manx customs officers 'took any notice of this trade'. Harley believed that 'if they had it would be easily prevented'. He concluded that, if he were given his own yacht, 'I don't doubt but with little trouble, in a short time, to break these great measures used in running goods'. He could provide 'some certificates of my way of living and behaving from my infancy, if your Lordship please to see them'. Unfortunately, the Earl did not respond to Harley's pleas and these certificates have not survived.[19]

In October 1713 John Blith, then master of the wherry known as the *Two Brothers* of Narrowwater, carried two miners, George Leech and Abraham Kidd, off the Island. Harley was one of several people who could prove that the same wherry, now with John Ivins as master, was back at the Isle of Man. The wherry was seized, because Leech and Kidd had owed money to several people, including two sums of £1 and 6d to Harley.[20]

Five years later, in September 1718, Harley was accused of taking Richard Quirk, Richard Caine and Henry Killey, all 'natives and inhabitants of this Isle' off the Island in a wherry belonging to William Harrison of Malew, without the governor's pass or licence. Neither Harrison nor Harley had anything 'material to offer why the wherry should not be condemned'.[21] One wonders how much money Harley had hoped to be paid for this.

Postscript

On 2 May 1705 Nicholas Harley and his wife Sarah drew up a joint deed of gift, which was accepted by the Consistory Court fifteen years later as Sarah's last will. Harley made his own will on 8 May 1720 and died only a few days later.[22] He had requested Captain Farrell to take care of all his 'effects and concerns' until his nephew Nicholas Cribb of Liverpool, could take over as his executor. As Cribb was in Virginia, his wife, Margaret, came to the Island and was accepted as executor in his stead. The inventory totalled only £11, including

At the late dwelling house of Mr Harley deceased an old brass furnace patched in a great many places and the patches very large, in several other places plastered with lime mortar	14s 0d
Two stone sledges, the weight to us unknown, (they had been sold) otherwise @ 2d per lb	4s 11d
An old cupboard apprised by us to	2s 6d

Margaret Cribb's expenses of £8 16s 10d included the costs of both funerals:

For funeral charges	£3 17s 6d
For lacquered nails for Mrs Harley's coffin	3s 0d
To the clerk for his dues of both the decedents	3s 4d
To John Costean for money given Mr Harley to pay for Mrs Harley's funeral charges	£2 0s 0d
To Mr Cosnahan junior for the remainder of the money due for Mrs Harley's funeral sermon	7s 1d
For Mrs Harley's burial money, copies of record, recording the inventory etc	5s 11d

This left £2, plus a mortgage worth £7, to be distributed amongst the creditors. One can only imagine the bitterness that Harley must have felt throughout his time on the Island, remembering the debt of £3,000 owed to his father by the crown.

Robert Harley, Earl of Oxford died on 21 May 1724, aged 62. His memorial at Brampton Bryan church in Herefordshire provides a detailed picture of his life. He was Speaker of the House of Commons for three parliaments in King William and Queen Anne's reigns. In 1704 Anne made him Secretary of State and in 1710 Lord of the Treasury and Chancellor of the Exchequer. In 1711 he became Earl of Oxford and Earl Mortimer and was appointed Lord High Treasurer of Great Britain. In 1712 he was installed as a knight of the garter. His decline was somewhat rapid. A few days before the Queen died in 1714, he gave up the post of Treasurer. On 10 June 1715 he was charged with treason by the House of Commons and 'other high crimes and misdemeanours' and on 16 July committed to the Tower of London. After two years in prison, he was tried and unanimously acquitted by his peers, 'not one article alleged against him' being proved. 'During his long and severe confinement he contracted so bad a habit of body that his health declined'.[23]

THE WILLIAMITE WARS

There was a Williamite garrison at Belturbet and a Jacobite garrison at Finea so that the surrounding land became 'a wilderness' with only a few uninhabited houses left standing.[24]

England and Wales pledged their allegiance to William of Orange but James II still had supporters in most of Ireland and parts of Scotland. In March 1689 he landed at Kinsale with 6,000 French troops, supplied by Louis XIV. The plan was to secure the whole of Ireland before returning triumphantly to England. He was opposed by William of Orange's army of 37,000 men from England and Scotland, Holland and Germany, and by the Protestants in Ulster. The Jacobites were finally defeated at the battle of Aughrim on 12 July 1691.

Figure 5: William III (1689 with Mary, 1694-1702)

Figure 6: The Battle of Killiechrankie 1689

John Graham of Claverhouse, Viscount Dundee, was James II's Lieutenant General in Scotland. He raised an army of 2,000 men, including the MacDonalds, Camerons, Stewarts and MacLeans, and Rob Roy MacGregor. They raided Perth on 10 May 1689 and then seized Blair Castle. A government army consisting of 4,000 infantry and two troops of cavalry under General Hugh MacKay of Scourie was sent from Stirling to recapture the castle and then garrison the fort at Inverlochy.

On the night of 26 July, Claverhouse was camped near Blair Castle. The next day MacKay advanced through the narrow Pass of Killiecrankie. Surprised by the Jacobites, he sent his men uphill through the woods. The Jacobites were on a higher ridge, however, and Claverhouse waited for sunset, when the light would be in the eyes of the government troops. At 7 o'clock he ordered his men to charge. Most of the government troops were 'swept away and routed in the fierce onslaught and the Jacobites overwhelmed the baggage train. The pass was choked with fleeing men'. MacKay attempted a last stand. Claverhouse led the attack but he was hit in the stomach by a musket-ball. It was reported that a looter killed him, 'as he lay wounded'.[25]

Spurred on by their victory, the Jacobites headed for Dunkeld but they failed to take the town. On 1 May 1690 they were attacked by the government troops at Cromdale, while they slept. The Williamite War in Scotland was over.

'Killiechrankey' Goods
It was legal for anyone to import into the Isle of Man goods that were classed as 'high duty and contraband' in Britain, provided he paid the duties due to the Lord. It was illegal, however, to run goods into the Island so bypassing the customs system. These goods could be seized and everyone who had been involved in transporting or storing them would be liable to prosecution. The smuggling run described here was in June 1713 and yet it was connected with the battle of Killiecrankie in 1689.

On Wednesday 10 June 1713, 'about an hour in the night time', John Wattleworth junior of Ramsey went to William Corkill senior of Port Lewaige's house, 'at which time he was in bed'. Wattleworth explained that he had some horses loaded with 'merchant ware' and asked Corkill to let him use a room in his house, with a lock and key, to store the goods.

As he had only one room that could be secured properly, and his things were in there already, Corkill suggested that Wattleworth should go to Karrow, where he might find something suitable. Wattleworth did not accept this proposal, explaining that, as it was raining, his goods might be spoiled. At last, Corkill offered him the use of a cowhouse, 'if that would serve his turn'.

Corkill was concerned in case Wattleworth's horses were allowed to wander into his cornfield. Although he was assured that this would not happen, he became convinced that Wattleworth and his men would not take sufficient care of the horses and his precious corn would be damaged. As a result, Corkill got out of bed and went outside.

To his surprise, he saw a 'considerable parcel of goods' lying at the cowhouse door. He also saw Wattleworth, Hugh Kerrush and a stranger not unloading horses but carrying casks from the direction of the shore. There was a boat at the seaside, 'being about a third part upon dry land and two thirds in the water, lying to the westward of the place'.

When Corkill asked Wattleworth what had happened to the horses, he was told they were 'gone up there'. He ran up the hill, 'for fear they might be in his corn. Nevertheless, when he came to the field he found no horses there nor anywhere else thereabouts. Returning down to them again, he saw some men thrust off the boat, with some haste, and [they] rowed away by the black rocks towards Ramsey'.

Now realising that Wattleworth had misled him, Corkill said to him, 'Johnny, see that these are not troublesome goods or <u>Killychrankey</u> goods that we may come to trouble about them'. Wattleworth tried to reassure Corkill, saying he would 'bear him harmless' and make sure that he was not implicated in any trouble. Presuming that he would call Corkill's bluff, Wattleworth added that he could go and tell Captain Michael Christian, the Manx customs officer at Ramsey, about what had happened in the morning, 'if he would'.

Wattleworth intended to take the goods to Ramsey the next day anyway and asked Corkill if he could hire a couple of horses from him. Corkill agreed, provided Wattleworth did not overload them with too many casks. Wattleworth then went home. He did not return to Corkill's house the next day to hire the horses or to remove his goods. A few days later Captain Christian junior seized everything 'in the cowhouse they lay in'.[26]

The exact meaning of Corkill's use of the word 'Killychrankey' is not completely clear from the context. He also referred to 'troublesome' goods so that by 'Killychrankey' he could have meant opposed to the government or laws of the Island. There is no real evidence about Corkill's political leanings but it could be supposed that he was a Whig.

Postscript

In November 1725 Edward Nash of Douglas charged John Bowdell with a debt of £10. As this related to freight of goods, the case was referred to the Admiralty Court. John Wattleworth junior was Bowdell's surety and so the new water bailiff, John Sanforth, charged him to be present when a jury was sworn in to consider the case, at 4 o'clock in the afternoon of 6 December 1725.

Sanforth had come to the Island as the collector of customs for the farmers Josiah Poole & Richard McGwire. When he lost that post, he became one of the Island's officers. Wattleworth did not believe that Sanforth had been sworn into his office yet and so he had no authority to call a jury. He ignored the summons.

When he did not appear, Sanforth sent Wattleworth a message. His first response was that he would meet Sanforth, and presumably the jury, half way to his house in Ramsey. Sanforth insisted that Wattleworth should be fined immediately for his non-attendance. When he heard about this, Wattleworth went straight to Castletown. Sanforth told him that he was too late and Wattleworth called him 'a rogue, a knave and a villain'. This type of verbal attack on an officer of the Island was against the Statute of Defamation of 1601 and punishable by having his ears cut off.

Wattleworth was imprisoned in Douglas Fort. He petitioned the governor, explaining that he had thought the jury was going to meet at 10 o'clock, when he had been in Castletown. This excuse was not accepted but Wattleworth was released, provided Gilbert Smith and William Curlett of Douglas were bound in the penalty of £100 that he would present himself as and when necessary.

Nothing happened for nearly six months and then Wattleworth was summoned to appear before the House of Keys. Sanforth had three witnesses, George Bennett, Kenny Morgan and William McGwire, who was Richard McGwire's son. Wattleworth's witnesses were dispersed in England and Scotland. He asked for more time to contact them and was given until 24 June and then 13 July 1726. Wattleworth did not prepare his case sufficiently and was shocked when the House of Keys found him guilty. Their sentence would 'overthrow his reputation and ruin his family'. Believing that the Keys had acted 'rashly', Wattleworth requested the governor to allow him to appeal to the Earl of Derby. This request was granted. However, by November 1727 Wattleworth had made no attempt to appeal, not even making copies of the papers relating to the case, ready to send them to the Earl. On the 27th he was fined £10, for not appealing, and sentenced to undergo his punishment. It is unclear whether Wattleworth did have his ears cut off.

He died, intestate, on 17 November 1728.[27]

TWO BORDERERS: JOHN HUNTER & ROBERT DOUGLAS

The reivers have been described as 'anything from Jolly Knights errant, robbing the rich to give to the poor, to a set of bloodthirsty scoundrels, whose sole delight was in robbery and mayhem, without any kind of justification or even a redeeming feature'.[Godfrey Watson *The Border Reivers* 1998 Preface]

During medieval times, pele towers were built on both sides of the Border to defend the people and their property from the reivers, who were also known as Borderers. After the union of the crowns of England and Scotland in 1603, in theory, the Borderers were less violent. The habit of generations continued, however, and in the early eighteenth century many people in the Borders were still expert horse thieves.

Both John Hunter of Shillah Hill, a pele tower above the Tarset Burn, a tributary of the North Tyne river in Northumberland and Robert Douglas, second son of the Laird of Fingland near Dalry in south-west Scotland, were described as 'Borderers' at the battle of Preston.

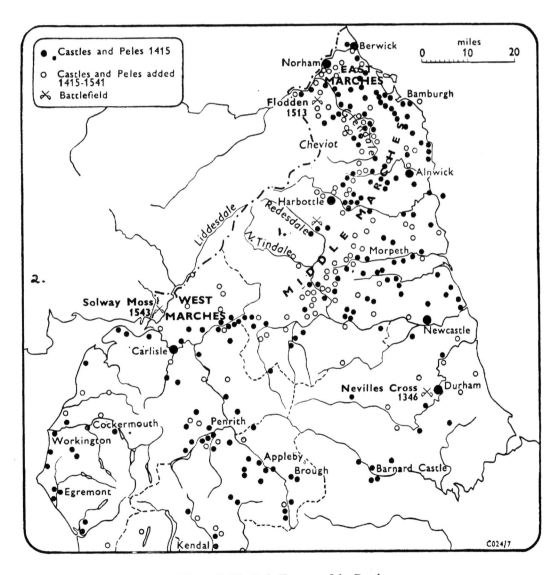

Figure 7: The Pele Towers of the Borders

1. Shillah Hill & 2. Fingland

Douglas in particular was recommended for his ability in stealing horses. 'When the Jacobites were in contact with General Carpenter's cavalry and were themselves short of horses [it] was suggested to the Jacobite leaders that, if Douglas camped in the vicinity of the enemy, General Carpenter's cavalry would have no horses at all in the morning'.[28] Before joining the 1715 rebellion, both Hunter and Douglas had connections with the Isle of Man in the tobacco and other running trades.

John Hunter of Shillah Hill, 1708-1711

When he joined the Northumbrian Jacobites, John Hunter was described as having 'rendered himself famous for running contraband goods'.[29] Shillah Hill was well placed near the Border route from the Solway to the north-east of England. At this stage, Hunter may have known Thomas Forster of Bamburgh Castle, the Earl of Derwentwater at Dilston near Hexham and Isaac Allgood of Brandon White House, Nunwick, near Simonsburn. Considering their lifestyles as country gentlemen, it is probable that each of these men would have been a customer for claret and brandy. In October 1715 they shared a bottle of wine before parting company, Forster and Derwentwater to raise support for the Pretender in Northumberland and Allgood to lurk on the Isle of Man until the new regime was established in London.

Hunter's main smuggling partnership was with Charles Dalrymple, a tobacco merchant in Glasgow. They were co-owners of the sloop *Joseph* of Sligo that, with Thomas Vance of Peel master, made regular trips from the Isle of Man to Galloway with tobacco and other goods. In 1708 Hunter became involved in a cargo of brandy and wine with Jacob Turner of Lurgan in county Armagh and John Bignall, an Irish merchant now living in Douglas.

Articles of Agreement between John Hunter, Jacob Turner and John Bignall

Know all men by this present writing that it is agreed upon by and between the abovesaid persons to load on the Ann *of Douglas £121 worth of brandy and one tun of claret, valued at £21. Whereof John Hunter is to be for his proportion in the goods liable for £61, Jacob Turner for £40 10s and John Bignall for £40 10s. It is further agreed upon by the abovesaid persons that they shall be equally concerned in loss or gain of the goods, according to each man's proportion. As witness our hands and seals this 9th day of November 1708.*

This agreement was witnessed by William Cosh of Donaghadee, one of the sailors on board the *Ann*, and John Bignall's wife, Mary. Before the partners parted company, Turner expressed his concern that they had omitted to include the wherry in the agreement. He wanted to insert words to the effect that if any misfortune or disaster should befall the *Ann* then the partners would be liable for the cost of the boat, sailors' wages and victuals, according to their proportions of the cargo. Bignall agreed that this was 'but reasonable' and shook Turner by the hand to confirm that he would be equally concerned in both the goods and the wherry etc.

Bignall supplied the brandy, although there is no evidence that he imported it into the Island himself, and Turner purchased the claret from Samuel Sisson, who had imported a cargo from Spain in the *Success* of Dublin, Robert Brown master, at the end of September 1708.[30] Daniel Hayton was appointed master of the wherry and Hunter, Turner and Bignall went with him. This may have been to introduce Turner and Bignall to Hunter's network so that they would be able to supply them with goods from the Isle of Man in future. Alternatively there might have been a certain lack of trust between the partners.

In the meantime, William Johnson, the collector at Dumfries, had received information that Jacob Turner was on the Island, planning to run goods in a creek near Abbey Holme in Cumberland (Figure 8). Johnson forewarned the collector at Carlisle and advised Mr Grierson, the riding officer[i] at Dumfries, 'to be upon his rounds on this coast, and all our other officers to be on their guard'.

---

[i] a riding officer had a horse and responsibility for 'riding' a section of the coast, usually covering about 10 miles. As he worked alone, he would send an express message for help, if he found any smugglers.

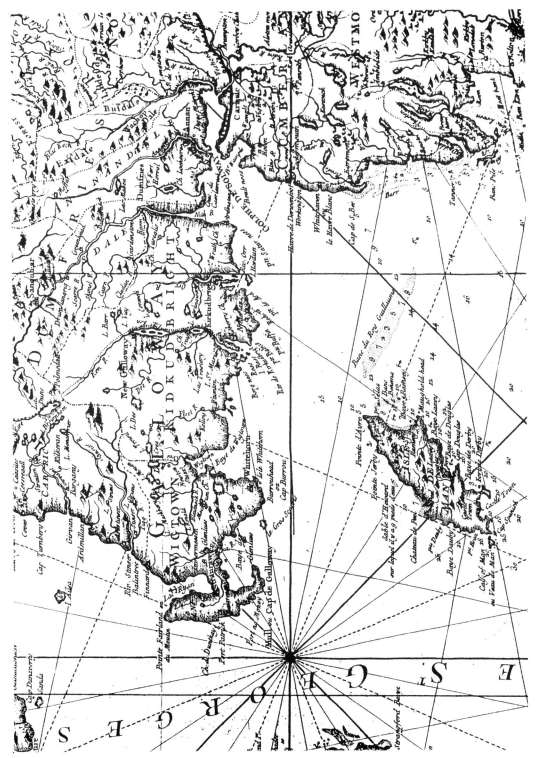

Figure 8: The Solway Shore

On Sunday, 2 December 1708 the *Ann* was stranded on a sandbank near Carsethorn, waiting for the tide. When Grierson and one of the Dumfries tidewaiters seized her there, they described the boat as Manx built, about 10 tons burthen, with 23 quarter casks and 20 small casks of brandy, four hogsheads of red wine and two packs of coarse Irish canvas on board. Because of the low tide, they could not move her up the river Nith to the safety of the customhouse quay at Dumfries that day.[31]

Hunter, Turner, Bignall and Hayton all found lodgings at Ruthwell, north of the Solway between Dumfries and Annan. They were safe here. In 1711 the collector was to inform the Board of Customs in Edinburgh, 'Ruthwell is the only place here we have the greatest difficulty to get an officer entertained [lodged] at'. His solution was to find an 'inhabiter' at Ruthwell, 'whom we shall search out for'. The collector could not find anyone, however, and Ruthwell continued as a smugglers' base.[32]

At 2 o'clock on the Monday morning, Hunter woke Hayton and took him to see Bignall, 'who was then in bed'. Turner was not present but the other two partners explained that they planned to rescue the goods still on board the *Ann*. They instructed the master to hire two boats in Cumberland and he would be given 'full satisfaction for my trouble'. Hayton managed to hire only one boat, for £3. She went to Carsethorn and stayed there several days 'to perfect the project, which was frustrated, and so returned back again'. In October 1711 Hayton complained to the Chancery Court on the Isle of Man that he was 'never yet paid' his expenses.

Once the customs officers had succeeding in moving the *Ann* to Dumfries, Hayton overheard Bignall say that he would be no further concerned in her and, despite his promise to Turner on the 9th November, he would spend no more money trying to claim the cargo. Hunter had moved on and probably Bignall realised the futility of spending any more time and money trying to persuade the customs office to relinquish their seizure. There is no information in the Dumfries letter books about the ultimate fate of the *Ann*.

Bignall went to Whitehaven, where he had business to conduct with Thomas Coates, the tobacco merchant. His correspondence has not survived but this reply from Turner gives an indication of what his letter contained. It has been quoted in full:

Newtown, near Carlisle, 5 January 1709. To John Bignall at Whitehaven. To be forward.

I received thine of the 3rd and noted the contents. Thou might have been so kind to have waited here or at Dan Hayton until I returned from Carlisle, that we might [have] consulted business. Since I see thou, I have been once at Carlisle myself and sent Anthony Watson to Dumfries twice to see what will be done in that business. For I am not free to leave this country until I know the end of the matter. I am now waiting for his return from Dumfries. If I get a good answer to my letters, that I sent myself, I will go myself before I come to Whitehaven. If not [I] will come next week.

But in the meantime I must tell thou thou art too hasty to draw on me for £30, the case being so at present that we cannot settle our accounts without some disadvantage either on one side or the other. For thou very well knows that if the wherry be not got again that I am to have satisfaction from thee, for one third beside men's wages and victuals, from the time the goods were shipped until they were taken.

But since thou has occasion, I will here state accounts and if thou accept of the same I shall pay the balance to Thomas Coates freely, or to any other thou think fit to order me to pay. In the meantime, I am with due respect thy real friend. Jacob Turner

The 'occasion' was because Bignall owed John Murray of Douglas for a cargo of wine from Bilboa and Murray was determined to destroy his credibility both on the Island and at Whitehaven, if he did not pay.[33] The £30 was owed on a separate account between Turner and Bignall. Turner reckoned that he had paid off this sum, and more, by his expenses on behalf of the Hunter, Turner & Bignall partnership. According to his account, Turner had paid for Bignall's proportions of the wine and of the loss of the wherry, sailors' wages etc. He had also paid Thomas Coates of Whitehaven £9 and given Hunter £4 in cash, which he had passed to Bignall. As this totalled more than £30, Turner had overpaid by 13s 3½d. The case was taken to the Chancery Court, who referred the account for detailed inspection by John Murray of Douglas, or if he felt unable to adjudicate because of the ongoing case against Bignall then to Thomas Martin, formerly a merchant in Glasgow but now living in Douglas, and Daniel Janson of Castletown. The verdict was that Turner could claim everything against the £30, except the £4, which he had 'no other credence or proof of but his own allegation' and which Bignall refused to confirm 'upon his affirmation (which is the usual oath taken by Quakers)' that he had received the money.[34]

The arguments between the partners continued. In September and October 1709 Bignall charged Hunter in the Chancery Court with a debt of £23 and 'putting to his own use', 12 empty casks, valued at 3s 6d each. In April 1710 Hunter attempted to counter-claim the sum of £20. He wanted the case heard quickly, not only because he believed that Bignall would 'speedily depart' from the Island but also because his business 'likewise requires him to go off the Isle in a little time'. When Hunter did not appear in Court on 5 October 1710, the case was dismissed.[35]

On 5 March 1712 all Bignall's identifiable goods on the Island were sold for £53, which Murray accepted as full payment of the £72 still due for the cargo of wine from Bilboa. This figure included the debts, which the Court had proved that Bignall was owed by Hunter and Turner on the final settlement of their accounts.[36] Turner was in difficulty with the Dumfries customs officers again in 1711 but on this occasion there is no information about his partners on the Isle of Man, if any.

Thomas Vance's wages as master of the *Joseph*, at the rate of 40s Manx a month, were due in mid-May 1710. When he only received one guinea, in February 1711 Vance charged John Hunter and Charles Dalrymple for his overdue wages.[37] Hunter also owed Philip Moore of Douglas £116. The creditors were particularly anxious to ensure that no goods belonging to Hunter were removed from the Island until their debts were satisfied.[38]

During the summer of 1711 Hunter's brother (his first name is not recorded) came to the Isle of Man with an order from Robert Douglas (see below) to receive some lead, tobacco and herrings that were in John Murray's custody. Murray would not deliver anything, however, until Dalrymple came to the Island. In October 1711 Dalrymple was instructed by the Chancery Court to pay Vance £8 18s 6d Manx, the balance of his wages.[39]

In December 1711 James Read was at Whithorn, where he met both Dalrymple and John Hunter. Having arranged with Read for his passage back to the Island, Hunter received a letter from Dalrymple, calling him to Wigtown, where James Laurie, the local notary public, was based. It is possible Dalrymple needed Hunter's assistance in his case against William Park (see pp. 24-27). Hunter did not appear at Whithorn the next morning and Read sailed without him.[40]

John Hunter never returned to the Isle of Man. Queen Anne gave him a commission, 'for raising an independent company [of men] for the service of the government'.[41] As a result, he was now referred to as Captain.

Robert Douglas of Auchenshinnoch, 1708 - 1712

James Douglas of Morton Castle was descended from Patrick Douglas, the illegitimate son of James Douglas, 7th Lord of Drumlanrig. His son Archibald of Morton had four children: William, Robert, Grizel and Sara. Although William wrote the first two verses of *Annie Laurie*, he married Elizabeth Clark on 18 August 1706 and she married Alexander Ferguson in 1710. William was also an expert swordsman, fighting for the Jacobite cause in both 1715 and 1745 – he died in 1755. Grizel married John Murray, a merchant in Dumfries and cousin of John Murray of Douglas in 1713 and Sara married William Johnson, the collector of customs at Dumfries on 12 June 1703. The castle was occupied until 1714, after which it fell rapidly into disrepair.[42]

Figure 9: Morton Castle, near Thornhill – August 2002

Figure 10: Fingland, near Dalry – from an old photograph

Through his marriage to Christian Lockhart, James Douglas obtained Fingland and Auchenshinnoch. His son Archibald became laird of Fingland and his son Samuel was laird of Auchenshinnoch. Remains of a pele tower were found a few yards in front of the house at Fingland. Over two hundred years later, the area was described as 'a large tract of fine wild moorland country', which was entirely used for sheep. Little has changed in the twenty-first century.[43]

Robert Douglas was given Auchenshinnoch by his uncle, Samuel in 1704. He married Margaret, the daughter of James Corbet, a merchant in Glasgow, on 16 April 1708 but there is no evidence that Robert and his wife ever lived there.[44] Despite his title to Auchenshinnoch, Robert was always referred to as the second son of the laird of Fingland.

It has proved impossible to trace Robert Douglas's career before he appears, aged 34, as the surveyor of landcarriage at Glasgow town with a salary of £40 per annum. This position suggests, despite his reputation as a horse thief, a certain level of education, and responsibility. Douglas had four staff under him, all landwaiters.[i]

Glasgow Town: Establishment from the 1st of August 1707 to the 29th September following

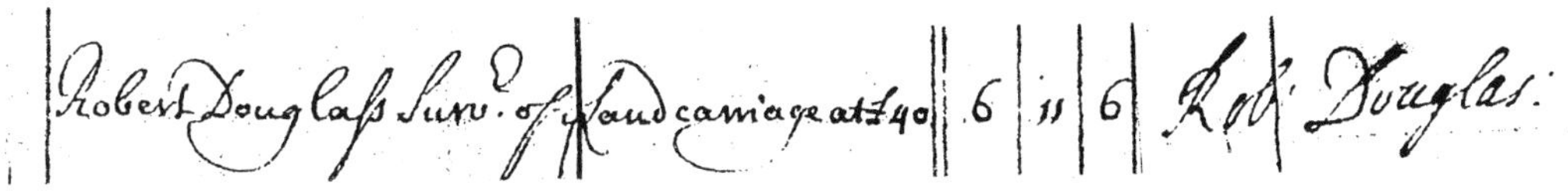

Figure 11: Robert Douglas's salary in 1707[ii]

The 'merchant traffickers' of Dumfries complained to the meeting of the Royal Burghs at Edinburgh on 5 July 1709 about the increase in smuggling along the Solway in general and the behaviour of Robert Douglas in particular. The Royal Burghs in Scotland paid a tax for the privilege of importing goods from the British Plantations and other ports overseas. Recently 'setts, partnerships and clubs of gentleman freeholders and others within this country' had swamped Dumfries's trade. These interlopers were running 'great and considerable' quantities of brandy and tobacco. A large smuggling ship had cruised along the Solway coast, threatening the customs boatmen and 'any other boats, except those of her own correspondence, that offered to come near her'. The smugglers were becoming more and more daring. 'In open daylight they are known to unload boats and carry off the goods both on the English and Scots side to a considerable quantity which, as is informed by all, has come from the Isle of Man'. What infuriated the burghers was that 'we have several times laid the same before the officers of the custom house here, yet we have found no effectual redress, but the foresaid encroachments still increase and grow worse and worse'.

At the end of June 1709 William Johnson, the collector of customs for Dumfries and Robert Douglas's brother-in-law, seized 24 packs of tobacco at Annandale. This tobacco never reached the custom house. The supposed owner, 'a person who is known not to be worth a groat', produced a certificate, signed by Douglas as surveyor at Glasgow, giving him authority to transport the tobacco overland to Dumfries. Johnson persuaded the Justices of the Peace in Dumfries to accept this certificate and issue their own warrant, permitting the 'owner' to keep his tobacco and transport it, presumably into the Borders.

---

[i] With the Union of the Parliaments in 1707 the customs system in Scotland was brought into line with that of England. There was a Board of Customs in Edinburgh and a series of outports, each with a customhouse, collector, comptroller and associated staff. Glasgow town was not on the coast and so instead of a collector of customs a surveyor, with an area under his survey, was the senior officer. The landwaiters had power to stop and inspect any goods carried by land to ensure that they had paid the appropriate customs on importation.

[ii] The letters from the collectors to the Board have survived for some outports, such as Dumfries, from 1707 onwards. The Glasgow records have only survived from 1807 so that it is not possible to recreate Douglas's time there, apart from his salary returns.

The Dumfries burghers were well-aware that the certificate signed by Douglas was only to be used in case the tobacco were stopped by customs or excise officers, because they could prove it had been 'carried from the sea'. They knew that 'a certain gentleman, both concerned in the trade and in the collection at Glasgow', in other words Douglas, had destroyed his record of the certificate, 'thinking the warrant to be sufficient'.[45]

Douglas was removed from his post as surveyor at Glasgow town at the end of 1710 and all the other staff at the collection were transferred to different posts in Scotland. From this point Douglas was referred to on the Isle of Man as 'late collector of Glasgow', thereby promoting him from surveyor to the more senior post.[46]

He was involved in trade not only through his father-in-law, James Corbet, but also with other Glasgow merchants, including Charles Dalrymple and John Peadie junior. It is probable that Douglas knew Hunter before their respective dealings with Dalrymple. As Dalrymple had 'good credit' on the Isle of Man, he agreed with John Murray of Douglas that he would act as security for up to £500 worth of goods to be purchased on the Island by Douglas, and subsequently smuggled into south-west Scotland. Murray probably supplied the tobacco seized by Johnson, which had so infuriated the burghers of Dumfries.

Soon Douglas owed Murray more than £500. He sent several bills to the Island in payment, but all these proved to be worthless. For example, Douglas claimed that A owed him £x and so should pay this sum to Murray. Yet when Murray applied to A for payment, it was discovered that he did not owe Douglas any money. Because of the very nature of the running trade, assets belonging to debtors were often 'in the hands' of merchants in the Isle of Man. These were arrested and once the amount of the debt had been proved they were sold to defray part, if not all, of what was owed. As a result, Murray needed to locate some of Douglas's assets on the Island. Alternatively, he could charge Dalrymple, as Douglas's surety, with £500 of the debt.

Murray sued Dalrymple, who appeared at the Chancery Court on 27 September 1711. The following day Dalrymple attempted to obtain the money from Douglas by charging him with the debt of £500. In Douglas's absence, Dalrymple requested the Court to authorise the arrest of 12 pipes of brandy in Murray's warehouse, because he claimed that some of these belonged to him. The resultant battle between William Park, described as an apothecary or chirurgeon from Beith in Ayrshire and at one stage the only owner of the brandy, and Dalrymple occupied the Chancery Court on eight separate occasions over the next nine months. In November 1711 Park suggested:

> as we that are North Britainers, particularly myself, are said to be by some very troublesome to this Honourable Court, by knavish and cheating pleas among ourselves, I propose a method for evading any such trouble by allowing us to go to Glasgow and be judged there in law.

The Glasgow magistrates would then inform the Island who were the villains so that they might be known as such 'in time hereafter'. The proposal was not accepted.

Twelve Pipes of Brandy
In 1710 Thomas Martin purchased 19 pipes and 11 puncheons of brandy from John Murray. Within days he had sold the brandy to William Park. The parcel was left in Murray's custody, as security against £915, the price of the brandy. On 25 November 1710 William Blackburn, a merchant in Glasgow, confirmed that he had received full payment from Park so that the brandy could be shipped off the Island. Several boatloads were removed, leaving 12 pipes still in Murray's warehouse.

Because Park owed money to Douglas's father-in-law, Corbet claimed an interest in half of the remaining brandy, as security against that debt. If Dalrymple could prove that Douglas was included in Corbet's share then he would be able to gain some redress. On the instructions of the Chancery Court all the brandy was arrested until it could be proved what proportion, if any, was owned by Douglas.

Certainly, John Murray thought that Douglas was involved in the brandy. In January 1711 two Greenock shipmasters, Hugh Crawford and John Wilson, came to the Island with instructions from Park to take some of the brandy to Scotland. Murray called them into his counting house and asked why they had not shown him any instructions from Douglas. Wilson wondered how Murray knew that Douglas was involved in the brandy. Murray replied that he had been 'so informed from Scotland'. Wilson then explained that, although Douglas was partly concerned, as only Park's name was on the purchase order from Martin, it had been supposed that his instructions alone would be sufficient for Murray to deliver the goods.

Wilson set out for Castletown to complete the paperwork at the custom house so that the brandy could be cleared for export. When Crawford refused to go with Wilson, Murray walked with him 'down towards the seaside'. He explained that the only security either he or Dalrymple had against Douglas's debt was this brandy. Crawford promised to swear before the water bailiff, William Ross, that Douglas was indeed one fourth part involved in the cargo. He hired a horse and they went to Castletown together.

There they found Wilson at William Thompson's house. Originally from county Cavan, Thompson and his brother John had moved to the Isle of Man, where they became deeply involved in the running trade. Now William was employed as an attorney for merchants who lived elsewhere whilst his brother had returned to Ireland. As he acted as Dalrymple's attorney, Murray would have expected Thompson to give the shipmasters good advice. Wilson and Crawford went into Thompson's yard, where they had 'some conference', before going with Murray to see Ross. Instead of confirming Douglas's involvement in the brandy, however, they refused to make any statement. Murray was 'left remediless'.

Later Crawford explained their reasons for this refusal to Ross and William Murray, John's cousin and partner in business. Douglas also owed Park's brother-in-law, the Glasgow tobacco merchant Robert Houston, £400. This meant that Park was anxious to reserve Douglas's share of the brandy against that debt.[47]

To this point, everything to do with the case is comparatively straightforward. Everyone, including Park, believed that Corbet had given half of his claim on the brandy to his son-in-law Douglas. Remembering that the whole parcel had cost Park £915, then three pipes were worth approximately £100 and so would have paid off 20% of Douglas's debt to Murray, or a quarter of what was owed to Houston.

In fact, Douglas had no share in the brandy. Yet it was in his interest to help Dalrymple prove that he was involved – and so pay off part of the £500 debt with someone else's goods, even if this involved cheating his father-in-law out of part of his security against Park. At the same time, because of the Houston debt, Park was anxious to prove on the Island that Douglas had nothing to do with the brandy. He objected to Dalrymple's evidence, hoping that he could prove it had no basis.

Dalrymple and Douglas helped Park's case by concocting their evidence somewhat naively. It was in the form of two affidavits taken in Scotland on 13 September 1711. Park described these affidavits as 'scandalous'. The two witnesses were not on the Island to be cross-examined 'nor anyone here knows them'. As it was 'ordinary in law' that both the claimant and the defendant should be present when affidavits were taken, Park and Corbet, should have heard the statements, 'we being all at that time in the same kingdom'. If these affidavits were accepted by the Chancery Court they would form a precedent that 'this age nor any other that hath been since the law was first made among men' had known, although there had been '10,000 [cases] to the contrary'.

The first affidavit was from John Creighton, supposedly a merchant in Glasgow, who claimed that in December 1710 he had been at Irvine with Dalrymple, Douglas and Park, when they used their 'utmost endeavours' to persuade the collector, Patrick Boyle, to give them a coast cocket for 12 pipes of brandy. Their scheme had been to transport the brandy from the Island to Irvine, use this cocket to transfer the cargo to the Clyde and then, using a permit written out by Douglas as the surveyor at Glasgow, carry it overland to the south-west. This sounded so farfetched that the Chancery Court supported Park's request for an opportunity to contact the magistrates in Glasgow, so that they could confirm that Creighton really was a merchant there, and to obtain collector Boyle's oath that he 'never seed' Dalrymple and Park together 'nor none of us ever asked a cocket off him directly or indirectly'.

On 8 December 1711 Alexander Johnston of Whithorn, who was currently on the Island, gave evidence to the Court that he had been present at Baillie John Brown's house in Sanquhar when John Creighton, who lived in that town, admitted Douglas had told him what to say in his affidavit. John Gray of the Cross in Glasgow confirmed on the 14th December that there was no churchman called John Creighton in the city, nor anyone of that name ever stented [the stent was a valuation or assessment of property for taxation] with the 'designation' of tradesman or merchant.

The second affidavit was from James Welch, who had been a landwaiter at Glasgow under Douglas and was now a tidewaiter at Port Patrick. He stated that Douglas was a fourth part concerned in the brandy with his father-in-law and Park but provided no evidence to explain how he had obtained this information. Both the affidavits were rejected.

Figure 12: Gate Slack, near Morton Castle – August 2002

On 22 October 1711 James Laurie of Wigtown attempted to deliver papers calling Douglas to attend the Chancery Court on the Isle of Man. He went to Gate Slack, described as the 'usual residence' of Mrs Douglas. She was not at home and the papers were delivered to Robert's father, Archibald, instead.[48]

Dalrymple had an equally strong case against Park's evidence that Corbet had now signed over all the brandy to him. Hugh Crawford, the shipmaster, had given Murray a letter from Corbet, dated 2 October 1711:

I desire that you may deliver to Mr William Park, or his order, the parcel of brandy, which remains in your hands, he having fully, and completely satisfied me in all that I can demand in the matter. Deliver said brandies without further advice.

Murray was suspicious about this letter, particularly when Crawford refused, yet again, to go to the custom house at Castletown with him. On 14 October he asked Corbet to confirm his order to deliver the brandy. Corbet replied that he had written to Murray, with just such an order, but on the 11th October. When he enquired on the quayside at Greenock if this could have reached the Island before the 14th he was informed that it 'went from this only upon Wednesday last, which was the 17th. This meant that the first letter was a forgery. It is unclear why Park took the risk, unless he was concerned in case some of the brandy, which was in a 'perishing condition', would be sold on the Island, against Douglas's debt.

When Dalrymple made other attempts to discredit him, Park stated, 'I am sorry the gentleman should trouble this Honourable Court and blot paper with such mean and frivolous arguments, being quite extraneous to the matter in hand'.

Both Dalrymple and Park claimed that they were suffering considerable business losses at home, because of their prolonged visits to the Island. The main problem was that all the 'evidence' was in Scotland and as it was the winter season boats were delayed by 'contrary winds and stormy weather' whilst crucial witnesses could not be contacted because the rivers were 'so very dangerous in travelling in North Britain towards Glasgow'. On 6 March 1712 Park reported that the boat sent to Scotland by William Thompson to bring Dalrymple to the Court had returned without him. The arrest on the 12 pipes of brandy was laid aside and the case dismissed.[49]

As Park was on the Island, on 6 March 1712 Murray charged him with a debt of £100, the balance of trading accounts between them. He requested that the brandy, which had just been released, should be re-arrested. The case was dismissed on 12 June 1712, however, when Murray did not appear to continue his prosecution against Park, suggesting that the dispute had been settled between them privately.[50]

William Park, and his son William, continued to trade with the Island. In 1730 George Moore of Peel claimed that the Parks owed him £30. That case was dismissed on 4 March 1731.[51]

Ten hogsheads of tobacco
Other attempts were made to secure the money from Douglas. On 20 February 1712 William Thompson, still acting on behalf of Charles Dalrymple, started a new case in the Chancery Court for the £500. He explained that John Peadie junior had died recently, supposedly with a considerable sum of money in his hands belonging to Douglas – the produce of a parcel of tobacco, which they had owned in partnership.

In 1710 John Warden, master a Greenock vessel, had taken 16 hogsheads of tobacco to Kirkcudbright, where both the boat and her cargo were seized by the customs officers. The case was heard at the Exchequer Court in Edinburgh, where John Wilson and Mathew Brown, acting as agents for Douglas, successfully 'claimed and recovered' everything. Brown was recompensed for his time and trouble with part of the tobacco, which he was allowed to sell for himself. Wilson was to sell the remainder of the tobacco for the partners. As his recompense, Douglas recommended Wilson for a burgess ticket, making him a freeman of Glasgow. Not satisfied with this, Wilson kept the money that he had received from a Mr Colquhoun in Glasgow, who had purchased the tobacco. Douglas charged Wilson with theft and he was imprisoned until he had returned all the money.

The Manx Court needed to prove that Wilson had paid this money to Peadie, not Douglas, so that it could be claimed from his executors. It is unclear whether this is the same John Wilson as the shipmaster referred to above.[52]

Peadie had been in partnership also with other Scottish merchants in a parcel of brandy. His share, 355 gallons, was now on board the *Rose* of Douglas, about to sail from the Island. This was arrested, and the *Rose*'s departure postponed, until the situation could be clarified. Dalrymple was instructed to put thirteen questions to John Peadie's brother James and John Tod, both merchants in Glasgow, in front of the Provost or some other Justice of the Peace there. Their responses were never received, the case was dismissed and the brandy on board the *Rose* was released from arrest.[53] There is no further mention of Robert Douglas on the Island.

Postscript

From 11 o'clock in the morning to 11 o'clock at night on 10 January 1711, Robert Stewart, a riding officer based at Dumfries, watched a small Manx boat hovering off the coast to the west of the Nith estuary. At last, she came into the 'very creek' where he was hidden, which was about half a mile from Arbigland house. The crew waited until the tide was out, when they started to unload the cargo. Stewart did not recognise any of the men but he saw Jacob Turner, 'a Quaker who formerly used to practice the running trade'.

Emerging from his hiding place, Stewart went on board the wherry and in the Queen's name seized the boat and her remaining cargo of 12 ankers (casks) holding about 10 gallons each. The smugglers disappeared, leaving him alone with the boat until about 4 o'clock in the morning. Then they returned with three horses and two of the servants working for the Laird of Arbigland, Adam Craik. Two of the boatmen 'laid violent hands' on Stewart and held him until the other three had unloaded the cargo.

Next day, with assistance from other customs officers, Stewart searched Arbigland house and found two ankers of spirits. The collector, John McDowell, wrote to the Board, 'we are heartily sorry that the gentlemen of the country give so much encouragement to these rogues, for if they had not their countenance they would not dare such insults. They [the gentlemen] are so far from discovering these practices that it's said this cargo did properly belong to them and that no merchant was concerned therein', apart from Jacob Turner, of course.[54]

There is further information about Adam Craik in the section on John Aglionby and about his son William in the section on the 'Forty-five and Appendix IV.

JOHN MURRAY'S VISIT TO THE ISLAND IN DECEMBER 1713

I am branded for a papist and traitor up and down this Isle on purpose to give the government an ill impression of me, though I thank God at the same time I was baptised into the Episcopal faith and communion of the church of Scotland and in which, by God's grace, I hope to live and die and never be guilty of treason or disloyalty against Her Majesty and the Royal Family, which shall be sacred to me in the worst of times and greatest of persecution. [John Murray of Dumfries to the House of Keys, 8 January 1714][55]

James II died at St Germains in September 1701, leaving a daughter, Anne, by his Protestant wife, Anne Hyde and two children, James Francis Edward and Louisa Maria Theresa, by his Catholic wife, Mary of Modena. Queen Mary had died in 1694 and in 1702 William of Orange's horse stumbled over a molehill, throwing him to his death. Anne was proclaimed Queen.

Although James Stuart was only 14 years old when his father died, both France and Spain proclaimed him King James III of England and VIII of Scotland. Convinced that there would be enormous support for him as King of the Scots, in 1708 Louis XIV of France funded an expedition of 6,000 French troops in 30 vessels to invade the country. They sailed from Dunkirk, headed for Burntisland on the Firth of Forth. Not only was the unfortunate James recovering from measles but he also suffered from seasickness. When the French arrived in the Forth, they were prevented from landing because of bad weather, and the unexpected arrival of a large fleet of English ships under Admiral Byng. In order to escape, the French ships scattered and returned to Dunkirk by way of the north of Scotland. The proposed invasion had been a disaster.

In 1700 the Austrian Charles II of Spain nominated Philip V, Duke of Anjou, as his successor. France's challenge to this appointment resulted in the War of Succession (1702-1713). James Stuart fought with the French, gaining a reputation for bravery. The war ended with the Treaty of Utrecht – Philip V remained on the Spanish throne and Louis XIV agreed to expel James from France. He went to Bar-le-Duc in Lorraine.

John Murray was a major merchant in Douglas during the late seventeenth and early eighteenth centuries. He had several cousins, who were also merchants and provided an effective family network. This involved England, Scotland and Ireland, with the Isle of Man as the central supply base for the running trade. His cousin, John Murray of Dumfries,[i] imported tobacco from Virginia, which was then exported, landed on the Island and finally relanded in Scotland.

In December 1713 John Murray of Dumfries visited the Isle of Man, essentially on business. This visit brought the Island into somewhat dramatic contact with the hunt for the murderer of the 4th Duke of Hamilton, who might have become one of the main leaders of the Scottish national party, and with the problem of defining the appropriate punishment for someone drinking a disaffected health.

James Black was a tobacco merchant from Alison Bank in Annandale. On 29 December 1709 the *Patience* of Whitehaven, William Smith master, arrived at Dumfries from Virginia. Black entered his cargo of tobacco, paid the customs charges and gave sureties that he would pay the duties within nine months. In October 1710 this tobacco was exported on the *Kirkconnell* of Dumfries for Londonderry and the *Intention* of Whitehaven for the Isle of Man. John Murray of Douglas agreed to keep 40 hogsheads of the tobacco in his warehouse until Black's customers arranged for its transport back to Scotland.[56]

---

[i] He is also known as John Murray of Barnhorrey (or Barnhourie), the name of his estate to the west of Dumfries on the coastal road to Kirkcudbright.

On 16 November 1711 Black went to the Dumfries custom house to pay his outstanding duties, with interest. As the collector, reported to the Board of Customs in Edinburgh, 'we had got the bonds written out and ready to sign but suddenly he was seized by a high fever and carried off in four days' time, without ever being capable to do any business'.[57]

Inevitably, Black's trading accounts were also in 'disarray'. There was some tobacco belonging to him still in John Murray's warehouse on the Island. His widow, Barbara, did not want a 'half pennyworth' of this but hoped that it could be used to discharge 'such debts as appear legally due'. To her great distress, several Dumfries merchants laid claim to the tobacco. They included William Rowe, Joseph Pearce and John Shepherd, who all stated that they had been in partnership with Black in the 40 hogsheads, and John Murray of Hydwood, who claimed that he had paid for eight hogsheads of the tobacco and simply awaited their delivery. John Murray of Dumfries could prove that Black had owed him £100 'due debt'. As he was the principal creditor, the widow appointed him as her attorney to go to the Island and ensure that no 'ill-disposed persons' took any advantage of her husband's effects in case any 'unworthiness' should be attached to his memory.

According to Manx laws, transmarines were allowed three years to enter their claims against an estate. In the meantime, two people resident on the Island had to ensure that none of the goods was embezzled or, if anything were sold, that the money would be available to the creditors. Barbara Black appointed the Wattleworths of Ramsey as her sureties.[58]

In December 1713 Murray of Dumfries went to the Island and borrowed from the Wattleworths several papers relating to the administration of Black's affairs, in an attempt to sort out the situation. They claimed that he refused to return the papers and threatened to 'carry off' all Black's effects. As this would leave them liable not only to be fined by the Consistory Court but also charged by any future claimants for what was owed to them, they took Murray to the Chancery Court on the 17th December 1713.[59]

The Murder of the Duke of Hamilton
James Douglas (1658-1712), 4th Duke of Hamilton, was described by Jonathan Swift as 'a worthy, good-natured person. Very generous, but of a middling understanding'.[60] His second wife, whom he married in 1698, was Elizabeth, daughter of Digby, Lord Gerard, and sole heiress to extensive lands in Staffordshire and Lancashire. Although in theory Hamilton was an ardent Jacobite, strongly opposed to the Act of Union between England and Scotland in 1707, he was accused of being too concerned about the safety of these estates to make use of this opportunity to unite his country against the English.

By his second marriage, Hamilton had five children, the third son named Anne, after his godmother, the Queen. He also had a natural son, Charles, who became a Colonel in the army. Lady Hamilton's uncle, Lord Macclesfield, had died childless, leaving all his estate to his other niece, wife of Charles, Lord Mohun. Hamilton disputed this will in the Chancery Court at London and the case continued for eleven years.

Whitworth, a former steward to the Macclesfield family, was giving evidence on 13 November 1712, when he contradicted himself. Hamilton exclaimed, 'there is no truth or justice in him', to which Mohun responded, 'I know Mr Whitworth. He is an honest man, and has as much truth as your Grace'. That evening General McCartney claimed that Hamilton had insulted Mohun's honour and offered to act as the Lord's second in a duel. Mohun, who had fought several duels in the past, and had stood trial for murder on two occasions, was unwilling to fight again. Encouraged by Colonel John Churchill and somewhat overcome by the large amount of claret, which he had consumed, Mohun was finally convinced that his honour had been slighted and that he should fight Hamilton. The next morning McCartney took Mohun's challenge to the Duke. Charles agreed to act as his father's second. The two men met at dawn on 15 November 1712 to fight with small swords, some sources claim at a pond in Kensington Gardens and others in Hyde Park (see below). The seconds fought at the same time and

Charles Hamilton succeeded in disarming McCartney. The Duke killed Mohun but, as he had been badly wounded, he lay on the ground. Charles ran to help his father but McCartney attacked the Duke, presumably with Mohun's sword, and killed him. On 12 December 1712 Colonel Charles Hamilton was called before the Privy Council for taking part in the duel but acquitted of any charges.[61]

Figure 13: 'My Lord Mohun was standing over him'.

Before this comes to your hands, you will have heard of the most terrible accident hath almost ever happened. This morning at 8, my man brought me word that the Duke of Hamilton had fought with Lord Mohun, and killed him, and was brought home wounded ... In short they fought at 7 this morning. The dog Mohun was killed on the spot; and, while the Duke was over him, McCartney, shortening his sword, stabbed him in at the shoulder to the heart. The Duke was helped toward the cake-house by the ring in Hyde Park, (where they fought) and died on the grass, before he could reach the house; and was brought home in his coach by 8, while the poor Duchess was asleep. McCartney, and one Hamilton, were the seconds, who fought likewise, and are both fled. I am told, that a footman of Lord Mohun's stabbed [the] Duke of Hamilton, and some say McCartney did so too. [Jonathan Swift, *Journal to Stella*, 15 November 1712][62]

Swift wrote to Stella on 16 November, 'I design to make the ministry put out a proclamation (if it can be found proper) against the villain McCartney'. The Tory government, convinced that the Duke's murder was part of a Whig plot, offered a reward of £500 for McCartney's capture. In December 1712 a gentleman, who had been waylaid by highwaymen, claimed that he was McCartney. They took him to a Justice of the Peace, 'in hopes of the reward, and the rogues were sent to gaol'. In fact McCartney was already in Ireland and by January 1713 he had reached Holland. Swift commented, ''tis hard such a dog should escape'.[63]

A short time before John Murray of Dumfries went to the Isle of Man in December 1713, McCartney was described to him as:

a middling size man with a red face, high nose and a set of good teeth, a little vacoule between them

Murray saw a man fitting this description at Mrs Thompson's house in Castletown. The man was going by the name of John Sabbarton. Before he could report his suspicions, Murray became involved in a drinking orgy, possibly celebrating in anticipation of receiving the £500 reward. As he was now in prison at Castle Rushen, Murray asked Dennis O'Bryan, described as 'of North Britain', to deliver a paper to the deputy governors, requesting that Sabbarton should be arrested and transferred to Kirkcudbright or Whitehaven, from where he could be delivered to the government in London. Murray encouraged O'Bryan to do this by stating several times that he could swear Sabbarton was McCartney. Not only did he fit the description currently circulated but also Murray had seen the man himself in Edinburgh about 12 years previously. He promised O'Bryan that, 'as soon as his own troubles were over', he would help him with the prosecution and pay half of all the expenses.

As O'Bryan was 'something doubtful' about this accusation, he went to see Sabbarton. They met in Mrs Thompson's little parlour, in the presence of both John Murray of Douglas and John Aglionby. O'Bryan said that if Sabbarton could prove, by a letter or some other means, that he was not McCartney, then he would not 'put him to any further trouble'. Sabbarton did not give O'Bryan a satisfactory answer, 'being very stiff on the matter'.

On 26 January 1714, based on Murray's certainty that he had identified McCartney, 'as also for the regard and honour that he had for the noble house of Hamilton', O'Bryan delivered the paper to the Island's deputy governors, John Rowe and William Seddon.

Lady Hamilton, learning that 'by good providence' McCartney was arrested on the Isle of Man, commissioned Lieutenant James Hamilton and Ensign Alexander Cleland to go there with 'such servants or other persons, as you shall think fit to employ', to confirm his identity. They took with them John Adams and George Miller, who had been sergeants in Queen Anne's 3rd regiment of foot guards for nine years. During this time, McCartney was first Captain, afterwards Major and then Lieutenant Colonel of regiment. Adams and Miller 'very well know his person and have frequently seen him since he left that regiment'. They stated that the man held on the Island was definitely not McCartney.

When William Wybrants was in London about 25 years before, he had known Captain George McCartney, often drinking in his company. Since then he had been informed of McCartney's promotion to the rank of General. He could confirm that this man was 'nothing like him'.

Other evidence was produced suggesting that John Sabbarton was probably not McCartney because he had made no attempt to hide himself. William Douglas and Samuel Cowle had been on board John Wilson's wherry with Sabbarton on a voyage from Dublin to the Island. The wherry had put into Killough because of contrary winds and remained there for 17 days. During this time, Sabbarton stayed sometimes in Killough, sometimes at Downpatrick and sometimes at Lisburn and 'always appeared in public', which he would not have done had he been attempting to disguise his identity.

A letter from Sabbarton's son, Benjamin, who was at school in Cheshire, provided further evidence that his father was not in hiding:

> *In obedience to your command in a letter to my master, I humbly offer these lines to your hands, which being the good news of my health and well liking of Budworth, particularly the school; and am easy and well satisfied to continue at Mr Poole's, where I now board, and beg not to be removed from my master till I am fitted for an apprentice. When we break up school for Christmas, I am to say a Latin Oration publicly in the presence of many auditors. Had you been then in Cheshire your company would have been very pleasing to me and acceptable to my master. Pray excuse my boldness in taking this opportunity of presenting you with the duty of, Sir, your most obedient son, Benjamin Sabbarton.*

At last Sabbarton was given an opportunity to prove his own identity. He produced a certificate stating that he was born in Hertfordshire and had spent several years in the navy - as secretary to Admiral Nevill in Carthagena and Virginia and as purser of the *Ruby* man-of-war.

In 1693 or 1694, Captain William Cross had seen Sabbarton on board Nevill's ship but did not know what post he had held. Since Sabbarton's arrival on the Island, the two men had spoken together frequently and Cross could confirm that Sabbarton had been on board warships, 'he giving an account of several remarkable passages that happened in the navy since that time, which he could not have done had he not actually seen the same'.[64]

On 28 January 1714 Rowe and Seddon reported what had happened to the Lord Chancellor, Robert Harley, Earl of Oxford (see the Introduction and the section on Nicholas Harley). They concluded, 'it appears to us that O'Bryan's information is groundless and we do not see any reason to take any further cognisance of the matter'.[65]

A month later O'Bryan was summoned before the court to explain his attempt to obtain money from Sabbarton, if he promised not to prosecute him. O'Bryan declared upon oath, 'as he shall answer before God, that he never spoke such words to him'. His denial was accepted.[66]

Postscript
In 1716 George McCartney returned to England where he gave himself up and was convicted of manslaughter.

The chief witness against him was Colonel Charles Hamilton. Because his evidence was not consistent with that previously given before the Privy Council, Hamilton was 'obliged to sell out of the Guards and quit the country to avoid a charge of perjury'.[67]

The First Disaffected Health
A disaffected health was a toast proposed not to the current monarch of Great Britain but to the Pretender, or one of his associates. As this was a treasonable offence, in England it carried the death penalty. Because this type of sedition was unknown on the Isle of Man, there was no law to deal with treason. As a result, the House of Keys were somewhat limited in the punishment they could recommend.

During the evening of Thursday, 10 December 1713 John Murray of Dumfries, Nehemiah Kemp, tobacco agent on the Island for Sir Thomas Johnstone of Liverpool, Robert Maddrell of Castletown, steward of the garrison, Captain John Wood of the Nunnery and Richard Brew, a soldier, were drinking a 'hearty glass' of punch in James Read's house at Douglas. Everything seemed peaceable and friendly. They all drank to the Queen, the church and the government of the Isle of Man. Murray, Wood and Brew continued drinking whilst Maddrell spent the night at Philip Moore's house and Kemp went to his own lodgings in the town.

The next morning Wood and Murray sent Brew, who claimed that he had not taken his clothes off all night, in search of the others so that they could continue drinking together. Maddrell realised that Brew was still 'concerned in liquor' and so 'went about his business', only going to Read's house about 10 o'clock. Here he found Wood and Murray so 'excessive drunk' that each was incapable of understanding what the other was talking about. He left the house without taking a drink. Kemp had been at the house an hour earlier but, as Wood and Murray were both 'ill drunk', he left and did not see them again that day.

Between four and five o'clock on the Friday afternoon Wood, Murray and Brew went to see Thomas Christian. Murray was 'concerned in liquor to a vast degree' so that two or three men had to support him as he walked along the street and another two carried the punchbowl behind him.

During that Friday evening, Murray accused John Christian, Thomas's son, of 'drinking confusion and damnation to the Prince of Wales', which was a name often given to the Pretender, as son of King James II. Christian replied, 'he would not drink damnation or confusion to any person. But if he did it was the effect of liquor and he did not remember it'.

As Brew was a soldier, he wore the Queen's uniform and 'ate her bread'. Taking exception to Murray's comments about the Pretender he asked, 'what is Queen Anne?' Murray replied, 'he (the Pretender) is the lawful son of King James and if he had his right he ought to have the crown of Great Britain'.

Figure 14: Queen Anne (1702-1714)

At this point Murray spat in Brew's face and, picking up a whip that was lying on the table, tried to strike him with it. Brew, taking the whip from Murray, hit him on the forehead with the butt. Wood intervened. 'What a noise you make!' he declared. 'What is he but an impostor? Let him alone'. Brew and Murray sat down.

Soon afterwards, however, they started to argue again, Murray still claiming that the Pretender was his King and Prince and, 'if he had justice done to him, he would be heir to the crown'. Brew said, 'the

Prince of Wales was a bricklayer's son and a bastard and was brought in in a warming pan'.[i] This time Murray spat in Brew's face twice and Brew slapped Murray across the face. They both stood up, young Christian helping Murray to his feet. Refusing to fight with a man who was not wearing a sword, Brew challenged Murray to meet him on Douglas Green by 10 o'clock the following morning, so that he could vindicate his Queen and country. If Murray failed to appear then Brew would have him declared publicly as a coward.

Dennis O'Bryan, having found Murray at Christian's house, went out into the street, calling for a barrow so that he could be carried to his lodgings – at John Aglionby's house. There he was helped into the room by two or three men and threw himself down on a pallet, complaining that his forehead was sore, but 'not knowing what had happened to him'.

The following day, instead of meeting Brew at Douglas Green, Murray was back at Thomas Christian's house with him and Wood and Maddrell. They drank the Queen's health together and seemed to be good friends. Maddrell asked Wood and Murray if there had been some trouble the previous night – they declared that they could not remember anything.

Brew did not report the incident to the deputy governors until 23 December, twelve days after the event. There is no information about why he kept silent for so long, or why he suddenly decided to make a complaint against Murray.

Murray described the subsequent events in his petition to the House of Keys. In late December, he was told that there was an order for his arrest because of the words he had spoken against the Queen. Shocked at this development, Murray asked his cousin, John Murray of Douglas, and John Wood, to find out from the deputy governors, if this were true.

When it was confirmed, Wood attempted to defuse the situation, explaining to Rowe and Seddon that Murray's words were merely the effects of 'excessive drinking'. Murray added that he had taken the oath of allegiance to Queen Anne on 17 October 1713, at the election of a Member of Parliament for the Stewartry of Kirkcudbright, and he was willing to take the oath again, if they would administer it to him. Finally, 'I begged no further procedure might pass upon such a foolish drunken story lest it should prejudice my credit as a trading merchant, the greatest support of my livelihood'.

The deputy governors would have imprisoned Murray on the spot but Wood and William Ross agreed to be bound 'body for body and goods for goods' that he would appear at Castletown on 23 December. When he reported to the castle with his bail, they discovered that the deputy governors were 'seated in judgement'. Murray claimed that nothing should happen, 'without knowing my crime, my informer and by what law I am to be judged'. Despite this, evidence was taken from both Brew and John Christian. Murray was obliged to renew his bail for another week. When Murray appeared before the deputy governors and Bishop Wilson on 30 December 1713, he was informed that the House of Keys would be meeting 'upon me' on 8 January 1714.[68]

The deputy governors explained to the Keys they had received information that Murray had referred to the Pretender as his King and Prince. They continued:

> *these words, gentlemen, seem to tend to sedition and the alienating of the affections of the people*
> *from Her Majesty, Queen Anne. As the Lords of this Isle have always distinguished themselves by*
> *their loyalty and fidelity to the crown of England, and the people of this Isle in like manner, so it*

---

[i] The warming pan story is described in detail by Hibbert Ware in *Lancashire during the Rebellion of 1715*. According to him, it was claimed by the Whigs that as a baby the Pretender had been 'clandestinely enclosed in a warming pan; that he had been thus introduced into the bed of the Queen Mother [Mary of Modena] during her pretended accouchement, with the view of being palmed upon the nation as a legitimate heir to the throne of England'. This story is referred to by Charles Sinclair in *A Wee Guide to the Jacobites* as a 'somewhat far-fetched and oft-used claim'. The warming pan story was clearly circulating on the Isle of Man by 1713.

behoves us to preserve that character and discountenance and discourage anything that may seem to bring any reflection upon us.

They asked the House of Keys to consider the evidence and proceed, 'according to your duty and the laws of this Island'. The Keys acknowledged that nobody had been accused of behaving in this way on the Isle of Man before. They agreed to join with the officers 'in discountenancing and punishing such offenders, according to their deserts, which, with humble submission, we take to be the usual and accustomed way of procceding in all new cases within this Island'. Twenty-two members of the House signed this statement.

The following day the Keys considered the evidence put forward by John Wood, Thomas and John Christian, Richard Brew, Henry Moore (who had heard O'Bryan calling for a barrow to carry Murray to his lodgings), Nehemiah Kemp, Robert Maddrell and Murray himself.

Murray put forward nine points in his defence, emphasising the fact that they were all drunk and highlighting flaws and inconsistencies in the evidence put forward by Brew and John Christian. Wood confirmed that Murray, in particular, was 'concerned in liquor to a vast degree' and Thomas Christian stated he was 'in the worst condition of the three'. Murray concluded by describing, 'the great trouble and concern I labour under' on the Island 'as my honour, loyalty, reputation and interest' were at stake.

Four days later, 'having deliberately perused the evidences', the Keys found that Murray's words did not amount to treason. They reiterated Maddrell's evidence that the following day Murray had shown himself to be 'a good subject by drinking very freely a health to the Queen, church and government of this Isle'. In addition Murray was known to most of the Keys and had previously behaved himself 'orderly and loyally at all times'. They concluded that Murray's words were not spoken 'either advisedly or maliciously but merely the effects of extreme drunkenness'. He was acquitted, provided he gave security for his good behaviour whilst he remained on the Island.[69]

Postscript
John Murray of Dumfries held Barnhourie from 22 March 1705 to 8 April 1721, when it passed to John Somerville. He was in partnership with John Cannon and Robert Gordon of Dumfries. In October 1711 both John Wattleworth junior of Ramsey and John Dickenson of Lancaster charged the partners with debt, claiming that they had some tobacco lodged with John Murray of Douglas.

On 4 February 1714 the Chancery Court dismissed the case between the Wattleworths and John Murray of Dumfries over James Black's effects, the parties having agreed.[70]

In 1724 the Board of Customs at Edinburgh instructed the collector and comptroller at Dumfries to explain why the paperwork relating to James Black's tobacco imported on the *Patience* in 1709 was still incomplete. They replied that it was not 'in our power to inform your Honours whether or not there hath been any fraud committed in the exportation of it'. Another enquiry from the Board the following year produced a similar response – the paperwork simply did not exist. William Johnson had been collector at that date.[71]

THE GOVERNOR AND THE HOUSE OF KEYS

Whether you did not think the times dangerous or what other consideration moved you is best known to yourselves. [Governor Horne to the House of Keys, 20 October 1715][72]

The governor was the Lord of Man's representative on the Island, responsible for ensuring that everything ran as smoothly as possible – that the Lord's interests were protected and yet at the same time the Islanders were happy.

There had been several problems on the Isle of Man during the seventeenth century. These had been exacerbated by the fact that the 7th Earl of Derby and his family had sheltered there during the Civil War. Only 60 years had passed and memories were long. This meant that both the Lord and the governor had to act with caution.[73]

The 24 Keys represented the Manx people. Although Governor Horne was on the Island from 1714 to 1723, he failed completely to elicit co-operation from the Keys, intensifying rather than defusing the situation between them. This meant that two issues of particular significance: a law against treason and arming the Island in case of a Jacobite invasion, became major issues.

The exchange of words between John Murray of Dumfries and John Christian marked the beginning of a new period in Manx history. The date was crucial. Governor Mawdsley had left the Island before Murray arrived in December 1713. In August and October of that year several boxes and casks and loose parcels of household goods, wearing apparel, linen and woollen bed clothes and one feather bed 'for private use' all belonging to him had been shipped on board the *Henrietta*, David Christian master and the *Rose* of Castletown, John Kewish master for England.[74] The new governor had not arrived and in his absence John Rowe, the comptroller and William Seddon, the water bailiff heard the evidence that had been put forward by Brew and others against Murray. This was then presented to the House of Keys for their consideration.

Both Rowe and Seddon provide the continuity because they collected the evidence for all the cases of disaffection that were heard on the Island between 1713 and 1720. When Seddon became a member of the House of Keys in 1708, his oath included these words:

> *Your allegiance to the King's Majesty of England reserved, you shall true faith and fidelity bear to the Right Honourable William, Earl of Derby, and his heirs during your life ... You shall use your best endeavours to maintain the laws and customs of this Isle. You shall justly and truly deliver your opinion and do right in all matters, which shall be put unto you, without favour or affection, affinity or consanguinity, love or fear, reward or gain or for any hope thereof but in all things you shall deal uprightly and justly and using no men.*[75]

Yet the House did not react to the threat of disaffection as Horne, Rowe and Seddon would have expected. Instead of instantly producing a new law to deal with acts of treason, they prevaricated. There were various reasons for this. Horne was incapable of managing people in general and the House of Keys in particular. He attempted to brow-beat them and when this failed he imprisoned them.[76] This was not the background against which he could expect their co-operation.

When Horne addressed the Keys on 5 July 1716, there had been other examples of 'speaking disrespectfully of the King's Majesty and present government of Great Britain and in favour of the Pretender'. These would have included Henry Butler, who is discussed in the next section. Horne had hoped that the 'strict examination and prosecution' carried out against these individuals would have 'discouraged and put a stop to such behaviour here for the future'. There were hints of continued disaffection, however.

Whether the favourable judgement you gave in that case or the defect of our laws be the occasion of people's liberty of speech, I find there is a necessity to make some further laws to punish offenders of this kind, to stop the growth of an evil that has lately been introduced into this Island and which it seems there was no necessity to provide against by stricter laws formerly.

Horne had informed the Earl of Derby about the problem and had received 'positive and particular orders to take the strictest course to punish and discourage offences of this nature'. He told the Keys:

Since you have said that our laws are defective in such cases, I know no better way at present to answer his Lordship's orders than by making more strict laws for the punishment of such crimes and offences for the time to come. For which reason I have now called you together, that we may all join in making such a law [as] will effectively suppress such offences.

The Keys agreed to think about the problem. In the meantime, they continued to hear cases against individuals who had been accused of disaffection. In February 1720 the accusation of disaffection was against a Manxman, Nicholas Christian. Horne exhorted the Keys to take real action on this occasion:

You cannot but be sensible how that nothing has been wanting in the governing part of this Isle to put a stop to offences of this nature and to preserve our character as a loyal and well-affected people to the crown and government of Great Britain. I doubt not but that you will so weigh and consider the case now before you and take such measures as may be effectual to prevent all such crimes and misdemeanours for the future, which may lay us obnoxious to a kingdom which is our chief support and protection.[77]

This time the Keys apparently had a genuine excuse:

We having no law to direct us in punishing crimes of this nature and the law for that end and purpose lately by us unanimously proposed and agreed to not being yet confirmed and published, we cannot inflict any punishment for the same.

When Thomas Christian of Marown was accused of disaffection in 1746, Governor Lindesay wrote to the Duke of Atholl, 'we have no laws for punishing treason against the king'.[78] This was repeated by Thomas Foley, a spy sent to the Island by the collector of Whitehaven during the same year, 'they have no law in that Island to punish such offenders'. In fact, no law against treason ever reached the Manx Statute books.[79]

Arming the Isle of Man
During 1715, Governor Horne was becoming more and more alarmed by the news reaching the Island about the unrest in England and Scotland. His first concern was in case refugees from the troubles swamped the Isle of Man. On 18 August 1715 he addressed the House of Keys at St John's Chapel, where he asked them to consider, 'if it be not necessary that we should at this time appear in a condition to defend ourselves from resolute, though unarmed men'.

He had inspected the garrisons on the Island and concluded 'I must say I yet never saw anything that bore that name so slenderly provided for with arms'. He had discovered that these arms were dispersed 'throughout the country' and when called in they were found to be 'in a condition that I am sorry to mention'.

His main concern was that the government of the Island would be blamed if the people suffered 'either in their persons or goods, for want of such arms and ammunition as is necessary'. As a result, he hoped that the Keys would consider with him 'proper means for raising money to supply these defects'.

They replied there was no necessity for raising money on the Island for arms. Horne wrote to the Earl of Derby, who was 'not a little surprised that a matter so plain and so often practised before should meet with any scruple'. He suggested that this was because of 'a want of due examination'.[80]

Figure 15: James Stanley, 7th Earl of Derby and Charlotte de la Tremoüille, His Countess

Horne addressed the Keys again on 20 October 1715. He suggested that, even if 'our allegiance to the crown of England and our duty to our Honourable Lord and master be not as good arguments', then surely the 'times are too parlous to use delays'. The Keys should provide for 'the preservation of our persons and goods'. He wanted their resolution about what to do 'with such expedition as the circumstances of the matter requires that I may discharge my duty in putting the Island in a necessary posture of defence or give his Lordship the reason why it is not'. The Keys asked for more time, until 23rd November, to consider what action was necessary, 'as it is like to be a precedent for the future'.[81]

As promised, the Keys presented their response to Governor Horne on 23 November 1715. They explained that, as the Island had been frequently 'variously and falsely alarmed with insurrections and dissents in Scotland of late years' it had been reasonable for them to think in August 'we might not be in so great danger as you then supposed'. They would have been more alarmed now, however, had it not been for the 'entire victory it has pleased God to give His Majesty's forces last week at Preston' and the fact that in the meantime the governor had 'replenished' the garrisons, presumably at the Lord's expense.

As the present Earl, 'God be praised', was not in such dire circumstances as the 7th Earl had been, they hoped he would help the Island to supply their own needs. The Earl's father and his brother had always provided them with ammunition, furnished and repaired the arms and paid the salaries of two armourers, which could be proved from the annual accounts submitted to the Lord. These accounts would also show that the Earl's increased income from customs duties, as a result of the major expansion in trade, more than compensated for the military and civil salaries and the cost of ammunition, which were subtracted from his rents and fines. As a result, he received 'very much more' each year than 'ever his illustrious ancestors had'. This should give him 'a great deal more reason' to provide the Island with arms and ammunition, to defend his own wealth.

They concluded, 'we have much more to offer in this matter, which would be tedious for his Lordship to read'. As the governor had told them that the Earl would be on the Island, 'as soon as conveniently might be' then they were prepared to wait so that they could lay all their papers before him and discuss the situation face to face.[82]

In marked contrast, also on 23 November 1715, the Bishop, Vicars General and the clergy assembled in convocation at Castle Rushen to consider the governor's 'call to arms'. Having considered their 'paper evidence' of precedents, they assured the governor that 'we shall cheerfully contribute towards the general defence of the country by giving such assistance for that service as ... shall bear a proportion with the rest of the inhabitants of this Isle'.[83] Despite this apparent co-operation, in 1722 Governor Horne claimed he had delivered prayers composed 'in the time of the Rebellion' to Bishop Wilson for use in all the churches and chapels on the Island. Although the Bishop had promised that these prayers would be said, the governor 'did not find they ever were'.[84]

At some stage in the early 1720s, Horne wrote notes on twenty-one members of the House of Keys. He divided them into two categories, the Tories who supported the Bishop and the Whigs who supported the Lord of Man, and his authority on the Island. The accusations against those 'in the Bishop's interest' included:

1. They were 'priest-ridden' and bigoted. This does not suggest that they were Catholic, unlike several of the English Tories, but that they believed the Bishop's power on the Island was superior to that of the Lord. This meant that anything Bishop Wilson proposed they would follow. He had the power to decide whether they used the prayers instructed by the King and to ban *The Independent Whig* from the Island's library.

2. Because the Bishop needed funds to help in his case against the Earl of Derby over Mary Hendrick's excommunication, several members of the Keys 'contributed'.

3. The governor believed that there was a high level of moral corruption within the Manx church. Provided someone did penance for any 'sin', they were easily forgiven. This explains his comments about being censured.

4. Possibly the most serious accusation related to William Murray. He had been sworn into office by John Sanforth, the collector of customs for the farmers Poole & McGwire despite the fact that he had been fined as a common juror for an illegal verdict in favour of parson Halsall. He was now 'screened without any acquittance from that imputation'.

The governor's detailed comments about each individual are listed on the next page.[85] A table of those present at six of the disaffection cases has been included. There are further comments about these cases in the Brief Review section.

Postscript

John Rowe and William Seddon appeared to act together, presenting a united front against those accused of disaffection to the English crown.

Between 1717 and 1722 they were joint comptrollers of the revenue on the Island and responsible for submitting accurate accounts to the Earl of Derby. On 6 August 1722 they stated a final account, which was audited the following day by Governor Horne. Seddon delivered up the keys of the Treasury and left the Island on his private business, 'without molestation'.

In his absence, Rowe, 'out of prejudices or other indirect motives' informed the Earl of Derby that Seddon had gone off without settling his accounts and 'considerably in arrears to the Lord'.

There were two problems. Bags containing £112 worth of money had been stolen out of Seddon's office 'in his Lordship's garrison of Castle Rushen (the proper place appointed for the comptroller to receive such money)'. The auditors had accepted that this robbery had taken place and adjusted the accounts accordingly.

Seddon and Rowe had sent to England the balance of what was due in 39 bags. They had not counted the contents of these bags but when they arrived with the Earl of Derby at Knowsley, they proved to be £66 short. Rowe claimed that this discrepancy was because Seddon had failed to bag all the money he had received. Responsibility for this debt was passed to him, as the only comptroller,

The Earl asked Richard McGwire, one of the farmers of customs on the Island, to prosecute Seddon for arrears of £500. The case started in the Chancery Court on 22 July 1723 and on 26 October 1724 Seddon was charged with a deficit of £406 – considerably more than the £178 discrepancy noted above. This was reversed on appeal from Seddon and on 31 December 1726 it was agreed that the audit taken on 7 August 1722 should stand.

When Rowe died in 1725 his son-in-law, William Mercer, was the sole executor. The case against Rowe re-opened in the 1730s and Mercer had to mortgage Rowe's estate to pay the 'great deficiency of cash in the Treasury'. In 1740 he wanted a recompense of £150 from Seddon, who rehearsed all the old arguments and refused to pay. Seddon died on 4 June 1758, aged 81 years.[86]

The 'honest' minority, for Lord and country – the Whigs

John Fargher	listed without comment
John Harrison	listed without comment
Daniel Lace	parish clerk of Kirk Andreas, turned some time ago from the majority. Yet was prevailed upon to sign a certificate in favour of the Bishop against the Lord's interest in the London business (the Mary Hendrick's appeal), of which he is said to have repented.
John Oates senior	over 70 years old, never appears in the House since the majority prevailed.
John Wattleworth senior	captain of Ramsey fort.

The majority, in the Bishop's interest against the Lord - Tories

James Banckes	has oftener than once been censured by the Spiritual Court and made penance. One of the contributors.
James Christian	the Earl's forester on the Island, yet a zealous bigot in the Bishop's interest, whereby some of his [word missing] have been screened from censure and penance. Said to be a contributor.
John Christian	parish clerk of Kirk Maughold, priest-ridden.
John Christian Junior	a hot headed, priest-ridden bigot ... tool to him [the Bishop] ... censured and made penance oftener than once. Attorney in the Bishop's cause. By reason of his poverty and idleness could not afford a contribution.
William Christian	much in years
Edmund Corlett	parish clerk of Kirk Christ Lezayre, censured and made penance. Said to be a contributor.
Thomas Corlett	the general sumner of the Bishop's court. Bigoted in that interest ... said to be an evidence finder wherever a Whig is to be crushed. An eminent tithe gatherer.
John Curghey	priest-ridden and foolishly bigoted ... a contributor.
Robert Curghey	one of the Bishop's proctors or tithe gatherers. Reported to have contributed.
John Garret	censured and made penance oftener than once.
Philip Moore	a Douglas merchant, priest-ridden and credibly said to be a contributor.
John Murray	the great Douglas merchant, priest-ridden. Reported to have contributed £50.
William Murray	censured and made penance oftener than once. A Douglas merchant ... reported to have contributed £30.
Silvester Ratclifff	parish clerk of Kirk Patrick, superannuated.
John Stevenson	premier of the opposing majority. Of a self-conceited, haughty and ambitious disposition, which talent he zealously, on all occasions, employs in the Bishop's interest against the Lord and not for the country.
John Wattleworth junior	censured and made penance. Subscribed to the contribution but afterwards refused to pay. Still of the majority but is now said to be declining it.

Members of House of Keys	Those accused of disaffection					
	Murray	Butler	Aldridge	Deale	Davies	Cross
James Banckes*	y	y			y	
Charles Christian		y				
James Christian*	y	y		y	y	y
John Christian*	y	y	y	y	y	y
Nicholas Christian	y		y	y		y
Robert Christian	y	y				
Thomas Christian	y					
William Christian*	y	y	y	y	y	y
Edmund Corlett*	y		y	y	y	y
Thomas Corlett*	y	y	y	y	y	y
John Curghey*	y	y	y	y	y	y
Robert Curghey*	y	y	y	y	y	y
John Fargher*	y		y	y	y	y
John Garret*	y		y	y	y	y
John Harrison*	y	y	y	y	y	y
Daniel Lace*	y	y			y	
Charles Moore	y	y	y	y		y
Phil Moore*	y	y	y	y		y
John Oates*	y	y	y	y	y	y
Silvester Ratcliff*		y	y	y	y	y
John Stevenson*	y	y				
Thomas Stevenson		y			y	
William Tyldesley	y	y	y	y		y
John Wattleworth senior*	y	y				
John Wattleworth junior*	y	y				
Unidentified 1 (folio tight bound)		y				
Unidentified 2 (folio tight bound)		y				
John Wattleworth senior or junior			y	y	y	y
	22	22	16	17	16	17

Table I: Members of the House of Keys Present at Six of the Disaffection Cases

* included in Governor Horne's notes

Various excuses could be given by members of the House of Keys for non-attendance at a trial, including ill health. On 4 June 1715 Robert Christian, Edmund Corlett and John Wattleworth senior were too sick to attend the trial of John Kewley. John Garret was fined 4s on 13 May 1717 for being absent from the trial of John Aglionby and Isaac Allgood without a legitimate excuse.[87]

Figure 16: Charles II (1660-1685)

How far the extraordinary corruption of private morals which has gained for the restoration period so unenviable a notoriety was owing to the king's own example of flagrant debauchery, how far to the natural reaction from an artificial Puritanism, is uncertain, but it is incontestable that Charles's cynical selfishness was the chief cause of the degradation of public life which marks his reign. [Encyclopaedia Britannica 13th edition]

THE JACOBITE REBELLION OF 1715

'What was the end of Robert Douglas is not recorded' [R Edgar *Introduction to the History of Dumfries* 1915]

When Queen Anne died in 1714, her cousin, the Hanoverian George I, became King of Great Britain.[i] At first, the Tory members of the government welcomed the new king but he spurned them in favour of the Whigs, thus losing an opportunity of stabilising the Kingdom and ending the unrest caused by the supporters of the Pretender.

On the Isle of Man, there were further examples of people's disaffection to the crown.

Good Friday	**Henry Butler allegedly proposed a disaffected health**
20 July	**House of Keys acquitted Butler**
17 August	**Horne asked the Keys to consider arming the Island**
16 September	Earl of Mar raised the standard for James VIII & III at Braemar
2 October	**Horne asked Bishop Wilson to announce penalties for disaffection in all the churches**
6 October	Northumbrian Jacobites met at Plainfield
20 October	**2nd meeting between Horne and the Keys over arms – they asked for more time**
October	**Lieutenant Cable stated anyone who fought for King George was a knave and a fool**
13 November	Indecisive battle between Argyll and Mar at Sheriffmuir
13 November	Battle of Preston
23 November	**The Keys presented to Horne their reasons for not arming the Island**

1715 on the **Isle of Man** and in Great Britain

Good Friday 1715

Henry Butler of Rawcliffe was descended from one of the oldest Roman Catholic families in Lancashire. 'Although he had deeply involved himself in the rebellion, it was his oldest son, and heir, Richard Butler, who actually appeared in arms'.[88] It is <u>probable</u> that the Henry Butler who was on the Isle of Man during 1715 and 1716 was this individual.

On Good Friday 1715 there were four men talking in Henry Harrison's parlour. Thomas Allen and Joseph Tapp started to argue about whether William Orange had landed in England on the 4th or 5th of November 1688. Henry Butler joined them and they asked his opinion. He replied that it was the 4th, adding, why did it matter?

Soon afterwards, Allen proposed a toast to the immortal memory of King William. Butler responded, 'since you are drinking healths to kings here is a health to the memory of King Charles'.

He added that Allen was 'upon the catch', trying to collect evidence against Jacobite sympathisers, and so he would 'say nothing that he should take hold of'.

Allen now drank 'confusion' to all those who were not for the Revolution.[ii] Possibly Butler was becoming reckless because he responded with 'confusion' to all those that rebelled against King

---

[i] Charles I's sister, Elizabeth, had married Frederick V of Bohemia. Their daughter, Sophia, married Ernest Augustus, Elector of Hanover. Their son, George I, was the only male Protestant heir to the throne.
[ii] William of Orange's arrival in England to replace James II.

Charles. Allen claimed he also said that William III had been a usurper and a rebel, who was 'undutiful' to his father.[i] The English were the rebels, not to accept James III as their rightful king. In a few years the nation would become weary of George I and regret their rebellious actions.

On 30 May 1715 Butler provided his own bond of £200 that he would appear at the next General Gaol Delivery. This was supported the following day by a further bond of £100 from John Sabbarton. Horne, Rowe and Seddon heard the evidence against Butler on 31 May and 16 June. Although the three witnesses remembered the conversation between Allen and Butler, they could not recall any reflections against King George, or any suggestion that the Revolution was a rebellion.

The House of Keys met on 20 July 1715. The governor explained that he had hoped 'the discouragement lately given on an occasion of this kind would have put a stop to any such like for the future'. According to the surviving records, the previous case had been John Murray in 1714. It is apparent, however, that there had been at least one other instance on the Island of disaffection to the crown in England. Horne noted that strangers coming to the Isle of Man caused the problem and it was 'a thing not known among any of the inhabitants'. As a result, the Keys ought to make an example of Butler, to prevent 'such irregularities hereafter'.

New evidence was taken on 26 July 1715. John Sabbarton and his son Joseph claimed that Thomas Allen was an untrustworthy witness, describing an occasion when he had declared something fact and then denied it a few days afterwards. This accusation against Allen appears to have been justified. In 1717 Captain William Cross was accused of making refractory remarks about the King of Great Britain. He was acquitted by the Keys, however, because Allen's evidence was 'various and uncertain in regard he is not certain whether the words were spoken by Captain Cross or his wife'. This somewhat vague evidence was not sufficient to convict anyone.[89]

At Butler's trial, Anthony Halsall suggested that Allen was partly deaf. They had been together at his mother's house in Castletown[ii] at Whitsuntide, when James Dymond had told a story about a tame otter, which was remarkable 'for some peculiar qualities'. Allen had added immediately that the hugest lion that ever was seen in England was now in London. Halsall, convinced that Allen had misheard Dymond's story, explained to him that they were talking about an otter and not a lion, to which Allen had replied 'Oh! Oh!'

The Keys concluded that Butler had proposed a toast to King William III and they could 'lay no weight' on Allen's evidence, that he had been reflecting on the present government. He was acquitted but 'for the peace and good government of the Island', he had to find sureties for his good behaviour in future, 'according to the practice in such cases'. On 10 August 1715 Butler was bound in the sum of £50 and John Aglionby a further £20 that he would be of good behaviour. This was released by the governor's order on 20 July 1716.[90]

Governor Alexander Horne's Solution, 2 October 1715
The governor was becoming concerned about the number of 'whispers' he was receiving of <u>Manx</u> people drinking disaffected healths, either 'encouraged therein by the ill-example of strangers or their own inclination'. As the House of Keys were still considering an appropriate law to deal with such offences, Horne imposed his own solution:

If any person or persons shall hereafter speak any reflecting words of the King's Majesty of England or the present government there, as by law established, unto which we owe our

---

[i] In 1631 William of Orange's grandfather, Frederick Henry, had made the title of stadtholder of Holland hereditary in his family. William's father died of smallpox a week before his son was born. This meant that William III was statdtholder of Holland from birth. When he became king of England, Holland was left without a resident stadtholder.
[ii] Margaret Thompson als Halsall had stayed in Castletown after her husband's death in 1713. Anthony Halsall was her son.

allegiance, or show their disaffections thereto by drinking the Pretender's health or the health of any other person or persons that are esteemed enemies to the crown of England, or attainted or outlawed by the law thereof, such person or persons so offending shall, upon proof made thereof, be fined and further punished at the discretion of the court, as their crime shall demerit.

To encourage witnesses to such disaffected healths to give evidence Horne added that, if anyone heard such expressions and did not report them within two days, either to him or another of the Island's officers, then they would be 'esteemed disaffected to the crown of England' and also fined or punished. The best method of ensuring that 'no person may plead ignorance' of this order was to ask Bishop Wilson to direct all the clergy on the Island to read it out at their services the following Sunday. The Bishop also told his clergy that they must exhort their congregations.

To study to be quiet and to mind our own business, to be subject to those whom God hath set over us ... remembering that whoever resisteth the power resisteth the ordinance of God ... these liberties complained of seem to take their rise from tippling and drinking [therefore] you will do well to discountenance these vices in particular and all others as may be an occasion of offence to Man or sin against God.[91]

In the liberal age of the twenty-first century it is difficult to imagine the impact of the governor's order and the bishop's exhortations on the Island's congregations on Sunday, 2 October 1715. Were these simply a 'licence' to make mischief by producing false evidence against one's enemies? The fact that the House of Keys acquitted each person who was charged to appear before them suggests that there was sufficient doubt in their minds, together with their other reasons for non co-operation.

Lieutenant Cable

Alexander Blain was master of the *Margaret* of Wigtown, which was frequently at the Isle of Man in 1715 and 1716. In October 1715 Blain was drinking at John Hendrick's house when Lieutenant Cable declared that anyone who took up arms to fight for King George was a knave and a fool. Blain reproved him for saying such a thing and Cable, clapping his hand to his side, said that if he had his sword he would run the master through. The next morning, 'the wind presenting fair for Ireland', Cable set sail and did not return to the Island.

Blain was with James McGuffock, a Galloway merchant, at Captain Nicholas Christian's house in Ramsey the following January, when he mentioned the incident. Christian reported the conversation to the deputy governors. The Keys rejected the accusation against Cable, however, as there was no case to answer – he was no longer on the Isle of Man.[92]

Postscript

William Agnew of Wigtown, Anthony McGuffock, formerly Baillie of Wigtown and a merchant in Whithorn, and his brother James, and John Pollock, a merchant in Baldone were equal partners in a cargo, which was taken by the *Margaret* from St Martins to the Isle of Man in 1716. McGuffock and Pollock received and disposed of Agnew's share, which included 1,448 pints of brandy, a hogshead of claret and one third of a hogshead of vinegar worth £1,568 Scots, but did not pay him. As a result, he charged them to appear at the Admiralty Court in Edinburgh to pay what was owed to him, together with interest from Candlemas 1717. The case was heard on 13 July 1717, when an order was given that all their ships and merchandise should be seized. As this order had been forwarded to the Island, Blain did not appear there again.[93] This is one of the instances when a case relating to events on the Isle of Man was heard in Scotland.

THE REBELLION

Scotland

John Erskine, 6th Earl of Mar, was a strong supporter of the Act of Union and had been Secretary of State for Scotland under Queen Anne. George I not only deprived him of this office but failed to offer him an alternative post. Mar returned to his castle at Braemar, where he declared himself a Jacobite and raised James VIII's standard. He managed to enthuse an army of 12,000 men, including George Keith, 10th Earl Marischal, Gordon, Earl of Huntly, the MacLeans, Mackenzies, MacRaes, MacDonalds, MacGregors and Mackintoshes. They planned to defeat the government forces in Scotland and establish the Pretender as rightful king. As a first step, Mar captured Perth and made it his headquarters.

Northumberland

The situation in England was entirely different. There were no clan chiefs to unite the Jacobite supporters. Instead their leaders, the High Church Tory Thomas Forster and the Catholic Earl of Derwentwater, were landed gentry with no fighting experience. They gathered together a small group of their friends and their servants and proclaimed King James III. The proclamation stated 'whereas George, Elector of Brunswick, has usurped and taken upon him the style of the king of these realms ... James III did immediately after his father's decease become our only and lawful liege'.[94]

Thomas Forster (c.1675-1738) lived with his sister, Dorothy, on their family's bankrupt estate at Bamburgh. One of the members of parliament for Northumberland from 1705, he succeeded his father as knight of the shire in 1708. Known locally as 'a popular sporting squire', he was a committed Jacobite, keeping in contact with other sympathisers in Northumberland, London and France. Forster's role was to mobilise the rural gentry in England, at the appropriate moment. He believed that thousands of men would join him.

Forster's physical appearance was described as 'of middle stature, inclining to be fat, well shaped, except that he stoops in his shoulders, fair complexioned, his mouth wide, his nose pretty large, and his eyes grey ... he speaks the Northern dialect'.[95]

The son of Lady Mary Tudor, a natural daughter of Charles II, James Radcliffe, 3rd Earl of Derwentwater (1689-1716), was born in London but brought up at the Stuart court in France, as companion to the Prince of Wales (the Pretender). Radcliffe did not live on his Northumberland estate at Dilston near Hexham until 1710. Once there he quickly made contact with the other Jacobite sympathisers in the neighbourhood.

Not all the Northumbrian Jacobites were 'out' in the 'Fifteen. Because he was lame and could not take part in active combat, Isaac Allgood from Brandon White House, Nunwick near Simonsburn in North Tyne went to the Isle of Man. The morning he left home, he drank a bottle of wine with his best friends, Forster and Derwentwater, and they had shared with him 'all their designs'. They were to set out in two days and he knew how many 'brave gentlemen were to rise with them'. There was 'not a gentleman in all Northumberland from the highest to those that were worth £600 or £700 a year but were engaged in the rebellion', except himself and Sir William Windham and Mark Strother.[i]

Forster and Derwentwater had reassured Allgood that 'though it was not in his power to do them any service, they would not forget him'. He was convinced that 'before they were half way to London, the most part of England would be on their side. For there was not a coffee house in all London, that ever he was in, that if there were but twelve men then ten of them were disaffected'. He was sure it would be 'impossible for King George to hold it out'. When James III was on the throne then he would have a place in the government worth £1,000 a year.[96]

---

[i] This may refer to Sir William Wyndham (1687-1740) from Orchard Wyndham in Somerset. Educated at Eton and Christ Church, Oxford, he entered parliament in 1710 and became secretary-at-war in the Tory ministry in 1712 and chancellor of the exchequer in 1713. He was closely associated with Lord Bolingbroke, and he was privy to the attempts being made to bring about a Jacobite restoration on the death of Queen Anne; when these failed he was dismissed from office. In 1715 the failure of a Jacobite movement led to his imprisonment, but he was soon set at liberty. [Encyclopaedia Britannica 13th edition.] According to Gooch, Wyndham was to secure Bristol for the cause [p 45]. Alternatively it might be Sir William Widdrington from Lancashire, who did join the rebels. The Strother family did not 'venture out' in 1715 [Gooch p 53]

On the Isle of Man

Before Allgood was allowed on board a ship at Whitehaven, he had to 'take the oath for King George'. On his arrival in Douglas he lodged with Mary Hendrick, wife of John Hendrick, who was a coastal trader and herring boat owner.[97] Mary made no secret of the fact that she was both a Whig and a strong supporter of George I.

It is not clear whether Allgood knew John Aglionby before he arrived on the Isle of Man. Aglionby, from Nunnery near Penrith in Cumberland, was the eldest son of the recorder of Carlisle. He had been somewhat wild in his youth. In July 1696 William Gilpin reported that Aglionby, 'of whose character I suppose you are sufficiently apprised' was frequently in the Whitehaven neighbourhood. As there were no innocent pleasures to be found there, young men like Aglionby and Christopher Lowther became involved in 'lewdness'.[98]

At some time in the early 1700s both Aglionby and Lowther went to the Isle of Man. There Aglionby set up house in Douglas with his wife, Dinah, and six servants. His home became a focal point for Jacobite sympathisers and Allgood would spend every evening there, drinking and talking about what was happening in England and Scotland, and on the Island. When he got back to his lodgings, Allgood would report part if not all of the conversations to his landlady, Mary Hendrick.

One night Mary said to him, 'what tickling work would be among you, if the governor should know of these things'. Allgood replied, 'damn the governor, who cares for him? He will not be long in the place for they are going to petition my Lord [the Earl of Derby] to have him out'. Mary asked him, 'who is going to have him out?' He said, 'Mr John Murray and all the heads of the Island, and the Bishop and all the heads of the town'.

Allgood claimed that all the Island were Jacobites, 'as well the clergy as your parliament and even the Bishop himself'. As a result, he was 'a happy man that he had the fortune to come into such a place, where they were all according to his own heart'. He added that the Earl of Derby had joined Mar and that 'all the best of the Island are glad of it'. Mary answered, 'God forbid, not all for sure'. He confirmed that it was everyone, 'except the governor, and him they value not'.[99]

John Campbell, 2nd Duke of Argyll, was appointed commander-in-chief of the government forces in Scotland. Having raised an army of 4,000 men, he met Mar at Sheriffmuir, near Dunblane, on 13 November 1715. The right flank of the Jacobites, led by MacDonald of Glengarry, MacLean of Duart and MacDonald of Clan Ranald, routed the left side of the Hanoverian army. Several of the Jacobites were killed in the process, however, and both armies withdrew so that the battle was indecisive.[100] The clan leaders were nearly all customers of the smuggling merchant Baillie Steuart of Inverness, whose Jacobite sympathies are apparent from his letter book. Steuart was also frustrated by competition from the smugglers using the Isle of Man as a supply base for customers among the Highland and Islands. John Bignall supplied customers on Skye in 1721.[101]

There was great rejoicing at John Aglionby's house over the supposed news that the Duke of Argyll had been defeated at Sheriffmuir. When Allgood got home he asked Mary, 'what have you to say now, you whiggish bitch?' She replied that she did not believe it. He said, 'no, damn you, you will believe nothing'.

Afterwards, the news came that in fact Mar was beaten and Argyll had 'won the day'. Mary told Allgood, 'if she knew that to be true she would put up lights in the windows and make a bonfire at the door and give drink to the boys to huzzah for King George'. He swore by God, 'if you do, you shall not have a whole window left in your house'. Muttering that she should be made to repent it, Allgood went to Aglionby's house 'in a great passion'. When he returned home, Mary asked him if he had told anybody there what she was going to do. Allgood replied that Aglionby was very angry with her and John Murray had called her 'many an impudent hussy, how durst she have the impudence to say or act any such thing, knowing that there was no one of her principles here [on the Island] but herself'.[102]

The Battle of Preston

Forster and Derwentwater, and their followers had agreed to meet at Greenrigg near Bellingham on Thursday, 5 October 1715. When Forster arrived there, however, he realised that it was not an appropriate meeting place and moved immediately to Plainfield. Table II outlines their subsequent somewhat disorganised meanderings, which ended at Preston on Wednesday, 9 November.

Thursday, 6 October	Plainfield to Rothbury
Friday, 7 October	Rothbury to Warkworth
Saturday, 8 October to Wednesday, 12 October	Warkworth (Sunday, 9 October)*
Thursday, 13 October	Warkworth to Alnwick*
Friday, 14 October	Alnwick to Morpeth (joined by Merse troop under Hume)
Saturday, 15 October	Morpeth to Hexham
Sunday, 16 October to Tuesday, 18 October	Hexham (Tuesday, 18 October)*
Wednesday, 19 October	Hexham to Rothbury (joined Scots under Kenmure)
Thursday, 20 October	Rothbury to Wooler
Friday, 21 October	Wooler
Saturday, 22 October	Wooler to Kelso
	(Highlanders, Lowland Scots & Northumbrians united)
	Now 1,400 foot soldiers & 600 horsemen
Sunday, 23 October to Wednesday, 26 October	Kelso (Monday, 24 October – James VIII)*
Thursday, 27 October	Kelso to Jedburgh
Friday, 28 October	Jedburgh
Saturday, 29 October	Jedburgh to Hawick
Sunday, 30 October	Hawick to Langholm
Monday, 31 October	Langholm to Longtown (some Highlanders deserted)
Tuesday, 1 November	Longtown to Brampton*
Wednesday, 2 November	Brampton to Penrith*
Thursday, 3 November	Penrith to Appleby
Friday, 4 November	Appleby*
Saturday, 5 November	Appleby to Kendal*
Sunday, 6 November	Kendal to Kirby Lonsdale*
Monday, 7 November	Kirby Lonsdale to Lancaster*
Tuesday, 8 November	Lancaster
Wednesday, 9 November	Lancaster to Garstang (foot) & Preston (horse)
Thursday, 10 November	Preston (foot arrived)
Friday, 11 November	Preston
Saturday, 12 November	Preston (preparing to leave for Manchester)

Table II: The Route taken by Forster and Derwentwater from Plainfield to Preston[103]

In Scotland Kenmure was in command but once they crossed the Border Forster took charge.
* James III (or James VIII) proclaimed

During this time both John Hunter and Robert Douglas joined the Northumbrians. They brought with them a somewhat ragged collection of Borderers. One farmer said 'now I can leave my stable door unlocked, and sleep sound, since Luck-in-a-Bag[i] and the rest are gone'. Despite this, Douglas was described as 'indefatigable in searching throughout the country for arms and horses – a trade which, it was said, he had followed out of the Rebellion, as well as in it'.[104]

The Northumbrians organised their force into five troops of horse:[105]
1. Earl of Derwentwater's, commanded by his brother Charles Radcliffe
   and Captain John Shaftoe
2. Lord Widdrington's, commanded by Thomas Errington of Beaufront
3. under Captain John Hunter
4. under Robert Douglas
5. under Captain Nicholas Wogan, who was Irish but descended from a Welsh family.

---

[i] a notorious horse stealer

Robert Douglas was not with his men for most of the perambulation. His main role was 'the medium of Mar's correspondence with the English'. On 1 November Forster opened the Earl's commission, appointing him General of the Jacobites in England, which had been brought by Douglas. Letters from Mar, dated Perth, 21 October, also arrived for both Kenmure and Forster on 1 November. At this stage the Earl was uncertain about Kenmure's plans and would have preferred to have him in Scotland, where he would be 'of great service'. He wrote to Forster, 'if you be in need of [Lord Kenmure's] assistance in England, I doubt not but you have called him there'. Both Forster and Kenmure took part in the battle of Preston.[106]

John Hunter's troop was given two distinct tasks. On 12 October the Merse troop were at Felton Bridge, when they received news that Sir Charles Hotham's regiment was marching from Newcastle to surprise them. An officer was sent to Thomas Forster to ask for reinforcements. Lord Widdrington suggested that John Hunter's troop should go with them. He appears to have stayed with the Scots force until they joined the Northumbrians at Morpeth Common on 14 October.

On 29 October the combined army was at Jedburgh when they received information that the government forces were nearby. They left the town immediately and stopped on a moor between Jedburgh and a small hill called Dunian, where they stayed for two hours, trying to decide what to do next. While there, they received the news that the enemy was at Yetholm and approaching Jedburgh. 'It was then resolved, though as a temporary expedient only, to endeavour to gain three days' march on the government forces by crossing the mountains and pressing towards England. In an evil hour, therefore … this miserable course of proceeding was resolved upon, and captain Hunter was ordered with a small detachment to go into Tynedale, and prepare quarters for the troops which would follow'. In the meantime, there was a near mutiny. The Scots were very unwilling to cross the border into England. As a result, Hunter's instructions were countermanded and the rebels marched towards Hawick.

At Lancaster on 8 November the rebels found a large seizure of brandy and some claret that had been run from the Isle of Man. No information has been found about the ownership of this brandy, the wherries that transported it from the Island to Lancashire or the intended customers. Some of the brandy was drunk in the town and the remainder put on a cart for Garstang – but it was consumed before it reached there, supposedly by the Highlanders.

When the rebels arrived at Preston on 9 November, they appear to have forgotten that they were supposed to be fighting a war. 'The ladies in this town, Preston, are so very beautiful and so richly attired, that the gentlemen soldiers from Wednesday to Saturday minded nothing but courting and feasting'. Although apparently Forster had been told that General Wills was only 12 miles away at Wigan, neither he nor the other officers made any attempt 'to prepare for a battle at Preston, march to meet the enemy or march away from them'.[107] Forster had two excuses for this inaction. His spies had been watching General Carpenter, who had gone to Newcastle looking for Forster and was now at Barnard Castle. At the same time he believed the Lancastrian High Church Tories would stand by their promise of keeping him well-informed of what was happening within a 40 mile a radius of the town. Everyone had ignored the significance of General Wills, who had been in charge of the garrison at Chester and had been allocated one regiment of horse, five of dragoons and three of foot. All these men were fast converging on Warrington.

Figure 17 shows the plan of the battle of Preston. The Jacobites were all deployed within the town, at rapidly constructed barricades, located according to a plan devised by Brigadier Mackintosh. On 12 November 1715, George I's forces under General Wills crossed the river Ribble by a bridge that Forster had left unguarded. Derwentwater was exercising his men on a marsh nearby. 'He seemed very joyful, put off his hat and shouted "they are all for us". He immediately put spurs to his horse, commanded his men into the town and rode to meet them. He met them with their swords drawn … a short mile out of town, in a great consternation, and cried "we are undone, they are against us"'.[108] The government forces effectively surrounded the town.

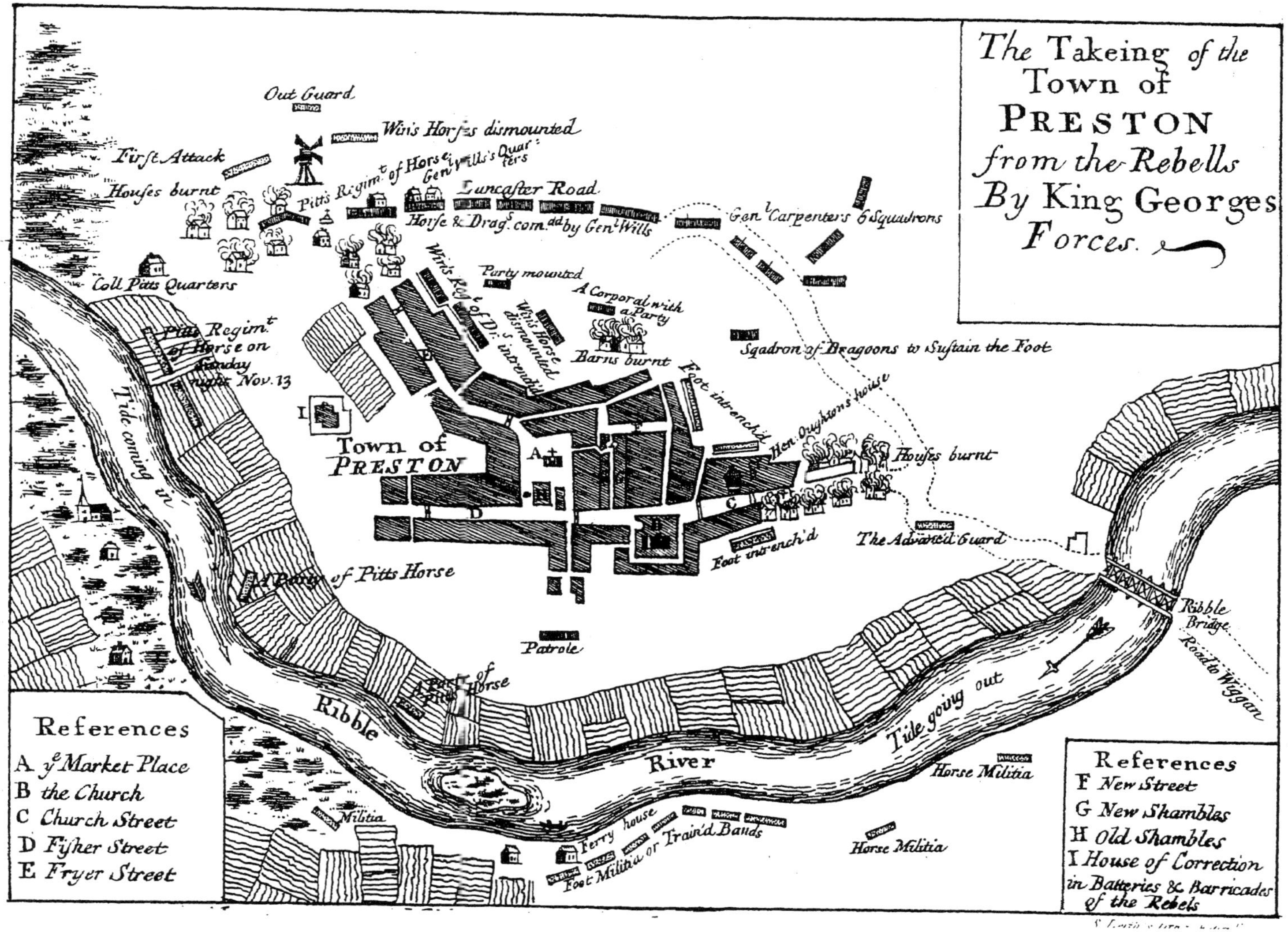

The map contains the following text labels:

Title cartouche:
The Takeing of the Town of PRESTON from the Rebells By King Georges Forces.

References (bottom left):
References
A ye Market Place
B the Church
C Church Street
D Fyker Street
E Fryer Street

References (top right):
References
F New Street
G New Shambles
H Old Shambles
I House of Correction
in Batteries & Barricades
of the Rebels

Map labels:
Road to Wiggan
Ribble Bridge
Horse Militia
Horse Militia
The going out
Horse Militia
River
Train'd Bands
Ferry house
Foot Militia or Train'd Bands
The Adveiled Guard
Hoyles burnt
Foot intrench'd after Oyfkin's turn
Squadron of Dragoons to Syfain the Foot
Foot intrench'd
Houses burnt
Barns burnt
Town of PRESTON
Ribble
Retreat of Pitts Horse
Pitts Horse
Patrole
Tide coming in
Coll Pitts Quarters
Pitts Regimt Horse on Sunday Nov. 13
Houses burnt
Out Guard
Furfe Attack
Pitts Regim of Horse & Wills's Quar Gen'
Winis Horfe dismounted
Dunglter Road.
Party mounted
A Corporal with a Party
Hoyle & Drag. com d by Gen'Wills
Winis Horse dismounted
Win's Reg of Dr. intrench'd
Gen Carpenters 6 Squadrons

Figure 17: Plan of the Battle of Preston 1715

The Jacobites created barricades across the four main streets:[109]

1. a little below the church, commanded by Brigadier Mackintosh. He was blamed for not placing this barricade at the extreme end of the town, to which he replied 'there were so many lanes and avenues that to defend such a barricade would have required more men than he possessed' (C).

   The Teviotdale, Berwickshire and Northumbrian gentry were on the north side of the church and the Borderers under Douglas and Hunter were on the southside (B).

2. at the end of a lane leading to fields, under Lord Charles Murray. Captain Wogan was on the street above Sir Henry Houghton's house, near here.

3. the windmill barrier, on the road to Lancaster was defended by the Mackintoshes under Colonel Mackintosh

4. Fishergate, leading to Liverpool, was held by Lord Strathmore's men under Major Rutter (D).

The rest of the Jacobites were in the Market Place (A).

12 November

12 noon	General Wills arrived at Ribble Bridge and planted all the horse and foot militia on the south side of the Ribble to defend the bridge and stop the rebels from escaping.
	Gained possession of both sides of the town – the roads to Wigan and Lancaster – and set fire to houses
2.00 p.m.	200 men entered Churchgate Street. The Highlanders, assisted by the Borderers, firing out of cellars and windows, killed 120 of them within ten minutes (other reports put the figure at 60 to 70 men). Derwentwater 'commanded in the churchyard and was observed to be pretty active the whole action through'. Hunter and Douglas were described as behaving with skill and bravery throughout. Next he attacked Lord Charles Murray's barricade
4.00 p.m.	300 men entered Back Street and attacked the Windmill Barricade. Houses were set on fire and the government troops suffered heavy losses. The Highlanders left Sir Henry Houghton's house unguarded and this was taken by the government troops. More houses set on fire
Night	General Wills's men camped round the town – Fishergate and the road to Liverpool was left unguarded and several of the rebels escaped by this route.

The Jacobites had 'repulsed the king's forces in all their attacks and maintained their posts', Mackintosh wrote to the Earl of Mar, expressing hopes of a victory.

13 November

10.00 a.m.	General Carpenter arrived and camped round the town. He took charge.
1 to 2.00 p.m.	unnerved by 'the horror and destruction they were witnessing', both Forster and Derwentwater discussed surrender – 'much to the surprise of the besiegers and the fury of the Scots'.

On 14 November the rebels laid down their arms. They were not treated with the compassion usually accorded to prisoners of war:

Goaded by bayonet and halberd, the mass of their men were driven like a herd of cattle into the old church of Preston; where, on a cold and bitter day, they were stripped of their tartans and other clothing by the soldiers of the cavalry, so that many of them were glad to tear the green baize linings from the pews to cover their nakedness.[110]

There was more than one John Hunter at the battle and therefore there is some confusion about the subsequent fate of Captain Hunter. According to one source he was hanged at Liverpool on 8 May 1716 but another states that both Douglas and Hunter escaped from prison - nothing is known about their future careers.[111]

It has been suggested that there were Manxmen fighting with Robert Douglas. This is virtually impossible to prove or disprove. Although it would have been expected that Douglas would be listed as Scottish, because he joined the Northumbrians he is on the English list of those captured. This list only includes the 'gentlemen' and main leaders. There were hundreds of others not named. Some of these escaped from Preston, through the gap left by the government forces, or from the makeshift prison arrangements, some died in prison, over 1,000 were transported to the colonies. John Murray of Hydwood, who is known to have taken part, does not appear on any of the lists.[112] In 1751 Bishop Wilson wrote to the King, George II, 'on the strictest enquiry I can not find that any one man of the natives was ever concerned against your Majesty or your late Royal Father'.[113]

Back on the Isle of Man
When news reached the Island that the rebels had been cut off at Preston, Isaac Allgood clapped his hands and cried, 'Oh, poor Thomas Forster'. He added, 'he never had reason to thank God for his lameness till now', because otherwise he would have been captured at Preston. When Allgood went to John Aglionby's house that evening, they shared their 'grief and sorrow' at what had happened. Having continued in a depressed mood for two or three days, Allgood 'began to take heart and said they lied, it was not so bad as was reported'. When the defeat was confirmed, John Murray and John Hale visited Allgood several times, 'pitying the lives of such brave men who were taken in the Rebellion'.

Adam Christian, another boat owner in Douglas whose wife took in lodgers, was at the Hendricks's house one night when Allgood asked him, 'where is your Lord?' Christian answered, 'I cannot tell', to which Allgood replied, 'he is missing and it's well if he is not gone over to the Earl of Mar'.[114]

It appears that after the battle of Preston the Jacobite sympathisers on the Isle of Man became more vociferous in their views. Allgood said repeatedly that George I had no more right to the crown than either his landlady or himself and he believed that James III should be king, 'as firmly as he believed his creed'. Mary Hendrick was shocked by this, remembering that, before he left Whitehaven, Allgood had sworn allegiance to George I. When she challenged him, asking 'how could his conscience let him talk so?' he replied that the oath had been imposed 'upon me against my will. Damn them, and their oaths too, for they are impositions upon men's souls and conscience'.

One night William Thwaites, Mr Davis from Dublin, John Hale, Aglionby and Allgood were drinking a bowl of punch in Mary's kitchen, when they told her to shut the door. After proposing a toast to the Pretender, Aglionby, 'in a passion', swore by God 'that fellow', meaning King George, had no more right to the crown than Tiger, 'pointing his finger at his dog'. He added, 'make the best of him he is but a poor cuckoldy fellow'. When Mary asked what Aglionby had meant, Allgood explained that the King had never claimed the Prince of Wales as his son until he came to England, when he was obliged to have an heir, 'upon account of the crown'. Madam Allgood had confirmed this, saying that 'two Turks that waited upon His Majesty King George in his bedchamber told her the same story'.

The Pretender landed at Peterhead in early November 1715. Shortly afterwards, four men came to Mary Hendrick's house and drank the Pretender's health with Allgood. When they had left the Island, he told her that they were priests.

The government forces in Scotland had been reinforced by 6,000 Dutch troops and the 'Fifteen rebellion was virtually over. The Pretender held 'court' at Scone, where Jacobite ladies were persuaded to hand over their jewels to make a crown.[115] After a few weeks in Scotland, he boarded a ship at Montrose to return to Europe.

In early February 1716, a ship came into Ramsey Bay and it was believed that the Pretender was on board. Inevitably, Mary asked Allgood about this. On the first, second, third and fourth nights he said, 'No'. A week later, the ship having sailed, she asked again and he confirmed that the Pretender had been on board, adding that several people on the Island knew this. When Mary asked, 'how they could be so sure of it', Allgood replied, 'the Boys[i] had a private letter and Mr Aglionby had another'. She now asked 'how did the governor not know of these things?' Allgood explained that Horne had 'sent several times to demand what they were and they sent word it was a French ship, bound for the north of Ireland, to the salmon fishery'. John Williams, the king's officer at Ramsey had been on board and he knew that the Pretender was there. This is the only reference to Williams in the Jacobite context. It is unclear whether his reaction would have been 'wonderful, the Pretender is with us' or 'terrible, should I attempt to arrest him?'

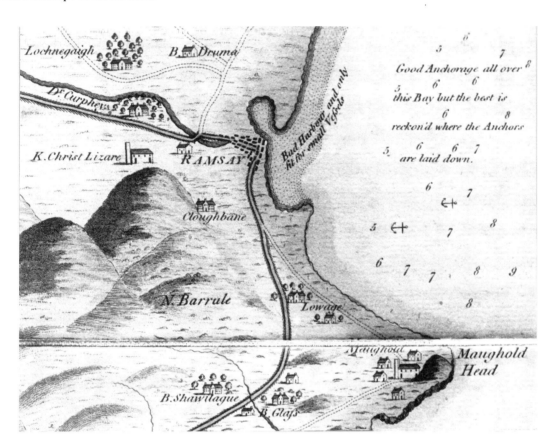

Figure 18: Ramsey Bay

Then a boat had come from Scotland with the message that the other two ships, which had sailed from Montrose at the same time, had arrived safely in France. Immediately the Pretender's ship 'hoist up sail and went away'. Allgood said, 'we have been very merry at Mr Aglionby's drinking his health and wishing him a good wind'. Mary wanted to know 'what good' the Pretender could do in France. He replied, 'a great deal of good for the thoughts of him being there will spirit the party'.

Mary asked who else was at Aglionby's house. Allgood said he would not tell her unless she would 'oblige herself not to tell it again'. When Mary promised she would not tell anyone he said that John Murray, Phil Moore and John Hale were there with him.[116]

It has proved impossible to confirm this story. No exact date is given for the presence of this ship in Ramsey Bay. According to all other sources there was not sufficient time for the Pretender to spend at least six days at the Island between sailing from Montrose and arriving in France. Yet all the rest of Mary Hendrick's evidence can be proved in historic terms.

The reader may choose his or her own conclusion.

---

[i] These are not listed but one imagines they include John Murray and Phil Moore.

Inspired by the victory over the rebels, Mary Hendrick erected the sign *Royal George* outside her house. When Aglionby saw this, he said it should have been the *Royal Cuckold*. Allgood 'swore by God she should repent' setting it up and that 'in a little time it would be pulled down about her ears'. He called her 'a grand fool', because 'there is no person of note in the town will come to your house again' so that she would lose a great deal of custom. 'By woeful experience', Mary found this to be true because 'nobody comes to her house no more than if the plague was in it'. A few days later the sign was pulled down and Mary charged ten people (Robert Davies, Charles Dalrymple, Dr Abraham Silk, Mr Magummery, Mr Simpson, William Jackson, Mr Moluin, Captain Young, Mr Wells and William Clark) with the offence.[117]

Dr Abraham Silk went to Mary Hendrick's house during the evening of Sunday 5 August 1716 and called for a bottle of beer. The servant, Ann Cowin, went upstairs to find her mistress, who was going to bed and said that she would not sell beer at that time of night. Silk would not accept this, sending the maid upstairs again with the message that he was there because he wanted to speak to Mary. This time she came downstairs and gave Silk a bottle of beer. The servant appears to have stayed in the room, or listened at the door. Silk told Mary that 'it was better for her to set [rent] or sell her house and get away to some other place, for there was no living for her here'. This was because she was 'as black as hell'. A papist in Douglas was telling any shipmasters or strangers who came to town that they must not go to her house so that soon she would have neither lodgers nor drinkers and her income would disappear. When Mary remarked that Esquire Aglionby was the only papist in town, who was 'so much her enemy', Silk replied, 'I name nobody'. He added, 'if she would bring his name into question for telling her this or reveal it to any body, he would stick her at her own door like a cat'.[118]

Despite the governor's foreboding, there appears to have been only one 'incident' involving the Isle of Man. After the 'Fifteen, Alexander, son of Patrick Gordon of Hallhead, became a merchant first in St Martins and then Bordeaux. He purchased a ship, the *Subtle* of Glasgow, at Rochelle. She was about 40 tons burthen with a woman as a figurehead. He appointed James Duncan as master. The ship was fitted out at Rochelle, including a few weapons for self-defence: four buccaneer fire locks, two blunderbusses, six pistols, two fowling pieces, four cutlasses, four half pikes and two old iron guns. Some stone ballast was put on board and on 8 August 1716 she sailed to St Martins. There the crew threw out the ballast and took in 26 tons of salt, 18 bundles of liquorice and 12 tons of wine, which had been brought from Bordeaux.

On 22 August they sailed for the Isle of Man. Stormy and contrary winds forced them to take shelter at Ramsey Bay on 1 September and they finally reached Douglas on the 9th. The following day Robert Wilson entered three tons of wine. Alexander Young, who was the supercargo on board, having travelled with the ship from St Martins, managed to hire a warehouse and on 29 September he entered a further 9 tons of wine, the liquorice and 6 tons of the salt.[119]

In the meantime, the Admiralty had received information that a ship of the *Subtle*'s description was carrying a large quantity of arms, hidden under her salt and to be landed in Scotland. The *Lively*, commanded by John Charlton, was ordered to cruise between the Isle of Man and Carrickfergus on the look out for the ship, which he was instructed to seize.

When he called at Ramsey on 30 September 1716 for any news, Charlton was told that a similar had been there for eight days earlier in the month and was now at Douglas.

As Charlton explained to the governor, 'lest she should endeavour to make her escape, upon the news of my arrival, I sent my Lieutenant to examine whether it were the same ship and to search for arms and was much surprised to hear from him that it was the same ship and no arms on board. I thought it necessary to give you this account, believing the arms may be landed on the Island, she not having stirred from hence since her arrival. I should not have offered to examine any ship in Douglas harbour without first acquainting you but from the reasons abovementioned and the great distance you live from Ramsey' – the governor was at Castletown

On 3 October William Seddon reported that the ship had been 'strictly searched'. He could confirm that there were no arms or ammunition on board 'save a few small arms in her cabin and two old iron guns without carriages in her hold and a small parcel of ammunition for those arms'. He had also examined the warehouse where her cargo had been put and found no arms. Young's papers, in his trunk, were also examined and produced nothing.[120]

Other Gordons who became merchants overseas were Alexander Gordon's brother Robert, who also became a wine merchant in Bordeaux. He had several customers who used the Isle of Man as their supply base. William, son of William Gordon of Farskane, went to Paris in 1716 and later became a merchant in Norway.

John Murray of Bankend

John Murray of Hydwood, also referred to as Townhead, in Bankend, to the east of Dumfries, was a merchant with several connections on the Isle of Man.

Early in the morning of 25 June 1711 the Dumfries customs officer, James Young went to Glenhowen on the Nith estuary, where the fishermen told him that Murray, 'one of the runners' had just come home from the Island. Young went to the parish constable and asked for his help in searching Murray's house for 'run goods'. Young found one large pack and two trusses of leaf tobacco. The constable was carrying the pack to the Queen's warehouse at Dumfries, when he was attacked by 'a multitude of women'. Young left the constable with the two trusses, which he had been carrying, and chased after the women. 'They laid violent hands upon me and carried me prisoner' into Murray's house, where Young was held until 'they got all the tobacco carried away'. On his release, Young hurried to Dumfries, where he collected ten men to help him search 'all the houses, field gardens etc.' They found one pack of tobacco in a dry dyke about half a mile from Bankend. They had carried this as far as the moor, when they were attacked by 20 women 'with clubs and pitchforks'. This time, however, the tobacco was delivered safely to the warehouse. When Young threatened the women that they would be 'severely punished for this deforcement', they answered that they would expect to be punished with those who had deforced Stewart at Arbigland (see p. 28).

The collector wrote to the Board in Edinburgh that his officers were discouraged from doing their duty because of 'the daily abuses' they received. The criminals were never punished and nobody could be expected to search for smuggled goods 'seeing that thereby they run the hazard of their lives'.[121]

Murray of Hydwood was in Ramsey during April and May 1713, when both John Wattleworth junior and James Read charged him with debts of nearly £45, relating to a cargo of hops and barley. Philip Moore of Douglas was bound as Murray's surety and it was claimed that Edward Casement of Ramsey had some of Murray's money in his hands.[122]

On 25 February 1714 John Murray of Douglas charged him with a debt of £100 and on 24 March Samuel Brown, of North Britain, charged him with the same amount. As neither of the plaintiffs appeared, on 4 March the cases were dismissed.[123]

There are no further references to John Murray of Hydwood, on the Island after March 1714. That year he was appointed as a tidesman for the port of Dumfries. This was part of the general policy of the Boards of Customs to employ former smugglers, who might be persuaded to provide excellent information about the activities of their erstwhile partners. In 1715 Murray left his post and 'went into the rebellion'. He managed to escape, either from Preston or from prison afterwards, and returned to the Borders where he 'betook himself to the smuggling trade' once more.

'The better to carry on that affair, [he] forged several excise permits'. In February 1723 he was arrested on information provided by Daniel Munro, door keeper to the Commissioners of Excise at Wigtown, for allegedly forging the excise officer's signature, and claiming to be him. Realising that if convicted he would be almost certainly be hanged, before his trial Murray escaped from Dumfries gaol, through the slate roof. He returned to 'the old smuggling trade' in the Borders. According to the collector of customs for Dumfries, 'it's a practice of his to personate our officers to strangers and get money from them to let their goods pass. He is such a villain, to them he knows, that he will bring them under some composition or threaten them with acquainting our officers where their goods lie'.

At last, in June 1727, the customs officers believed that they had caught him. 'From the general character Murray has, and what consists with our particular knowledge, there is little credit to be given to his oath'. His accuser claimed he was 'able to prove all the facts sworn in his affidavit by a great many witnesses'. [124]

The end of this story is not known.

Postscript
In 1736 the Dukes of Atholl became Lords of Man. James, the 2nd Duke and the first Lord of Man, was a confirmed Whig. Three of his brothers had joined the Earl of Mar during the 1715 rebellion. Lord George Murray and William Murray, Marquess of Tullibardine, fought in Scotland – and then escaped to France.

Lord Charles Murray marched south with some of the Higlanders. Described as one of the officers who distinguished himself by assimilating his manners to those of his men, 'he would never be prevailed upon to ride or even mount a horse to cross rivers, but, in his Highland dress, without breeches, kept at the head of his regiment on foot'.

Murray defended the second barricade at Preston, on a lane leading to fields, behaving 'very gallantly' despite two separate onslaughts from the government troops.

After his capture, Murray was tried for desertion from the army, where he had fought abroad as a cornet of horse. His defence was that before he entered into the rebellion he had made over his commission to a relative and that he had never received any pay from, nor sworn allegiance to, the government of England. As he could not provide any exculpatory evidence, Murray was condemned to be shot. The Court-Martial, 'who were much interested with his youthful and gallant demeanour', postponed his execution for a month.

'When he was sensible he was to die, being removed to the house of Mr Wingilby with the other half-pay officers, he kept a true decorum suitable to the nobleness of his mind, and the bravery of his soul, and not unsuitable to the circumstances he was in'.

In the meantime, through 'the interest of his friends' Murray's life was saved.[125]

MARY HENDRICK: 1716 TO 1722

Mrs Hendrick came in a short time down and after her Mr Galbraith, both in a disorderly dress. Upon which Mr Owen and Mr Wallis, looking upon one another, fell a laughing, and suspected that they had been naughty together. [Evidence from Peter Lancaster, chaplain of Douglas, to the Chapter Court, 29 May 1716][126]

When Isaac Allgood, his wife Hannah and their maid Ann Cottam came to the Isle of Man, they lodged at Mary Hendrick's house in Douglas. Mary's reaction to the defeat of the rebels at both Sheriffmuir and Preston caused problems between them, which were exacerbated by her reaction to the story that the Pretender had been in Ramsey Bay. In February 1716 the Allgoods moved to live with John Hale, the king's officer in Douglas.

The year 1716 was somewhat eventful for Mary Hendrick. These events touched the lives of several other people on the Island. She accused Isaac Allgood and John Aglionby of disaffection to the English crown. If this had been proved to the House of Keys, and if there had been a Manx law to deal with treasonable offences, then they should have been punished by the death sentence. This level of antagonism towards a former lover, someone with whom Mary had planned to elope from the Island, provides a somewhat dramatic example of the dangers of spurning someone, who was previously the most important person in the world. In the present context, Mary's accusations formed an invaluable contribution to the section on the Jacobite Rebellion of 1715.

Hannah Allgood learned that her husband had been unfaithful with their landlady. According to the Allgoods's maid, Ann Cottam:

> *Some time in February last, being in the next room to that wherein Mr Allgood and Mrs Allgood lay together, she plainly heard him own to his wife that he had several times lain with Mary Hendrick, 'at which words Mrs Allgood, being much grieved, fell a weeping'. When the maid asked what was the matter, Allgood answered, 'she has extorted a secret from me, and now she knows it, it makes her uneasy and she is such a fool as to cry'. Mrs Allgood was 'very much indisposed for some days afterwards'. The maid 'desired to know the reason for her illness, which she owned was Mr Allgood's criminal familiarity with Mary Hendrick'.*[127]

This distress is fully understandable. It <u>may</u> have been exacerbated by the fact that Hannah was not in fact Mrs Allgood (see below).

Bishop Wilson was fined for not accepting that the Earl of Derby had any jurisdiction over spiritual matters, such as excommunication, and for refusing to attend a hearing of Mary Hendrick's appeal before the Earl's commissioner at London. Although this fine was subsequently remitted, the argument between the Island's officers and the Bishop intensified the division within the House of Keys between those 'for' and those 'against' the Bishop.

On 25 February 1716 William Kempsey imported at Douglas on the *Success* of Dublin, Thomas Dickson master, 31 pipes of wine, 214 casks of raisins and 88 casks of figs. Between 29 February and 31 March these goods were exported to Dublin on board the the *Mable* of Donaghadee, John Stewart and the *John & Ann* of Carnarvon, John Williams, and for Liverpool on board the *Margaret* of Douglas, James Corlett. Kempsey was on the Island all this time.

The *Concord* of Greenock, Captain Patrick Galbraith master, was at Douglas on 3 April 1716, when James Dymond landed tobacco and six barrels of herrings brought by her from the Clyde. On 23 April Dymond imported more tobacco, at Derbyhaven, and the following day Galbraith entered on board his vessel 24 pipes of canary wine and 24 barrels of herrings for the Baltic. This means that Galbraith was on the Isle of Man from the 3rd of April until the 24th.[128]

These dates are significant because when Kempsey and Galbraith were on the Island they both spent time at the Hendricks's house in Douglas. Apparently disgusted by what he saw there, Kempsey accused Mary of being a whore. In return, she said that if he told any of the spiritual officers about this then she would go to London, where she would inform the government what had happened on the Island during the 'Fifteen. She would tell them about the disaffected conversations that she had overheard at her house and that had been reported to her by Isaac Allgood, as having taken place at John Aglionby's house. Alarmed by what he might have started, Kempsey persuaded Allgood to write 'such a letter … as silenced her', presumably threatening to tell the world about their adultery.

This letter did not halt the subsequent revenge and counter-revenge, which is summarised below. Because this summary includes both spiritual and civil actions, the events relating to the Ecclesiastical Courts and instructions from Bishop Wilson to the clergy etc. are indicated in *italics*.

1716

February	Isaac Allgood confessed to his wife that he had lain with Mary and that they were planning to run away together and live in Dublin. He explained that by the laws of the Isle of Man she had a title to half her house, which she would pawn or mortgage for £30 or £40.
4 March	Mary wrote to Hannah Allgood, who was now living at John Hale's house, begging her not to change an old friend (Mary) for a new (William Kempsey). In other words Mary hoped that Hannah would not believe any gossip that she might hear.
	John Hendrick hired a horse to ride to Bishop's Court and complain against Kempsey for calling Mary a whore.
5 March	Mary persuaded her husband not to make the complaint.
12 April	Mary gave evidence that she had not heard John Hale propose any disaffected healths against the government of Great Britain.
13 April	Mary changed her evidence, now accusing Hale of disaffection.[129]
April	William Kempsey was at John Hale's house with the Allgoods, Ann Cottam their maid, and Richard Gripton. He told them that William Deale, formerly a Dublin merchant, was 'lurking' on the Island because of his Irish debts. He owed money to Hugh Gregg, who was now living in Douglas. Gregg had asked Kempsey to find out if Deale had left any goods in Dublin. With the compliance of Deale's landlord, who was also a creditor, Kempsey had broken open his cellar but only found some old empty casks (see 28 October).[130]
26 April	*Mary was presented to the spiritual officers on John Hale's information that he had heard she had been 'naughty' with Patrick Galbraith, 'master of a Scotch ship'. The Concord had sailed from Derbyhaven two days before.[131]*
27 May	*The wardens of Douglas presented Mary and Isaac Allgood for the 'common fame of adultery'. She was given until 5 June to produce witnesses, who could prove that Allgood was 'the person that first gave forth this slander' and that it was not true.*
29 May	*Allgood gave intimate details of his adultery with Mary.*
	Evidence was taken from the men who were at the Hendricks's house, when Mary was reputedly 'naughty' with Galbraith: Thomas Edmonds, James Dymond, Thomas Wallis and Mr Owen. The story had been repeated by Owen to Sir James Poole, Henry Butler, Hannah Allgood and Ann Cottam, the Allgoods's maid. Wallis had told Peter Lancaster, the chaplain of Douglas. Despite the weight of this evidence, Mary cleared herself of the slander.

5 June	*Further evidence was taken from John Hendrick, William Murray, Captain John Wood, John Hale, Daniel Curghy, Ann Cottam and Mary Aiscough, the Allgoods's maids, and Mary and Isabel Cannell, Mary Hendrick's servants, all confirming Allgood's adultery with his landlady.*
	Both Allgood and Mary were found guilty and instructed to perform public penance at Kirk Braddan.
4 July	William Callin was fined 13s 4d for calling John Hendrick's boat 'cowcow', insinuating that he had been cuckolded. Callin had to find sureties for his good behaviour towards Hendrick in future – his own bond of £5 and a further £5 from Edward Killey of Castletown.[132]
26 July	John Hendrick charged Allgood with a debt of over £5. He made the standard claim that Allgood should be arrested because he was planning to 'speedily depart' from the Island. The case was dismissed.[133]
	Bishop Wilson wrote to the vicar of Kirk Braddan, John Curghey, with the following instructions:
	1. Allgood had failed to perform his penance the previous Sunday – he must do it the following week either in Douglas chapel or at Kirk Braddan.
	2. Mary must be told that her obstinacy in refusing to perform her penance would lead to excommunication.
11 August	John Hendrick gave detailed evidence to Horne, Rowe and Seddon about Allgood and Aglionby's disaffection to the English crown.[134]
17 August	Mary, Ann Cowin, John Hendrick's servant, Isabel and Mary Cannell, Mary's servants and Adam Christian gave evidence against Allgood and Aglionby.
	William Huddleston claimed he never heard either of them speak disrespectfully of the king or government. Allgood had told Robert Maddrell that he might have been prevailed upon to be at the battle of Preston. Nevertheless, Maddrell never heard him 'speak anything reflecting' about the king or government.[135]
20 October	*Thomas Corlett, general sumner and a member of the House of Keys, charged Mary to appear before the Bishop and Vicars General at Kirk Braddan.*
21 October	Robert Davies went to the Hendricks's house, where he verbally abused and beat both John and Mary. He pushed Mary several times in the belly with his cane. She was so bruised and wounded as a result of this attack that she was unable to get out of her bed for three days.[136]
22 October	*Presumably in her absence, Mary was excommunicated from the church until she agreed to do penance. This excommunication was to be made public at Kirk Braddan, Kirk Onchan and Douglas chapel. Should Mary die before doing the penance, then her body would not be buried in a church or churchyard.*
24 October	Recovered from Robert Davies's beating, Mary asked the governor to give her a token to charge the ten people who had pulled down her sign, the *Royal George*. Only Dalrymple failed to appear in court.
	Robert Davies was fined 10s for each 'battery' upon John and Mary. He had to find good security that he would behave himself peaceably in future – his own bond for £10 and Sir James Poole of Liverpool and Henry Butler £5 each.
	These sureties confirm Davies's social standing, as well as his political leanings.[137]

27 October	*William Ross published Mary's excommunication at Douglas chapel.*
28 October	*The Bishop informed all the church wardens on the Island that if Mary tried to attend a church whilst she was excommunicated then the service must stop until she was removed from the building.*
	John Curghey reported that when Allgood came to be received 'into the peace of the church' he did not have a plain habit to wear, as the law required. The vicar had suggested that Allgood should use the communion table cloth instead.
	William Deale went to the Hendricks's house, where Thomas Vance and Richard Lawson were drinking. Deale used provoking language and, pulling off his cravat, threatened Vance and challenged Lawson to fight him 'without any manner of provocation' (see April). He was fined 13s 4d.
	When Hendrick advised him to stop quarrelling and leave his house, Deale struck him in the face with his head. He was fined 11s and committed to prison until he could find security for his good behaviour in future – he gave his own bond of £5 and William Oates, a merchant in Douglas, provided a further £5.[138]
5 November	Mary handed the governor's token, given to her for charging the people who had broken her sign, to the deputy searcher at Douglas, pretending that it gave her permission to leave the Island. She was allowed to board a ship but the ruse did not succeed and she had to disembark.
9 November	Mary was fined 20s for misemploying the governor's token and she was committed to prison until she could provide 'good security not to depart the Island without a pass'. Robert Davies complained that Mary had used very scandalous and provoking language to him. She was fined 13s 4d.[139]
11 November	*John Curghey published Mary's excommunication at Kirk Braddan and William Gell published it at Kirk Onchan.*
19 November	Captain William Collier of Kirk Marown and Thomas Stoale of Ballasalla were bound in the sum of £5 each that Mary would not attempt to leave the Island again without permission. She was released from prison.[140]
11 December	*Because Mary had been excommunicated, she had 'forfeited' her body to the Lord of Man. The Bishop and the Vicars General ordered the sumner of Kirk Braddan to commit her to St German's prison.[141]*
20 December	The governor gave Mary an opportunity to appeal to the Earl of Derby against her excommunication, provided this appeal was submitted before May 1717.[142]
22 December	*Unaware of the governor's actions over Mary's appeal, Bishop Wilson and the Vicars General informed him formally of their proceedings in Mary's case.*
1717	
5 January	*There was a second part to Mary's excommunication – she also forfeited her goods to the Earl of Derby. John Hendrick made a statement about all the money owed to them. This included £3 10s from Squire Allgood and some bills worth 8s.[143]*
7 January	*William Cannell, David Christian, William Corlett and John Corris took an inventory of Mary's goods. These included a feather bed and bolster with bedstead and curtains, a blanket sheet and coverlaid; a feather bed and bolster with a bedstead and curtain, two blankets and a coverlaid, a trunkle bed, 10 coarse sheets, one pair fine sheets, eight pillow cases, 10 towels, 14 chairs, two looking glasses, a dozen napkins and five tablecloths. See also John Hale's inventory on p. 67.*

	John Hendrick and John Clague senior were bound in the sum of £150 that these goods would be forthcoming if necessary. Their bond was cancelled on 19 February 1719.[144]
9 February	*Allgood was presented for adultery with Henrietta Summers, 'who went under the denomination of his wife for some time in this Island'. Unless he could prove that they were married, 'his profligate and licentious course of living with this woman, even after his censure for adultery with Mary Hendrick, deserves a most rigorous censure'. In the meantime, he was committed to St German's prison for 28 days.*[145]
	In 1707 Isaac Allgood had married <u>Hannah Clark</u> at Newcastle and their son, Lancelot, was born on 11 February 1710. There is no information about Lancelot's whereabouts while Isaac and 'his wife' were on the Island. No further mention of this case, or of Allgood himself, has been found yet.
30 July	*The Earl of Derby accepted Mary's appeal and appointed 23 December for a hearing in London, at which Mary and the Bishop and the Vicars General would be given an opportunity to present their cases before him.*[146]
23 December	*Neither the spiritual officers 'nor any in their behalf' appeared in London.*[147]

Note: Unless otherwise indicated, the Presentments for 1716 (MS 10194) are the source of information.

The next stage in the story was between Bishop Wilson, the Earl of Derby and the governor.[148]

1718

19 February	Bishop Wilson was fined £10 for contempt in not appearing at London.
28 July	Wilson appeared before the Earl at Knowsley with a copy of an Act of Henry VIII, outlining the Bishop of Man's jurisdiction. This appeared to confirm that Mary's excommunication was indeed the province of the church and not of the Lord of Man. The £10 fine was respited until the governor and his officers could consider this new evidence. They claimed that the Bishop's copy of the Act was not authentic.
7 August	Bishop Wilson produced new evidence in the form of a printed book, 'wherein there is the Act of Henry VIII that annexes the Bishopric of Chester to that of York and the Bishopric and diocese of the Isle of Man to the Bishopric of York, after the same manner as Chester'. His fine was respited a second time, until the Earl and the governor had time to consider this.
16 August	Horne, Rowe and Seddon together with the deemsters, Daniel Mylrea and Charles Moore, 'having viewed and considered of several precedents of record touching appeals from church censures to your Lordship', believed that the Earl of Derby could require the spiritual officers not only 'to surcease any further proceedings' against Mary but also 'to absolve her from the excommunication' so that she could plead her case.
20 August	The Earl remitted the Bishop's fine.
17 September	The Earl ordered his officers on the Island 'not to molest her in body or goods and to protect her from abuse' until Mary's appeal was heard. This was to be published in the open market at Douglas, at Kirk Braddan after morning service the following Sunday and then affixed to Douglas market cross on Saturday, 27 September.
3 October	The governor and officers summoned the Bishop 'to give his reasons why our Lord Derby's order was not complied with' and he had refused to attend at London. He replied, 'there lay no appeal in that case and that he always thought so'.

Mary Hendrick continued in her refusal to do penance and despite the dispute raging between the governor and Bishop Wilson her excommunication was not lifted. Finally, in January 1723 Mary described her 'great extremity and want, being forced to wander from place to place in a miserable, destitute condition' because even her closest friends were 'no manner willing' to give her relief or a lodging. She appealed to Bishop Wilson, asking to be restored to the church. He was prepared to take her appeal seriously, provided her penance should 'in some nature answer the nature of her faults'. This involved 'standing in penitential habit and manner', just inside the door of six churches (Malew, Santan, Onchan, Lonan, Braddan and Douglas Chapel) and reading out a signed petition, admitting that she had been instigated by the devil and the enemies of the church to behave as she had done and begging the congregation to pray for her conversion. On 7 April 1723, the sentence of excommunication was lifted.[149]

Postscript

On 3 June 1726 John Hendrick was lost at sea on his passage from Ireland. In December 1727 and in early 1728 Mary charged John Tobyn and Charles Cosnahan in the Chancery Court for debts of £3 and £15 respectively. The cases were dismissed for want of prosecution. Subsequently Mary went to Liverpool, where she married Dr George Smith, and disappears from the story.[150]

Inevitably, there were recriminations amongst the Jacobites who were imprisoned after the battle of Preston, awaiting either their trial or execution, against the High Church Tories who had not joined them. A conversation was reported between some of the prisoners held at Wigan. Brigadier Mackintosh was charged with incompetence by Lord Widdrington, who claimed that he should have guarded the bridge over the river Ribble and placed the barricades within Preston more effectively. The Earl of Derwentwater, 'taking little or no notice of the Brigadier' turned to a gentleman who was in the room with them and said:

> You see what we have brought ourselves to, by giving credit to our neighbour Tories, as Will Fenwick ... and _Allgood_. If you outlive this misfortune, and return to live in the North, I desire you never to be seen to converse with such rogues in disguise, that promised to join us, and animated us to rise with them.

The gentleman replied, 'My Lord, I promise to obey you'.[151] On this occasion Allgood was only one of four people mentioned. Thomas Forster was quoted as making similar remarks in London, although he did not mention Allgood by name.

Considering Allgood's protestations that only his lameness had prevented him from joining with the others, Derwentwater's accusation seems somewhat unfair. This lameness was confirmed by independent evidence on the Island. On 29 May 1716 Daniel Curghy helped Allgood, 'who is infirm in his legs', to walk to the Court House. Shortly after the Allgoods arrived at the Hendricks's house, Mary had promised that she would get his lameness cured 'by a charm'. She had spoken to a man called Robert, 'who lives nigh Bishop's Court, but his surname I know not, who sent me some herbs by his niece, which herbs he used, as she said, only as a colour for his charms, to avoid punishment'.[152] The charm was not successful.

After the public enquiry surrounding the Mary Hendrick affair and the new charges relating to his 'wife', Isaac Allgood appears to have left the Isle of Man. It is highly likely, however, that Allgood would not want to return to Northumberland.

DISAFFECTED CONVERSATIONS IN 1716: JOHN HALE AND WILLIAM ALDRIDGE

King George had no right to the crown anyway because there were fifty other people before him that had a greater claim. [Paul Gelling of Braddan's evidence against William Aldridge, 8 November 1716][153]

This was not the end of the rebellion from the viewpoint of the Isle of Man. Strangers living on the Island continued to show disaffection to the government in London.

12 April 1716: John Hale

John Hale, who was the king's officer at Douglas, helped to support his wife and nine children by taking lodgers. Isaac Allgood, his wife and maids went to live with him after they left Mary Hendrick's house in February 1716. Other lodgers included Samuel Gorrell, John and Isabel Kissage and Richard Gripton.

Hale was accused by William Rushton, a watchmaker from Liverpool but currently living on the Isle of Man, of drinking the Pretender's health, by the name of King James III, hoping he would 'obtain his desire and come to the crown'. This had happened during the winters of 1714 and 1715, when 'he has pledged the aforesaid health several times'.

The governor met with Rowe and Seddon on several occasions to take evidence. Hale's lodgers and others, who had known him since he came to the Island, all declared that they had never heard him drink these healths. On 12 April 1716 Mary Hendrick stated that, although she had never heard Hale actually drink the Pretender's health, he had been in company with strangers at her house when they drank to the 'good old cause', hoping that 'every honest man had his right and every rogue a halter'.

Overnight Mary reconsidered her evidence, claiming the next day that when she and Isaac Allgood had been discussing people on the Island, who seemed disaffected to King George and his government, he had remarked, 'above all men he wondered at Mr. Hale that he would take the liberty of talking publicly, since his dependence lay that way'. Hale had felt secure whilst at her house, because more than once, when he arrived there with friends, he had put his hand on her neck and said, 'Mary is a good girl for that she will not tell what she hears'.

When Allgoods left Mary's house and went to live with Hale, she had said that she would find a time 'to be even with Mr Hale and that she would sit on his skirts' for taking them away from her. This suggested that her accusations might be out of pique or malice, but Mary declared that her evidence was given purely 'from the discharge of her conscience, being thereunto required by the government here'.

Possibly the most significant evidence should have come from the Douglas merchants John and William Murray and Philip Moore. It was unusual for people of their standing on the Island to give evidence about disaffection. In addition, Moore was a member of the House of Keys and so duty bound to disclose anything that he might have heard tending towards sedition. In theory, the merchants should have been hostile towards Hale, as a king's officer and therefore committed to spying on their trade and reporting their plans whenever possible.

William Murray stated that he had never heard Hale drink either the Pretender's health or that of James III but that he had often heard him drink a health to King George and the royal family, 'particularly that night that Mr. Rushton now mentions'. When asked if he had heard Hale drink Job's health, meaning the Duke of Ormonde, Murray declared that Hale was with him in company when that health was drunk 'but cannot particularly say that Mr. Hale drunk it'. On 17 April 1716 John Murray and Philip Moore created their own precedent by refusing to give evidence to the deputy governors (see Figure 19).

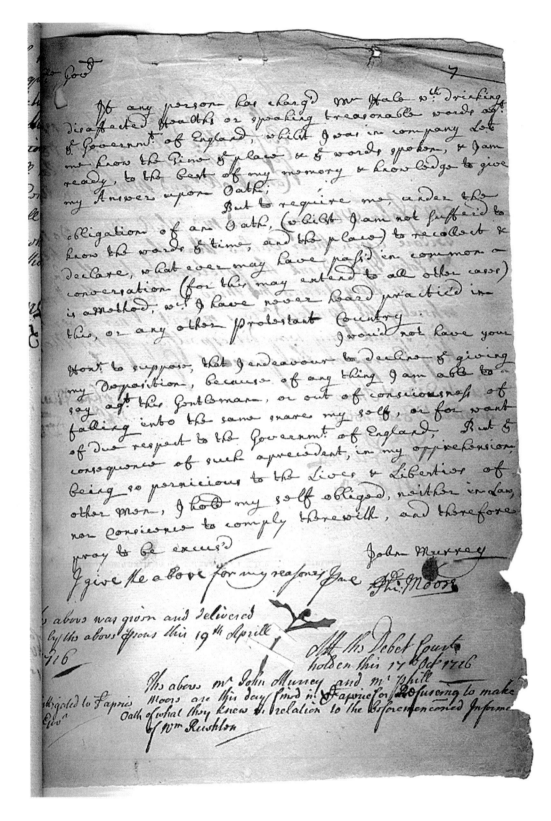

Figure 19: Philip Moore and John Murray's Statement[154]

On 11 August 1716 they declared, on oath, that they had never heard Hale drink a disaffected health. The same day John Hale was bound in the sum of £30 and Captain William Cross and Anthony Halsall both in £20 that he would appear before the House of Keys. Their verdict has not survived.[155]

If any person has charged Mr. Hale with drinking disaffected health or speaking treasonable words against the Government of England whilst I was in company, let me know the time, the place and the exact words spoken and I am ready to the best of my memory and knowledge to give my answer upon oath. But to require me under the obligation of an oath (whilst I am not suffered to know the words, the time and the place) to recollect and declare whatever may have passed in common conversation (for this may extend to all other cases) is a method which I have never heard practised in this or any other Protestant country. I would not have your Honour to suppose that I endeavour to decline the giving my deposition because of any thing I am able to say against this gentlemen or out of consciousness of falling into the same snare myself or for want of due respect to the government of England. But the consequence of such a precedent, in my apprehension being so pernicious to the lives and liberties of other men, I hold myself obliged neither in law nor conscience to comply therewith and therefore pray to be excused.

Postscript

William Rushton died on the Island in 1722. According to his will, he had appointed Captain John Wood of the Nunnery as his executor. Wood refused to 'see him buried' and so this task became the responsibility of Rushton's principal creditor, William Oates a merchant in Douglas. He wrote to Rushton's four sisters, Ellinor, Ann, Mary, and Alice, in Liverpool, telling them what they had each inherited but explaining that Rushton had left several debts on the Island. They replied that they understood the situation. 'But we desire you'll if possible send his clothes and the silver seal with his coat of arms on'. They believed that John Kewish, master of the Earl of Derby's vessel, the *Henrietta*, would help Oates if necessary.[156]

John Hale was already dead. The inventory of his goods, taken on 28 April 1718, included:

In the parlour
1 clock, 1 screwtore, 3 oval tables, 1 large armed chair, 9 cane chairs,
1 grate & brass fender, 2 punch bowls, 2 cruets & 3 salts, 2 old sconces, 10 old pictures,
1 large bible, 1 hackle, 1 tanned calf skin   £8 11s 0d
In the kitchen
1 table dresser & rack, 1 dressing glass, 8 old chairs, 1 warming pan, 2 coffee pots etc., 10
white ware plates, a white dish & basin, 5 candlesticks, 2 prs. snuffers, 1 mortar & pestle,
1 griddle & stone mortar, 1 smoothing iron & iron belonging to it, 1 brass saucepan, 1 iron
kettle, parcel iron stands for dishes, 1 parcel wooden ware, 1 sieve, 1 pr. bellows, 140 lbs
pewter @ 9d per, 39 lbs old brass @ 6d per, 104 lbs old iron @ 2d per   £8 10s 10d
In cellar
9 tubs, 2 barrels & 1 churn, 3 pails & 1 kissen, 1 close stool pan, 12 lbs of pewter   £1 13s 2d
In Little Room
Bedstead, curtains, 2 blankets, 1 rug, feather bed, bolster & pillows, 1 old chest & box, 1
cane chair & grate, 1 case for glass   £2 18s 4d
In pantry
1 chest, tub, 1 box, 1 chair, 1 side saddle, bag & hamper   10s 0d
In room over parlour
1 bedstead, curtains & window curtains, 1 feather bed, pillow & bolster, 1 chest drawers
& 1 square table, 1 armed chair & 1 glass, 1 grate, 5 small pictures   £5 17s 4d
In a little room
1 bedstead & curtains, 1 feather bed, 1 pillow & bolster, 2 blankets, 1 grate & 1 chair   £2 3s 4d
In room over kitchen
1 bedstead, curtains, feather bed, pillow, bolster, 2 blankets & a coverlet, 3 cane chairs, 2
armed chairs, 2 looking glasses, 6 small pictures, 1 old box, table & 2 stools   £4 3s 10d
In another room & garrets
1 bedstead etc. feather bed & curtains, 2 blankets, coverlet & parcel feathers, 1 bed &
furniture & 1 chair, 10 prs. sheets, 20 napkins   £11 18s 8d
                                                                                                     £46 6s 6d

The securities were Robert Davies and Ambrose Wall. This list should be compared with Mary Hendrick's belongings (see p. 62). It appears that Hale could provide more comfortable lodgings than those at Mary's house. There is no information about whether or not the Allgoods were still at Hale's house when he died – and if so where they took new lodgings. It is unfortunate that no details are given about the subject matter of the pictures.[157]

June 1716: William Aldridge

The historical background to this conversation was in seventeenth century Germany. In 1682 George Louis, the future King of Great Britain, married his cousin, Sophia Dorothea.

> *The marriage was not a happy one. The morals of German courts in the end of the 17th century took their tone from the splendid profligacy of Versailles. It became the fashion for a prince to amuse himself with a mistress ... George Louis followed the usual course. Count Königsmark – a handsome adventurer – seized the opportunity of paying court to the deserted wife. Conjugal infidelity was ... a privilege of the male sex. Count Königsmark was assassinated. Sophia Dorothea was divorced in 1694, and remained in seclusion till her death in 1726.*[158]

Their only son, George Augustus was born in 1683. Once he became Prince of Wales, the scandal became ammunition for those opposed to the Hanoverians – the counter to the warning pan story.

In November 1712 William Aldridge imported into the Isle of Man on the *Anne* of Liverpool, John Sergeant master, several parcels of old household goods, wearing apparel and old utensils for private use. He lived with his family first in Douglas and then in Ramsey. Aldridge was in partnership with various Manxmen in mills producing linen cloth.[159]

On 30 October 1716 Paul Gelling and his son John were charged with beating Aldridge, without any apparent provocation, and bound in the sum of £25 each to keep the peace towards the miller in future.

In early November Gelling told his brother-in-law, Thomas Tubman,[i] that he could have injured Aldridge, 'if I had been an ill man', because he had spoken treason. He would only give Tubman the details, however, if he promised not to tell 'any man'. Tubman said that he would keep silent.

Gelling had been in Aldridge's parlour the previous June when his host had claimed that the Prince of Wales (the future George II) was 'as great a bastard as the Pretender'. When Gelling asked, how? Aldridge explained that while he was still in Germany, the King had found a man with his wife in her room. Having told the man to say his prayers, George had thrown him over the balcony, breaking his neck. Gelling had asked what the King did with his wife. Aldridge reckoned that she had been sent to 'a monastery or nunnery, which of the two words he does not particularly remember'. Aldridge had added that King George had no right to the crown anyway.

Tubman had sworn that he would serve the Earl of Derby.[ii] He was concerned in case, if he did not report what Gelling had said, it might be a breach of his oath. In order to clarify the situation, Tubman asked the comptroller, John Rowe, 'how far his oath was binding upon him'. Inevitably, Rowe asked why he wanted to know. Tubman repeated what Gelling had told him about Aldridge. The comptroller advised him that if he heard anything spoken against the King, or the Prince of Wales or the royal family, then he was duty bound to 'discover it'. Tubman made his formal statement on 8 November 1716.

The Keys gave their verdict on 14 May 1717. As Gelling had concealed this information about Aldridge for nearly five months, they believed that the accusation was merely based on malice and revenge. They concluded that the case against Aldridge was not proved sufficiently and he was acquitted.[160]

Postscript

Aldridge died in May 1719, leaving a widow and five children. Thomas Lewn of Onchan claimed a new bible with the apocrypha, which had been promised to him by Aldridge, because of the injuries he

---

[i] In 1701 Paul Gelling married Thomas's sister, Ellinor Tubman.

[ii] It is unclear in what capacity Tubman actually served the Earl. The fact that he went to see the comptroller suggests that he was employed at Castle Rushen.

had sustained when quarrying millstones. Aldridge's other debts totalled over £40 and when these were paid only £10 was left. This should have been available for 'pious uses' because the church had paid for the administration of his will. Instead the money was given to the widow and her children, who were 'miserably poor', so that they could return to their 'own country'.[161]

Figure 20: James Butler, 2nd Duke of Ormonde (1665-1745) an Irish statesman and soldier, known as Job

With little of his grandfather's ability, and inferior to him in elevation of character, Ormonde was nevertheless one of the great figures of his time. Handsome, dignified, magnanimous and open-handed, and free from the meanness, treachery and venality of many of his leading contemporaries, he enjoyed a popularity which, with greater stability of purpose, might have enabled him to exercise a commanding influence over events. [Encyclopaedia Britannica 13th edition]

THE ACT OF GRACE AND THE DUKE OF ORMONDE: 1717

The severities of Government retribution suffered by the captured rebels had done nothing to mitigate the unpopularity of the King. By the Spring of 1717 it was clear that enough was enough ... [Noel Woolf, *The Medallic Record of the Jacobite Movement* 1990]

The aim of the Act of Grace was to stop all the secret meetings, like those at Mary Hendrick, John Aglionby and John Hale's houses, by giving people freedom of speech. News leaks existed even in the eighteenth century so that it was public knowledge that after 6 May 1717 anyone would be at liberty to express their true feelings, without fear of punishment. In fact, the Act did not become law until 17 July 1717, so creating a time lapse of over two months, when seditious words were still deemed to be seditious words.

Extract from an Act for the King's most Gracious, General, and Free Pardon

17 July 1717

The King's most Excellent Majesty having already shewed his Royal Inclination to Mercy, by many particular Instances of Grace, extended to such as had rendered themselves Obnoxious to the Laws, by being concerned in the late Unnatural Rebellion, that nothing may be Wanting in His Majesty to Quiet the Minds of all His Subjects, hath therefore, upon mature Deliberation, Resolved and Determined to Grant his General and Free Pardon in a Large and Bountiful manner; And however it may be Received by those who are Obstinately bent on the Ruin of their Country, His Majesty Promises Himself, that it will Raise a due Sense of Gratitude in all such as have been Artfully Misled into Treasonable Practices against His Person and Government, and Preserve them and others from standing in need of the like Mercy for the future, when such an Instance of Clemency may not be so Expedient for the Public Welfare, as it would be Agreeable to His Majesty's Inclination: And therefore His Majesty is well Pleased and Contented that it be Enacted by the Authority of this present Parliament; And be it Enacted by the Authority of the same, in Manner and Form following, (that is to say) That all and every His Majesty's Subjects, as well Spiritual as Temporal, of this His Majesty's Realm of Great Britain, their Heirs, Successors, Executors, and Administrators, and every of them, and all and singular Bodies Politick and Corporate, and their Successors, and all Cities, Boroughs, Shires, Stewartries, Ridings, Hundreds, Laths, Rapes, Wapentakes, Towns, Villages, Hamlets, and Tythings, and every of them, shall be, by the Authority of this present Parliament, Acquitted, Pardoned, Released, and Discharged against the Kings Majesty, His Heirs and Successors, and every of them, of and from all and all manner of Treasons, Dismissions of Treasons, Felonies, Treasonable and Seditious Words or Libels, Dismissions of Felony, Seditious and Unlawful Meetings and Conventicles, and all Offences whereby any Person may be charged with the Danger and Penalty of Præmunire [believing in papal jurisdiction]; and also of and from all Riots, Routs, Offences, Contempts, Trespasses, Entries, Wrongs, Deceipts, Misdemeanours, Forfeitures, Penalties, and Sums of Money, Pains of Death, Pains Corporal, and Pains Pecuniary; and generally of and from all other Things, Causes, Quarrels, Suits, Judgements, and Executions, in this present Act hereafter not Excepted or Foreprized, which have been had, made, done, committed, omitted, perpetrated, incurred, or forfeited, before and unto the 6th day of May, in the Year of Our Lord 1717.

The Act continued with several exceptions, covering over 11 pages. These included anyone who on 6 May 1717 was employed or in the service of 'the person who, since the death of the late King James, hath taken upon himself the style and title of King of England, or King of Great Britain'. Also 'all offences committed by any person or persons of levying the war against His Majesty, which began in this Realm in the year of our Lord 1715, who have been since beyond seas, and have, before the 6th May, returned into the Kingdoms of Great Britain or Ireland, without his Majesty's licence under his Privy Seal, or shall, on or after the 6th May, return into either of said kingdoms without such licence as aforesaid'. In other words neither Robert Douglas nor John Hunter were pardoned, wherever they were now living. Alexander and Robert Gordon of Bordeaux and William Gordon of Christiansand in Norway were unable to return to Scotland.

Certain other individuals were named, including all members of the Clan MacGregor, Robert Harley, Earl of Oxford and Earl Mortimer, Simon, Lord Harcourt, Mathew Prior, Thomas Harley (who was the Earl of Oxford's cousin and a director of the South Sea Company), Arthur Moor, James, Duke Crispe, Butler Nodes, Daniel Obryan (an Irishman, apparently not related to Denis O'Bryan), William Redmayne and Robert Thomson, late factor to the Viscount Arbuthnot. Also excepted were Robert Blackburn and the other people currently in prison for an attempt on the life of William III.[162]

Robert Davies

There was considerable support for the Jacobite cause in Cheshire. During 1715 the 'Cheshire Gentlemen' met at Ashley Hall to decide whether they should join the rebellion, and decided to stay at home.[i] There is no evidence that Robert Davies was with them.[163]

Davenport Davies was christened at St John the Baptist church, Chester, on 15 November 1715, two days after the capture of the English Jacobites at the battle of Preston. His parents were Robert Davies of Manley Hall and Salisbury née Lee of Darnhall in Cheshire. There were two other children, Thomas and Salisbury.

It is not known exactly when the Davies family arrived on the Isle of Man. They lived in Douglas and at some stage may have lodged at Adam Christian's house. Robert Davies's Jacobite inclinations are indicated by the company that he tended to keep – he was one of the sureties for John Hale's inventory and one of the several people charged with knocking down Mary Hendrick's inn sign in October 1716.[164]

At the end of May 1717, Lieutenant Farrell arrived in Ramsey from England. He told Captain James Christian, John Aglionby's former Cumbrian companion Christopher Lowther, Robert Davies and John Williams, the king's officer at Ramsey, that there was an Act of Grace passed that 'did clear all that was in or concerned in the late rebellion'.

On 5 June 1717 Davies was drinking a bottle of wine at the house of Captain Nicholas Christian junior in Ramsey with Captain Nicholas Christian senior, Christopher Lowther and Dr Abraham Silk. Lowther was asked to propose a toast and he named the Church of England 'as by law established, according to Magna Carta'. It was Davies's turn next and he named King George, the Church of England and the Duke of Ormonde.

Christian senior stated that he was 'much concerned to hear such words' spoken by Davies, because he was obliged by his oath, as a member of the House of Keys, to inform the governor. Davies explained there was now an Act of Grace, allowing him to drink to the Duke of Ormonde. Lowther disputed this, saying they only had Farrell's word that the Act was now law.

Both Lowther and Silk were summoned to give evidence before Horne, Rowe and Seddon. Silk stated that, 'being much concerned in liquor', he could not give 'a particular account of the words that passed. Only he heard Mr Davies express himself very passionately'. Despite this, the officers believed that there was a case to answer. Davies had to find security that he would appear before the Keys. His bond for £100 was accepted, together with a further £100 from Captain John Wood of the Nunnery. The Keys were convinced that Davies had drunk to Ormonde 'upon the assurance given by His Majesty's Act of Grace' and he was acquitted from the charge of treason.[165]

Christian senior had put forward a second accusation against Davies. During the same drinking session he had stated that he would pay £500 to see the governor 'out of his place', even if he had to

---

[i] These gentlemen included Thomas Assheton of Ashley, James, 4th Earl of Barrymore, Edward Berrisford, Robert Cholmondley of Holford, Sir Richard Grosvenor of Eaton, Charles Hurlestone of Newton, Henry Legh of High Legh, Peter Legh of Lyme, Amos Meredith of Henbury, Alexander Radclyff of Fox Denton, John Warren of Poynton. Their portraits, painted individually in 1720, now all hang at Tatton Park.

pawn his estate to raise the money.[i] Davies claimed that in October 1716 Horne had imprisoned him for his assault on the Hendricks, 'without anybody swearing the peace against me'. Christian reckoned that Davies had also claimed that 'some of the inhabitants' on the Island had told him that the governor was 'but a scoundrel and a rascal, as soldiers are' and that if they had been in England he would tell Horne so to his face.

Lowther corrected the words from 'some of the inhabitants of this Isle' to 'some people in this Isle'. This certainly changed the aspect of what Davies had said – it was well known that most of the problems in the Island came from 'strangers who are lately come into this Isle'.[166] Lowther added that Davies had said, 'Captain Christian do not mistake me, I do not say that the governor did me any injustice in it'.

Davies apologised to Horne:

> *Being truly <u>sensible</u> that I've given your Honour just cause to <u>resent</u> my ill manners, in taking liberty to talk so rude and unbecoming of your Honour's person. That I must confess was a great fault and <u>insults</u> the penalties of the law, the which I hereby acknowledge and affirm was altogether the effects of too much liquor and not the least of my inclination, when sober or sensible. For which great offence I earnestly beg your Honour's pardon, the granting of which will ever oblige Your Honour's most humble servant.*

Because of this submission and 'upon the intercession made by his friends', Davies was pardoned for his outspokenness by the governor.[167]

In February 1718 Captain John Wattleworth senior of Ramsey complained against Robert Davies's servant, William Haselden, because of 'the barbarous and inhuman usage' he had received from him 'by assault and battery in common highway'. Wattleworth had been confined to his bed for six weeks 'insomuch as [he] could not turn himself without help nor could he move his back for twenty days after the assault'. He also wanted Davies fined £500 as an accessory because he had claimed, 'in a boasting manner', that he had brought Haselden to Island 'on purpose to thwart or abuse people there'. Robert Davies and Robert Curghey of Kirk Christ Lezayre were bound, body for body, that Haselden would appear at the Court of General Gaol Delivery - the case was dismissed.[168]

Postscript

Davenport Davies 'fil' of Robert Davies Esq was buried at Kirk Braddan on 18 September 1718. In 1737 a man called Robert Davies was accused at Kirk Michael of having 'used Catherine Corteen junior after a rude and indecent manner … in the public road as she was about her lawful occasions'. He was to give bonds of £3 for his good behaviour in the future and to perform a public penance by asking Catherine for forgiveness 'upon his knees'. There is no evidence that this was the Robert Davies of Manley Hall.[169] Salisbury Lee also married John Townsend, of Darnhall in Cheshire. No date is available for this event so that it is impossible to know whether this marriage precedes that to Robert Davies or not.

The Duke of Ormonde
John Murray of Dumfries had been accused of drinking to the Prince of Wales. There were various other ways of referring to the Pretender and the Jacobite cause – the Duke of Ormonde (or Job) was also included in this category.

James Butler was born in Dublin on 29 April 1665. After an education in France and at Christ

---

[i] An inventory had been taken of Manley Hall on the death of Robert's elder brother, Davenport, in 1699. It included a great parlour, little parlour, hall, kitchen and buttery, best chamber, six other chambers, a brewhouse, dairy and stables plus horses, cattle, sheep, pigs and poultry. No value was placed on this. When their father died in 1685, his half of the state was valued at over £500. [Cheshire County Council Archives WS 1700 Davenport Davies].

Church, Oxford, he commanded a cavalry regiment in Ireland. In 1688, he succeeded his grandfather, as the 2nd Duke of Ormonde. One of the first to join William of Orange when he arrived in England, Ormonde was appointed a member of the Order of Garter and High Constable at the coronation. He was colonel of a regiment of horse-guards during the Williamite wars in Ireland and, after the battle of the Boyne in 1690, Ormonde entertained the King at his castle in Kilkenny. He served in Europe, first under William III and then Queen Anne. In 1702 he commanded Sir George Rooke's expedition against Cadiz. Now appointed as a privy councillor, Ormonde was Viceroy of Ireland between 1703 and 1707 and Lord Lieutenant from 1703 to 1705 and 1710 to 1713. When the Duke of Marlborough was dismissed by the Queen in 1711, Ormonde became captain-general in his place, continuing the fight against France and Spain in the War of Succession. The Tory government, whose public policy was war against the Netherlands, gave secret orders to Ormonde not to support the allied forces under Prince Eugene.

Ormonde appears to have become a Jacobite during the last years of Queen Anne's reign. He signed the proclamation of King George I but was soon deprived of his appointment as captain-general. On 21 June 1715 he was impeached for high treason and fled to France. As it could be proved that he had taken part in the Jacobite invasion later that year, in 1716 his estates were confiscated and a £10,000 reward was offered for his capture. Ormonde spent the rest of his life in Europe, where he received a pension from the Spanish court, for his role in the War of Succession. He was based mainly at Avignon, where he continued to intrigue with the Jacobites. He died on 16 November 1745 and was buried in Westminster Abbey.

It is uncertain why he was nicknamed 'Job'.

William Deale

In January 1717 the merchant, William Jackson, was drinking at John Hale's house, when he told Patrick Gelling that he had heard the Quaker, William Deale, say, 'here's Ormonde's health to you'. Jackson had seized the glass out of Deale's hand and thrown it to the ground. On this occasion Hale and William and Thomas Oates confirmed Jackson's statement. Deale's response was that he did not mean the <u>Duke of</u> Ormonde's health. This somewhat flimsy excuse was accepted by the House of Keys, who concluded on 14 May 1717 that the evidence did not confirm the information against Deale and he was acquitted.[170]

Postscript

The Irish merchant, William Jackson, was a regular visitor to the Isle of Man at this stage. During 1717 he imported large quantities of brandy, claret and prunes on the *Love* of Workington, Thomas Dawson master, and the *Robert* of Belfast, Robert Steward, and some tobacco on the *George* of Belfast, Ninian Stewart master, all from Europe. He also entered 220 empty casks from Scotland and Ireland. These would not have been sufficient for the goods that he sent out of the Island:[171]

Goods	Vessel	Official Destination
Brandy, empty casks and tobacco	*Agnes* of Loughlairne	Fort William
Claret and white wine	*Ann* of Portaferry	Kirkcudbright
Brandy and empty casks	*Jane* of Greenock	Londonderry
Brandy and claret	*Margaret* of Ballantrae	Londonderry
Brandy	*Mary* of Saltcoats	Bergen
Brandy	*William*	Wicklow
Brandy and wine	*William* of Derry	Bergen

During this time Jackson was either a lodger at the house of John Hale, the king's officer in Douglas, or a regular visitor there.

Date	Accused	Accusation	Verdict
1713	John Murray	Claimed that the Pretender was his King and Prince	He had spoken not advisedly or maliciously but merely from the effects of extreme drunkenness
1715	Henry Butler	The English were the rebels, not to accept James III as their rightful king.	No weight given to Thomas Allen's evidence
1715	John Hale	Hoped James III would 'obtain his desire and come to the crown'.	Not available
1716	John Aglionby	Innumerable examples of disaffection	Not available
1716	Isaac Allgood	Innumerable examples of disaffection	Not available
1716	William Aldridge	Prince of Wales a bastard and King George no right to the throne	Not sufficiently proved
1717	Robert Davies	Proposed a toast to the Duke of Ormond	believed an Act of Grace law
1717	William Deale	Proposed a toast to the Duke of Ormonde	The depositions did not amount to an information
1717	William Cross	Refractory remarks about George I	Evidence various and uncertain
1720	Nicholas Christian	Damned King George	No law on the Island to punish him

Table III: Details of Disaffection Cases: Accusation and Verdict

The Accused	Nationality & religion (if known)	The Accusers
John Murray	Scottish, Episcopalian	Richard Brew, soldier, & John Christian of Douglas
Henry Butler	English	Thomas Allen
John Hale	English	William Rushton, watchmaker in Liverpool
John Aglionby	English, Papist	John Hendrick, boatman & herring fisherman
Isaac Allgood	English	John Hendrick – see above
William Aldridge	English	Paul Gelling, miller
William Deale	Irish, Quaker	William Jackson & Patrick Gelling
Robert Davies	English, Protestant	Nicholas Christian senior & junior
William Cross	English	Thomas Allen
Nicholas Christian	Manx	William Henderson, king's officer at Ramsey

Table IV: Details of Disaffection Cases: Nationality and Religion of Accused, and Accusers

DISAFFECTION: A BRIEF REVIEW

This section provides a brief review of all the cases of disaffection to the crown in England considered so far. Table I listed the members of the house of Keys present at each of the disaffection trials. Tables III and IV summarise the cases in terms of the accusations and verdict of the Keys, the nationality and religion of the accused and details of their accusers. Table V compares the number of seditious words (disaffection) cases in three English counties with those on the Isle of Man. Finally, Table VI lists the sureties for those accused.

The population on the Isle of Man was small, though constantly changing because of the influx of merchants and other visitors from elsewhere. There was a high probability that individual members of the House of Keys had personal knowledge of all those accused of disaffection. Governor Mawdsley had been aware of this in 1711, when he exhorted the Keys to expose anyone disaffected to the Island's government, 'without favour or affection to any persons whatsoever'.[172] The 'strangers' accused were often regular visitors to the Island. The Keys claimed that John Murray of Dumfries (John Murray of Douglas's cousin) was 'for some time known to most of us to have behaved himself orderly and loyally at all times heretofore'.[173] John and William Murray and Philip Moore were regularly at John Aglionby and John Hale's houses. They were asked to find their friends guilty of a crime that should result in the death penalty.

Data exists on the number of seditious words (disaffection) cases heard in three English counties.

	Lancashire	Staffordshire	Gloucestershire	Isle of Man
1689-1714	22	7	32	1
1715-1752	37	38	22	13
Total	59	45	54	14
Population 1801	670,000	240,000	250,000	
Per thousand (1801)	0.09	0.18	0.22	
Population 1726				14,500
Per thousand (1726)				0.96
Population 1757				20,000
Per thousand (1757)				0.70

Table V: Comparison of Seditious Words Cases in three English Counties and on the Isle of Man

Notes:
1. The figures used for the Isle of Man represent the minimum number of cases.
2. The population figure for 1757 is from A W Moore *A History of the Isle of Man* pp. 412 & 413
3. The English data is from Paul Kléber Monod *Jacobitism and the English people 1688-1788* p. 249

It could be argued that the Island was not comparable with either Staffordshire or Gloucestershire. Thousands of High Church Tories were expected to join the rebellion from Lancashire, however. The impression when studying the cases of disaffection tends to be that the governor and his officers expended a large amount of time and effort over what appears to have been a handful of cases. When placed in the English context, however, Governor Horne becomes more justified in his concerns.

Although those giving evidence <u>against</u> people came from a wide range of occupations: from a soldier, a watchmaker and the keeper of a drinking and lodging house in Douglas to the king's officer in Ramsey, the people who were 'bound' for the accused tended to be gentlemen. This may simply have been because of the sums of money involved but it is also probable that it indicates the network of Jacobite sympathisers.

Accused	Surety 1	Surety 2
John Murray Scotland	Captain John Wood of the Nunnery	William Ross former water bailiff
Henry Butler Esq. Lancashire	John Sabbarton gentleman (£100) ex Royal Navy	
John Hale king's officer	Captain William Cross (£20) ex Royal Navy	Anthony Halsall (£20)
John Aglionby Cumberland	John Murray (£50) merchant	Phil Moore (£50) merchant
Isaac Allgood Northumberland	Christopher Parker (£100) Former receiver	
William Aldridge Lancashire	no information	no information
William Deale Ireland	William Oates (£10) merchant	Edward Cannell (£10) Cooper
Robert Davies Esq. Cheshire	Captain John Wood (£100)	-

Table VI: Sureties for those accused of disaffection

There are two final questions, which have been discussed previously, in passing:

What would have happened if there had been a law against treason already in place on the Island? One imagines that, considering the general mood on the Island at the time, the Keys would still have acquitted those charged with disaffection.

What would have happened if there had not been a clash between the Keys and the governor and unrest over the Earl of Derby? The answer is probably the same.

THE LITTLE RISING: 1719

Figure 21: Eilean Donan Castle – June 2002

The Pretender returned to Lorraine in 1716 and the following year he went to Rome. From there he contacted Charles XII of Sweden, who counted the Hanoverians as his enemy. They planned a joint invasion of Britain but this was foiled by the death of Charles on 12 December 1718. His army was besieging the Norwegian fortress of Fredriksten and when the King looked over the parapet of the front trench he was shot through the head by a bullet.

In 1719 Philip V of Spain invited James to lead a Spanish force, which would invade both England and Scotland, where the local Jacobites would rush to join them. Over 300 Spaniards set sail in two frigates headed for Scotland. They were to be followed by a further 29 vessels carrying 5,000 men and arms for another 30,000. This fleet was wrecked during a terrible storm in the Bay of Biscay. In the meantime, the first two ships reached Stornaway with 2,000 muskets and a large quantity of ammunition on board. Having made contact with some of the Jacobite leaders, they now sailed to Loch Alsh, where they captured Eilean Donan castle and established their supply base. Within a few days three frigates arrived and bombarded the castle from the sea. The powder magazine exploded.

A government force of 1,600 men under General Wightman approached from Inverness. On 10 September 1719 a battle was fought at Glen Shiel. Although there were equal casualties on both sides, the local Jacobites disbanded. The Spanish troops escaped over what is now known as Coirein nan Spainteach (Spaniard's Pass)[i] into the next valley. There they surrendered and were sent home to Europe. The Jacobite leaders returned to the continent through the Highlands.

---

[i] OS Map 1:50 000 No. 33 Grid reference 995150

ON THE ISLE OF MAN IN 1720: NICHOLAS CHRISTIAN AND CHARLES RADCLIFFE

All the King's Men: a revenue officer and a soldier

Both these stories fall into the aftermath category. Nicholas Christian was not accused of drinking a disaffected health – it was <u>claimed</u> that no drink was present in the house at the time. He had been disrespectful to the English government. Charles Radcliffe, brother of the Duke of Derwentwater, had escaped from Newgate prison in 1716 and now lived in Europe. He was so short of money, however, that he risked returning to England, using aliases, so that he could beg from his former Jacobite friends. He was on the Island in 1720 – when he was charged with a debt of £10.

Captain Nicholas Christian

The king's officers on the Isle of Man were discussed in the section on the running trade. In 1720 the customs establishment at Ramsey appears to have included Nicholas Christian junior, Manx deputy searcher of the customs, William Henderson, the king's officer, assisted by the Manxman Robert Kneale and his crew, including David Kennedy and a government appointee, Thomas Freeman, who had previously served in Ireland, all of whom were called 'tidewaiters'. Inevitably, there would be tensions between these men.

On 1 January 1720 Thomas Bridson, Edward, Elizabeth, John and Thomas Christian, Mary Harrison, David Kennedy and Margaret Kneale were playing cards quietly at Robert Kneale's house in Ramsey. They were not drinking alcohol.

About nine o'clock at night Thomas Freeman and his wife Ann came into the house. Freeman sat on a chair at the end of the table. Shortly afterwards Nicholas Christian junior arrived and 'in an abuseful way, which surprised them all', demanded to know what the noise was all about. Turning to the stranger, he asked, 'is your name Freeman?'

When Freeman said 'yes', Christian ordered him to 'get up out of the chair, you pitiful beggarly fellow'. Freeman refused and Christian had to sit 'above the table'. As Freeman was cursing the Manx people and their Manx manners, a few minutes later Christian suddenly jumped up, threw him out of his chair and 'fell atop of him, where they for a while struggled, but were parted by those that were by'. Freeman then called Christian 'a lousy dog, a fat bellied dog and a scoundrel dog'. Freeman's wife told Christian 'to kiss her breach, whereupon he called her an impudent whore, and called Freeman a runagate'.

Freeman asked Christian, 'what authority do you have to abuse me, a stranger, in this manner? Is it because you have a commission under my Lord Derby that you take that liberty?' He added that he held King George's commission, which was the better of the two. Christian declared, 'God damn your King, and your commission'. Freeman responded that if he cursed the Earl of Derby, 'after that manner', then it was probable he would be hanged for it.

The next morning, 'it was noised about that the waiters and Captain Christian was quarrelling the night before'. Michael Bridson found David Kennedy having breakfast at his father's house and asked what had happened. Kennedy replied that he had been present the whole time and swore that there were 'no reflecting words spoke or mentioned of either the King or the Lord'.

In the meantime, Freeman had reported the incident to Henderson. He would not have taken the matter further, if Christian had come to him voluntarily and acknowledged 'his fault and asked his pardon'. When Christian made no attempt to apologise, Henderson reported him to the governor for speaking disrespectfully against George I. Detailed evidence was taken from all the card players, and the servants in the house. The case was presented to the House of Keys.

One way of acquitting Christian was to provide evidence against Freeman. Nicholas Murphey, had lived near Freeman in Ireland[i]. About six years ago, Alderman Quinn of Dublin had refused to take Freeman's affidavit because it was known that he was prejudiced in the case under consideration and would not give fair evidence. Thomas Wogan confirmed this.[ii] The Irish merchants, Andrew and Patrick Savage, knew nothing about Freeman when he was in Ireland. Since he came to the Island, however, they had heard Captain Hayes of Dublin say several times in a coffee house at Douglas, and in other places, that Freeman was 'a rogue and guilty of many ill and base actions'.

Freeman acknowledged in Court that towards the end of Queen Anne's reign he had carried 12 men, called 'Irish Bullocks',[iii] on board Peter Gerard's ship in Dublin harbour. He was told afterwards that these men had been sent to France, 'for the use of the Pretender'. He should have reported this to the appropriate authorities.

On 3 February 1720 the Keys acquitted Christian. They gave three reasons for this:

- Freeman was 'a person of a very indifferent character';
- he had not reported the matter to the Island's officers, 'within such reasonable time as is required in matters of this kind in other parts of His Majesty's dominion';
- they had 'no law to direct us in punishing crimes of this nature'.

The Keys suggested that Christian and Freeman should be punished for their <u>drunkenness</u>, cursing and abusive language to each other, 'where such matters are properly cognisable'.[174]

Charles Radcliffe

Having defended the second barricade at Preston, Charles Radcliffe was one of the Jacobites captured on 14 November 1715. Three months after the execution of his brother, the Earl of Derwentwater, Radcliffe was found guilty of treason and sentenced to death. He succeeded in escaping, however, on 11 December 1716, by leaving Newgate prison with the visitors who had attended a party there. Having hidden in London for several weeks, Radcliffe managed to reach the continent.

Before his execution, the Earl had instructed his son, John, to give his uncle an allowance of £100 a year. This contribution and his small pension as a Jacobite agent in Paris were insufficient, however, to support Radcliffe's lifestyle. He returned to England regularly, using aliases such as G. Thompson (1721) and Mr Johns (1733), in attempts to raise money.[175]

Radcliffe was on the Isle of Man in July 1720, using the name Cornet[iv] Hanlon. Possibly he was trying to contact his fellow Northumbrian Isaac Allgood. Cornet Peter Renant, now of Castletown, charged Hanlon, 'who sometimes went under name of Charles Radcliffe', in the Chancery Court with a debt of £10. Radcliffe had moved on and the case was dismissed.[176]

Postscript
In November 1745 Radcliffe and his son James were taken prisoner on board the *Esperance*, a French privateer bound for Montrose with stores, ammunition and men. Because he was a French citizen, James was released but his father was tried for his part in the 'Fifteen. He denied that he was Charles Radcliffe - neither the barber nor the head-keeper at Newgate gaol could identify him positively. Two Northumbrians, Thomas Moseley and Abraham Bunting, recognised him, however, from a scar on his face and on 8 December 1746 he was beheaded on Tower Hill.[177]

---

[i] Although Charles, John, Mathew and Peter Murphey are listed in the Customs Ingates and Outgates of this period, no mention has been found of a Nicholas.
[ii] There is no evidence to link Thomas with Nicholas Wogan.
[iii] bullies (1716) but also Irish labourers, particularly with no land to work.
[iv] the 5th commissioned officer in a troop of cavalry, who carried the colours. It is not clear why Radcliffe had used this alias.

Figure 22: James I of England (1603-1625) & VI of Scotland (from 1567)

Although England accepted him [James I] *as the alternative to civil war, and although he was received and surrounded with fulsome flattery, he did not win the respect of his English subjects. His undignified personal appearance was against him, and so were his garrulity, his Scottish accent, his slovenliness and his tolerance of disorders in his court.* [Encyclopaedia Britannica 13th edition] In 1604 he convened a conference between the High and Low Church representatives at Hampton Court. This resulted in the *Authorized Version* of the Bible.

WHIGS: 1722 & 1724

It is disfigured by sentiments which are deserving of great reprobation. It was more immediately directed against the hierarchy of the church of England; but it was also meant, or at least has a direct tendency to undermine the very foundation of a national religion, under any circumstances, and to bring the sacred profession, if not religion itself, into contempt. The sacerdotal office, according to this book, is not only not recommended in scripture, but is unnecessary and dangerous; ministers of the gospel have ever been the promoters of corruption and ignorance, and distinguished by a degree of arrogance, immortality, and a thirst after secular power, that have rendered them destructive of the public and private welfare of a nation. [Thomas Murray *Literary History of Galloway* 1822]

Bishop Wilson and *The Independent Whig*: 1722

On 20 January 1720 Thomas Gordon (related to Robert Gordon of Douglas) from Kirkcudbright and John Trenchard of Somerset published the first issue of *The Independent Whig* in London. This was a weekly political newssheet, which included letters from Daniel Defoe on the merits of the clergy and the importance of Gibraltar to the British Empire. It was printed for one year only. When Trenchard died on 23 December 1723, Gordon produced a new edition, which appeared in two volumes.

Richard Worthington brought a bound volume of *The Independent Whig* to the Island in 1722 so that it could be placed in the library but first he lent it to John Stevenson of Balladoole. Stevenson showed the book to the Bishop, who was alarmed that it was being 'industriously handed about, with a manifest intent to beguile ignorant and unstable souls and to render the doctrine, the discipline, and the government of this church contemptible'. He claimed that the journal had

> *one continued design, in which the devil and the authors have shewed the utmost skill to lay waste the church of Christ, to overthrow all revealed religion, to reduce men to a state of nature and to bring all things to confusion, both sacred and civil.*

Because Stevenson tended to be used by the Bishop as 'an instrument to pursue anything he shall think fit to put him upon', he refused either to return *The Independent Whig* to Worthington or to produce a note from William Ross, the library keeper at Castletown, to acknowledge that it had been deposited there. When the governor imprisoned Stevenson until he returned the book, Bishop Wilson wrote a lengthy remonstrance, claiming that he should not be punished for assisting him in his bounden duty. The statements and counter-statements made by Bishop Wilson and governor Horne provide further evidence of the Island's standpoint during the 'Fifteen.

The Bishop claimed that he was obliged by George I's directions, forwarded to him by the Bishop of London, and by his consecration vows 'to banish and drive away all erroneous and strange doctrine contrary to God's word'.

The governor was not convinced by the Bishop's apparent zeal to follow the King's directions. In 1715 he had been convinced of an unwillingness on the part of the clergy to declare 'their affection and loyalty to His Majesty and government and his right to the crown of Great Britain, as established by law against all Pretenders'. They seemed content to let the Bishop appoint vicars to vacant parishes, instead of applying to the Lord of Man to have them filled, thus showing another example of disrespect.[i]

The Bishop was convinced that *The Independent Whig* was full of 'damnable errors', which were 'capable of doing more mischief than the very plague we are so justly afraid of'.

The governor knew that the publication had not been included in the King's list of books to be banned. He believed the Bishop was using this excuse to suppress something that he, personally, did not want on the Island.

---

[i] James Knipe, a schoolmaster, was licensed by Bishop Wilson in 1712 as chaplain of Ballure. [Canon John Gelling *A history of the Manx Church* p 244]

Figure 23: Bishop Wilson

To ensure Stevenson's release from prison, Bishop Wilson gave the book to the governor, protesting about 'the evil consequences which may attend the forcing it out of my hands'. On 21 February 1722 John Rowe and John Quayle took *The Independent Whig* to William Ross, who refused to accept 'the vilest book that ever he saw'. He would 'as soon take poison as receive [it] into the library upon any other terms or conditions than immediately to burn it'. He was imprisoned.[178]

Although at this stage Ross was clearly 'of the Bishop's party', in 1734 Wilson wrote to him, 'since you left off housekeeping [looking after yourself], you have given yourself too much to keeping company and drinking to an unbecoming excess ... In the meantime you will take my friendly intimation as 'tis meant for your soul's good and for the sake of the church for which we both pretend to have a great esteem'.[179]

Postscript
When George Hussey died in 1746 the inventory of his belongings included 27 books of various kinds, valued at £1 12s, *Camden's Britannica* in folio,[i] the 1st volume of *Bayle's Reflections*[ii] , the 2nd volume of *The Independent Whig* and 83 pamphlets, valued at 1d each.

In November 1720 there was a serious threat of the plague being brought to the Isle of Man by ships from the Mediterranean. According to the collector at Dumfries, 'I am pretty well informed that there have been three large ships hovering about that place these three weeks past and have in all the landing places of it endeavoured to force themselves on shore but have been repulsed by the inhabitants, who have all that time been in arms night and day upon the coast'.[180]

Ewan Curghey: 1724
On St Luke's day, 18 October 1724, William Corlett, the coroner of Michael Sheading, was standing at John Cannell's door when Ewan Curghey from Kirk Christ Lezayre came along the street. They exchanged words, which emphasise the strong links in people's minds between the political and religious components of Whig and Tory parties. The conversation only makes sense if Curghey was not a Whig:

Curghey:	What religion are you of?
Corlett:	If your religion is as good, let me alone.
Curghey:	I am a Whig.
Corlett:	Suppose I am another.
Curghey:	Damn you, as the son of a bitch.

Cannell stepped into the highway, to distance himself from the conversation. Curghey, stripping off his coat, pursued him along the road, giving him 'all the ill language possible'. Not wanting to quarrel with Curghey, Corlett went into his house - Hugh Cowley and William Kelly were there already. No sooner had he sat down than Curghey came in and 'upbraided him and his family'. He claimed that there was only one 'honest' Corlett on the island – Thomas Corlett of Ballaugh. All the other members of the family had 'stood against' Bishop Wilson and the church.

Curghey dared Corlett to use his rod of office, as the coroner, to command him to keep the peace. He claimed that if Corlett attempted to caution him, then he would kick him to pieces 'with several other provoking expressions'. When eventually Corlett did hold up his rod, in the Earl of Derby's name, Curghey took it from him – and hit him with it.[181]

Postscript
William Kelly was unable to give a detailed account of what had happened, because Curghey and Corlett were speaking in English so that 'he did not understand them rightly'. It was clear, however, that Curghey was provoking the coroner.

---

[i] Figure 3 is reproduced from this volume.
[ii] Pierre Bayle was one of the most important sceptical thinkers of the seventeenth century. His most famous work was the *Dictionnaire historique et critique* (1697), which was translated into English as *An Historical and Critical Dictionary by Monsieur Bayle* and published in London in 1710, posthumously. No reference has been found to his *Reflections* published in English but there were several French editions of his *Pensées diverses*. [Sally L Jenkinson ed. *Bayle Political Writings* Cambridge University Press 2000]

Figure 24: The Pretender: James III of England & VIII of Scotland

As to James's personal character, there is abundant evidence to show that he was grave, high-principled, industrious, abstemious and dignified ... Although a fervent Roman Catholic, he was far more reasonable and liberal in his religious views than his father. [Encyclopaedia Britannica 13th edition]

The Pretender was born in London on 10 June 1688.

THE PRETENDER'S BIRTHDAY: 1725 & 1726

The Pretender's birthday was celebrated by Captain John Doran in Douglas harbour on 10 June 1726, 'by setting forth and hoisting his colours and firing off guns'. [Chancery Court, 15 June 1726][182]

William Henderson, the king's officer at Ramsey, claimed that Richard McGwire,[i] one of the farmers of the Lord's customs on the Isle of Man, celebrated the Pretender's birthday on 10 June 1725 with a party at Castle Rushen. In 1726 John Doran held his own celebration in Douglas harbour 'contrary to the peace of this Isle'.

Richard McGwire and William Henderson – 1725

In 1721 Josiah Poole, a merchant in Liverpool, and Richard McGwire, a banker in Dublin, were appointed as farmers of the Earl of Derby's customs on all imports of goods and exports of Manx produce. This system of farming the customs had been used in England until 1688. The theory was that, if a wealthy merchant or group of merchants paid a fixed price, estimated to be not more than the value of the customs, then they were responsible for staffing the collection of these duties. It was in the farmers' interests therefore to make the collection system as efficient as possible to ensure the maximum profit.

Poole & McGwire agreed with the Earl of Derby for the lease of the Manx customs for 21 years, at the rate of £1,000 (sometimes this figure is quoted as 1,000 guineas) per year. Their motives and frustrations were described in a report from the Collector of Customs at Liverpool to the Court of Exchequer at London in 1764:

> Poole & McGwire made this contract in hopes of disposing of it to the Government, to great advantage, and accordingly offered it to Sir Robert Walpole, for £3,000 per annum, which was rejected, and they continued in the management of the Island, and got money, but not without much murmuring from the natives, who made many complaints to his Lordship of the tyrannical proceedings of their new masters.

> In 1726 a Bill was brought into the House [of Commons] to prohibit the importation of all goods [into Britain], except the produce of the Island, Poole & McGwire went up to oppose it, and had made interest for that purpose, but Sir Robert told them there would be a clause in the Bill giving him power to treat with the Trustees of Lady Ashburnham[ii], for the purchase of the Island, and that in consequence thereof, he should be enabled to treat with them; which satisfied them

> The Bill passed into a law. Sir Robert thought the Island was demolished, and neglected Poole & McGwire's repeated solicitations, who returned big with despair, and immediately flew to Lord Derby, complaining of the ill treatment they had met with, and that the Act just passed would ruin the Island, and that they were not able to fulfil their contract, and prayed His Lordship to release them from it. His Lordship, having been very much teased with complaints from the natives against them, granted them a surrender.[183]

It is possible that Poole & McGwire had misjudged the situation on the Isle of Man. They could not browbeat the merchants and they paid insufficient attention to another group of government-related people resident there: the king's officers.

In 1722 Poole & McGwire employed Joshua Robinson as a clerk under the direction of John Sanforth, their first collector of customs. Robinson would know where all the goods on the Island were coming from and their final destinations. This was exactly the sort of information that the collector at Dumfries was trying to obtain about the *Queen Anne*'s tobacco on board the *Lachmere*.

---

[i] There are several spellings of McGwire's name: this is the one on Richard McGwire's will.
[ii] Lady Harriet Ashburnham was the granddaughter of the 9th Earl of Derby (see Appendix I).

George Tollet was sent to the Island, presumably with government backing, to find out as much as possible about what went on there. He was in close contact with the collectors of both Dumfries and Whitehaven and his main contact on the Island was William Henderson, the king's officer at Ramsey. They persuaded Robinson to undertake 'many indirect practices'. He not only removed 'sundry writings of moment' out of Poole & McGwire's office and Sanforth's house but also defrauded the collector of 'several sums of money', which had been collected as customs duties.

Robinson was taken to England with Poole & McGwire's books. The collector at Whitehaven was able to estimate from these how much duty had been lost to Great Britain by the Island's low customs duties. He reckoned this amounted to at least £1,000 per year. The collector at Dumfries was able to confirm his worst fears about the Lutwidges and their tobacco movements.

Once all the information had been copied from the books, Tollet 'did most audaciously presume, in defiance to law and justice, to treat with Mr. Sanforth touching the bringing back of Robinson' to the Island. He promised to do this on the condition that Poole & McGwire took no action against their clerk 'for his enormous offences, in which it since appears Tollet himself was principally and deeply concerned'. The farmers had no alternative. They needed the books 'to prevent the great detriment' that both they and Sanforth faced because of the confused state of the paperwork and a total inability to sort out the accounts.

Although Robinson did return, his position was untenable. He could not account for 'the great deficiency of cash expended', according to Poole & McGwire 'in supporting Tollet and others in their extravagances'. He escaped from the Island, before the accounts had been adjusted with Sanforth.[184]

In the meantime, Richard Dutoral, Hendrick Toren and Thomas Harley had replaced Poole & McGwire's first collector. Possibly, they believed that three people would be in a stronger position to control the situation and keep the accounts accurately. Their overheads had increased.

There was another attack against the farmers, this time aimed at Richard McGwire personally. During the last week in March 1726, William Henderson went to McGwire's house in Castletown and demanded a dram of brandy. When he was told by the maid, Catherine Costene, that she had none to sell, Henderson became enraged. He 'damned her for a bitch', adding that her master was 'a villain'.

Having tried unsuccessfully to hit her, Henderson chased the maid 'in the way before the house'. Fortunately a man came to her rescue or 'she verily believes she could not have escaped his hands with safety or without blows'.

When the other servants appeared, Henderson asked them, 'who are you for – the King or the Pretender?' They replied that they were as loyal as he was. Henderson claimed, 'they were for the Pretender and so was their master, McGwire, and that he was a rogue and kept nobody about his house but rogues'.

On 8 September 1726 Henderson was called before the Court to answer McGwire's complaint against him for mistreating his servants and accusing him of being a Jacobite. Instead of explaining his behaviour, Henderson produced 'a most scandalous paper', which he called his 'Remonstrance'.

When this was read out, the Court was surprised to discover that it 'not only reflected on McGwire himself but also arraigned the judgement, justice and honour of the Lord of this Isle'. This referred to McGwire's long-term court case following the bankruptcy of the Liverpool merchant, Alderman John Earle. McGwire had attempted to seize Earle's ship, the *John & Mary*, and her cargo when she arrived at Ramsey. Part of the ship and cargo belonged to the merchant Robert Jackson, who was the King's Consul in Oporto, and his brother. William Murray had represented the Jacksons and the master, James Jolly, on the Island. On 14 October 1719 the Manx Court found in favour of Murray. McGwire appealed to the Earl of Derby and he passed two decrees in his farmer's favour, dated 5 March 1722 and 14 May 1723, reversing the sentence of the Manx Court. William Murray appealed to the King in Council and on 25 November 1725 the Earl's decrees were set-aside and the Manx Court's ruling was affirmed. Henderson claimed that McGwire had misrepresented the situation to the Earl, making him his 'tool'.[185]

The case was adjourned until 6 October 1726. Henderson was required to give security - his own bond for £100 and two bonds of £50 each - that he would appear at the next General Gaol Delivery. In the meantime, McGwire was given an opportunity to respond to Henderson's allegations.

<u>William Henderson's Remonstrance and Richard McGwire's Replies</u>

1. McGwire had been involved in 'a scandalous and notorious riot in Dublin', resulting in a censure from the Irish Parliament.

<u>McGwire's reply</u>: there had been a dispute in 1723 during the election of members to the Irish Parliament. Several people had been arrested. He had made 'such acknowledgment [of having done wrong] as satisfied the House and was soon released from his confinement'.

2. McGwire had violated the rights and privileges of the Parliament 'by infringing the immunity of a member of the house, contrary to law'. As a result, about twenty months ago he had left his house in Dublin and fled to escape the 'reach of the law of that kingdom for the offence'.

<u>McGwire's reply</u>: in 1725 his lawyer had advised him to serve a subpoena on his father's only executor, who was a Member of Parliament, 'for a considerable sum of money long due'. Whilst McGwire was on the Island, the executor had complained to Parliament about a breach of his privilege and 'obtained a vote' that he should be arrested. McGwire had been assured, however, that 'upon application' he would be discharged from this arrest.

He challenged the suggestion that he had been away from his house in Dublin for twenty months. McGwire came to the Isle of Man on 5 August 1725, 'upon his most lawful occasions, as one of farmers to my Lord Derby'. As he had purchased a considerable estate on the Island (Newtown McGwire), he needed to spend some time giving directions about its improvement. He was in England for four months from 25 February 'on account of the lease of the customs' (see the Collector of Liverpool's report). This meant that he had been away from Dublin for not more than fourteen months.

3. McGwire had 'surreptitiously endeavoured to procure and cultivate a character of sanctity' by donating to the Island 'some bibles of a blind and paltry kind'.

Then on 10 June 1725, without the Earl of Derby's knowledge or permission, he had given a public entertainment in Castle Rushen, 'on account of the day being the supposed birthday of the spurious Pretender to the crown of Great Britain'. This demonstrated his disrespect not only for the Irish Parliament but also for 'the most happy and glorious prospect of a long succession to the throne of Great Britain in the illustrious house of Hanover'.

<u>McGwire's reply</u>: his bibles were not paltry but one of the best editions, subscribed to by most of the bishops, nobility and gentry of Ireland, 'for the propagating and advance of the Protestant religion'. They were esteemed 'as good and correct as any extant', which was why he had given copies to every parish church on the Island, 'for the glory of God, the good of his church and the benefit of the poor'. The governor could see a copy, which had been presented to the comptroller's office.[i] McGwire believed that Henderson had called the bibles paltry because the common prayer of the Church of England was bound up with them and this would not have been acceptable to the conventicle[ii] he had tried to establish at Ramsey.

McGwire could not have organised an entertainment at Castle Rushen in June because, as already stated, he had not arrived on the Island until 5 August.

4. McGwire had attempted to pervert the course of justice by laying false information before the Earl of Derby, so inducing him to pass a decree, which had been reversed by His Majesty in Council.

---

[i] No copy of this Bible has been located on the Island in the 21st century.
[ii] Non-conformist meeting house

McGwire's reply: his dispute with William Murray had been 'wholly conducted by those who understood the laws here and by counsel in England'.[186] This Court was not the venue where the Lord would expect to have his judgements 'called into question'. The governor might consider whether to charge Henderson with this accusation against the Lord, for which he should receive a severe sentence.

5. McGwire had slandered John Murray, one of the 24 Keys, by suggesting that he had used 'felonious and dubious stratagems' to deprive him of his 'just dues'.

and

6. When told that 'his exorbitant and illegal' demands in this case were to be considered on the Island, McGwire had answered, 'what care I for that? I can make the Governor do what I please'.

McGwire's reply: he denied slandering John Murray and 'the arrogant expression' he had allegedly spoken about governor Horne.

Henderson submitted that 'a person whose actions have been so openly notorious can't assume the character of a just, an honest man'. He claimed that the current prosecution was contrived by McGwire as part of his 'insatiable revenge' on Henderson for doing his duty and as part of his scheme 'to ruin and destroy the substance and character of all honest men that are faithful friends to His Majesty, the present establishment of Great Britain and the Right Honourable the Lord of this Isle'.

McGwire's reply: he hoped that he could assume the character of 'a just and honest man'. He had not been in contact with Henderson before he abused McGwire's servants and slandered his character so that an accusation of 'insatiable revenge' was inappropriate. Finally, he hoped that neither his defence nor prosecution of this affair could be misconstrued as 'an attempt to attack either the government in England or on the Island'.

When Henderson appeared before the Exchequer Court on 17 November 1726, he declared that he was 'heartily sorry' for his Remonstrance and asked McGwire 'to pardon him for his offence'. McGwire was persuaded by the Court to accept this apology so that 'the same is past by and forgiven', Henderson promising 'never to do the like in future'.[187]

Despite McGwire's denial of any previous contact with Henderson, he had already accused him of conniving in Robinson's disaffection (see above). It should be noted that at no point in his replies did McGwire attempt to deny that he was a Jacobite.

From the events described above, it would be presumed that Henderson was a Hanoverian. On 28 June 1739 he drank Oliver Cromwell's health. Mr Davies, a merchant in Ramsey, apparently not related to Robert Davies of Manley Hall, heard about this toast. He accosted Henderson the following day and asked:

'What have you been doing last night? You were drinking the devil's health'.

'No', said Mr. Henderson. 'But I am told', said Davies, 'You were drinking Oliver Cromwell's health'.

'Yes,' said Henderson, 'I have drunk that health many a time, upon my knees'.

Davies replied, 'You had as good have drunk the devil's health as have drunk an health to Oliver Cromwell'.

Henderson had to appear before the Consistory Court to answer this charge. He would not acknowledge that he had drunk any inappropriate healths but he declared 'in the face of the court' that 'he glories in drinking to the memory of Oliver Cromwell'. The court was obliged 'to condemn the drinking such a health or memory as an action vile and impious, an affront to government and a reflection upon the wisdom of the legislature'. They admonished Henderson to behave himself in future 'as becometh a good Christian and a loyal subject to His Majesty King George'.[188]

Figure 25: Oliver Cromwell (1649-1658)

Captain John Doran: 1726

In comparison, John Doran's celebration of the Pretender's birthday the following year was both public and in blatant defiance of being told to desist. He was imprisoned 'under close confinement' for 21 days and before he could be released he had to pay 13s 4d 'in respect of his crime' and provide bonds for his good behaviour in future.[189]

<u>Postscript</u>

When Richard McGwire died in 1727, he owed the Earl of Derby 2,000 guineas 'upon account of the rent due for the customs of ingates and outgates of this Isle and other demands'. His goods on the Island were arrested, including two trunks now in the custody of Thomas Harley, 'within them unknown', and McGwire's money in Harley's hands relating to the customs.[190]

THOMAS HARLEY: 1727

Big Tree House, Malew Street, Castletown:
'Harley spared no money on the building and it possessed much elaborate panelling and a grand staircase'.[191]

Poole & McGwire were only farmers of the customs payable on goods imported into the Island and any Manx produce that was exported. When this did not prove as lucrative as they had expected, they instructed their collectors, James Poole and Thomas Harley, to collect any other customs and dues normally payable to the Island's water bailiff, John Brownell.

Harley and Poole targeted the herring customs for the parishes of Kirk Christ Rushen and Kirk Arbory. They made an announcement at the two parish churches, explaining that now they were the only people authorised to levy these customs. When the boat masters complained that they normally paid the water bailiff, Harley and Poole threatened that if anyone refused to pay then a soldier would take them to prison at Castle Rushen. They visited each parish in turn, collecting the herring customs from all the masters, except those attached to Harley's own boats and a few people who resisted.

Brownell was going round the Island collecting the herring customs in the normal manner. When he reached Rushen and Arbory, to his great surprise, he was told that Harley and Poole had been there already. Because they claimed to be aware that 'the crime and irregularity they had committed could scarcely pass with impunity', Harley and Poole assured Brownell that they would pay him what they had collected, 'without further trouble'. When he did not receive any money from them, Brownell ordered the masters, who had not paid their herring customs to him, to be arrested. All the details of Harley and Poole's scheme were exposed in Court.

In the meantime Brownell discovered that Harley and Poole, 'without any colour or foundation of law or authority', had also collected other fees and prerequisites belonging to the Island's water bailiff. Their defence was that McGwire had told them the herring customs and other dues belonged to him so that 'by virtue of their oath and duty they were obliged to collect and receive them, as had been constantly done by their predecessors and accounted for by them annually in their books of the customs and paid to the farmers'. Despite this, Harley and Poole were arrested. They now submitted a petition to be allowed to appeal to the Lord against their imprisonment

> *as being injurious and destructive to that right and property of the farmers, highly injurious to His Majesty's subjects, who trade to this Isle and of the utmost ill-consequence to all concerned in the trade and commerce thereof.*

Governor Horton claimed that he was

> *as far from having an intention of obstructing or giving any disturbance to the farmers of the customs ... in the proper or regular collection and enjoyment of the same ... as long as they, the farmers and their collectors, do not transgress or infringe upon any known law, custom or practice to prejudice the rights and privileges of the Lord of the Island, the authority of his courts or the properties of his people.*

They were both fined £2 6s 8d for 'taking upon them the exercise of the office of water bailiff without a proper authority or being sworn to that purpose' and released from prison.[192]

Postscript

No evidence has been found about Harley's activities when he was off the Island amassing his fortune. When he died in 1741, Harley wanted to be buried 'in the grave where my late dear wife was laid under the alabaster stone in the chancel of Kirk Malew'. This stone no longer exists.

WHAT HAPPENED NEXT? JOHN AGLIONBY AND JOHN BIGNALL

It was possible to be a partner with one person for a venture or two, and to be partners with different individuals or groups at the same time in different ventures. [David Hancock *Citizens of the World: London Merchants & the Integration of the British Atlantic Community, 1735-1785* 1995 p. 11]

John Aglionby's house in Douglas had been a meeting place for Jacobite sympathisers and his own views about the rightful king of Great Britain had been expressed very clearly. John Bignall had been in partnership with the Jacobite John Hunter, who was captured at the battle of Preston. After the Rebellion of 1715, they both stayed on the Island, until their respective deaths in 1729 and 1736.

John Aglionby 1725-1729

When Aglionby first arrived on the Island, he was a man of independent means. After the death of his father, however, he became dependent on his son for money. This meant that, in theory, Aglionby would have £40 a year 'to maintain his own large expense and his family'. His son had other interests, however, as Aglionby senior explained to his friend, Edward Nash:

> *As you have entrusted me with some secrets, which none but the great God of Heaven and ourselves ever shall know of, so at this time I entrust you with an affair which, beside yourself, no soul breathing shall be let into. At this time, I am truly pinched for money. By the end of the next quarter, my son will be the whole year in arrear to me. He has only returned me 20 guineas, protesting that what with building an expensive house, elections and other cross accidents he could not pay me till about Michaelmas next ... Besides I am in hopes since he has quitted parliaments to see him here this summer.*[193]

Figure 26: Nunnery, rebuilt by John Aglionby's son during the 1720s

There was a solution. Aglionby could become involved in the running trade. Although he had no money to invest, one of Aglionby's attractions to any would-be partner was his 'intimacies' with merchants in Whitehaven. Despite their protestations to the contrary, many of these merchants were deeply involved in the running trade. One of Aglionby's contacts was Walter Lutwidge. In 1729 he wrote to his 'partner' Nash:

> *Mr Lutwidge was here. I got him to be quiet and indeed he was very civil. He left a letter but I did not think it convenient to send it for fear of miscarriage.*

One of the problems about sending letters referring to orders for contraband goods by sea, either to or from the Isle of Man, was the ease with which they could be intercepted by the revenue cruisers. When the Peel based *Rose* wherry was seized on her return from a smuggling run to Culzean bay in 1748, Captain Dow of the *Sincerity* revenue cruiser found on board not only new orders but also an insurance policy for her previous cargo.[194] Dow also seized David Ross's wherry in Ramsey Bay on the strength of these letters, and the intention to smuggle that they indicated.

As Nash explained to the Consistory Court, Aglionby succeeded in procuring for him 'several consignments to my great emolument, who therefore thought myself obliged sometimes to gratify him with part of the commission'. The types of payment made by Nash are indicated in Table VII. The exact amounts have been listed to emphasise the indignity of Aglionby's position.

		£	s	d
1725				
May 18	cash lent to Aglionby in his room	21	0	0
June 4	cash lent Aglionby at Mr Murray's yard	9	0	0
June 15	cash sent Aglionby by his servant	1	0	0
June 26	cash lent Aglionby at the shore	4	11	0
July 22	cash sent Aglionby at the barbers	5	5	0
July 28, 6 & 14 August	cash sent Aglionby by his servant	7	5	0
August 27	cash lent Aglionby in his room	3	3	0
	cash sent Aglionby by his servant	1	0	0
September 3	cash paid Charles Murphy on Aglionby's account	1	3	0
September 10	cash paid Aglionby's servant	1	12	6
	cash paid Lamb on Aglionby's account	1	3	2
Dec 10	cash sent Aglionby by his servant	1	0	0
		57	**2**	**8**
1726				
January 3	cash sent Aglionby by his servant	6	0	0
February 8	cash lent Aglionby in his room	1	1	0
February 18	cash lent Aglionby at my home	1	0	0
March 12	cash sent Aglionby by his servant	1	0	0
March 23	cash lent Aglionby in my parlour with Mr Creagh	1	0	0
April 15	cash paid McNally for Aglionby's account	0	16	11
	cash lent Aglionby in my kitchen	1	0	0
April 27 & June 8	cash sent Aglionby by his servant	3	7	0
June 14	paid Pat Dempsey for Aglionby's part of the wherry	20	17	0
		36	**1**	**11**

Table VII: Payments made by Edward Nash to John Aglionby in 1725 and 1726[195]

Another of Aglionby's 'good connections' was 'my brother Arbigland', Adam Craik, whose second wife was Marjery Aglionby. With properties on both the north Solway shore and at Flimby on the Cumbrian side, Craik was a useful contact for those involved in the running trade. If a boatload of goods could not be landed on one side, because of stress of weather or the presence of revenue boats, then it would be landed at the other property, to be stored safely before being shipped across the Solway to its rightful customers.[196] Craik's Jacobite son William, by his first wife, was to become a surveyor of customs, like Robert Douglas.

In addition to his connections in Cumberland and south-west Scotland, Aglionby possessed an exceedingly useful skill, which was convincing people that his intentions were genuine. He used this skill in a variety of schemes with Nash:

> *The most practicable of these schemes was Aglionby's insinuating himself into the friendship of all strangers and inveigling some of them to put their money into my hands, with the most direful*

curses on himself that he would deposit the like sums, to be employed in trade. Although he never deposited one single shilling, yet he received a part of the profit ... Some paper resembling company accounts between your petitioner and John Aglionby [was] calculated to assist his schemes on the purses of strangers ... From these dealings, which were mutually advantageous, there grew the most strict league, which prompted Aglionby by all methods to promote my interest, which was at the same time so gainful to himself and swayed him to project new schemes to advance our profitable commerce.

One of these schemes was a partnership formed on 12 June 1725 between Nash, Aglionby and Francis Browne. According to the article of agreement, which Aglionby kept in his hands, each of the partners would give Nash 100 guineas to purchase brandy on the Island. Then Nash would sell this brandy to his network of customers and every three months he would pay out the profit gained. At the end of five months, any of the partners could withdraw their initial capital.

The timing of this partnership was unfortunate. After only four months Nash told Browne that the brandy trade was 'almost lost by reason of the Act of Parliament passed against this Isle in England and that he could not tell how to dispose of his money to get bread for his family'. He returned Browne's 100 guineas.

When Browne told Aglionby what Nash had done, he seemed 'displeased'. Then, as he claimed there was now no need to keep the agreement, Aglionby took a piece of paper out of his pocket, tore it into pieces and threw these into the fire. Browne was concerned because Nash had only repaid him the original investment and had not accounted with him for the profit. When he explained this to Aglionby, he shook his hand, promising that Nash would pay him, honestly, whatever money he was owed from the brandy that had been sold. Browne was convinced that this burning of the 'agreement' proved that Aglionby had not invested 100 guineas himself, because if he had then he would have kept the paper in case he needed it in any future dispute with Nash. When Browne told Andrew Savage what had happened, Savage said that in his opinion Aglionby, 'never had so much money [as 100 guineas] to spare, since he knew him'.

Another scheme was between Aglionby, Nash and the shipmaster Daniel McNally, described as a 'merchant' in Douglas. The memorandum setting up that partnership was dated 22 June 1725:

That it is mutually agreed between John Aglionby Esquire, Edward Nash and Daniel McNally, merchants all of the town of Douglas in the Isle of Man, that they shall be equally concerned and be sharers alike both in the profit and loss of a cargo of wine now sent for to Bordeaux in a ship belonging to Charles Murphy of Wexford. Whosoever shall fall from this agreement shall forfeit 20 guineas to the other two with £5 more to be levied according to the nature of all fines in this Island.

The signatures were witnessed by Aglionby's servant, Nicholas Fitzsimmons. Both Murphy and McNally are mentioned in Nash's list of money paid for Aglionby (see Table x).

One of Aglionby's letters to Nash, dated July 1729, provides further information about their style of conducting business. The reference to McNally confirms that he was a shipmaster and not a Douglas merchant.

I hope you will not be angry with me for taking a lot of about 1,400 gallons of brandy, to be paid when you return, at 2s 2d English per gallon. Patrick Savage takes another lot ... Forget not to write to McNally for I ordered him to stay to receive your commands. A prodigious quantity of tobaccos are landed from Glasgow, London and Liverpool but little or none from Whitehaven ... None of your customers have been in the Island, so I fancy I shall recover little money for you. I could have sold brandy upon credit but I had not your orders for that. If you come not home soon fail not to write to me what you would have done and depend upon it I shall carefully secure your orders ... I can think of nothing more but never fear trade will still flourish.

Despite the need from time to time for some form of company accounts, Aglionby could not risk leaving a paper trail, indicating that he received any money. This was because he was 'indebted to divers persons in England', so that he could not appear to be in trade and therefore have assets that could be arrested against these debts.

When John Grierson of Dumfries was due to arrive on the Island, John Grant commented that he presumed they were in trade together. Aglionby replied, 'with imprecations, that he was never concerned one farthing in trade in his life'.

Thomas Coates of Whitehaven owed Aglionby £50. As he did not want to receive this money publicly, on 26 December 1725 Aglionby drew a bill on Coates for the £50, payable to Nash, who received the money in full. In return, on the 28th Nash gave Aglionby a promissory note for the £50. The subterfuge was not successful, however, because the note was still unpaid by Nash at Aglionby's death.[197]

The management of Aglionby's business affairs was always in Nash's name. For example, in 1726 when Aglionby, Edward Nash and Patrick Savage formed a genuine company, Aglionby paid his contribution of £150 to Nash, who then gave £300 to Savage. Similarly, no receipts were given for money exchanged between the partners, 'it being contrary to Aglionby's orders'.

Nicholas Fitzsimmons, Aglionby's servant, was his sole executor. He claimed that he had found 'divers memorandums or journals contained in a book', articles of agreement, accounts and 'other authentic testimonies'. As a result, he could prove that Nash's circumstances, which had been 'very inconsiderable' when he first met Aglionby, were now 'somewhat advanced' so that he should be in a position to pay what he owed the estate. The lack of detailed accounts, however, made it virtually impossible for Fitzsimmons to prove to the Court that Aglionby was owed any money by either Nash or Savage. His battle with these two men continued for nearly fifteen years after Aglionby's death.

Although Nash once claimed that he was Irish, the majority of his customers appear to have been in Wales, where he spent a lot of his time. These customers included Morgan Floyd, Thomas Godfrey, Evan Jones, Thomas Lloyd and Lewis Williams. Nash collected large sums of money from them and 'sundry other people' – in October 1727 £495 and in November 1731 £372.[198]

Aglionby was extremely fond of Nash and found his absences hard to bear. He wrote, 'for God's sake return home as soon as you can, for I am perfectly dead for want of your company ... For you are sensible none loves you more sincerely than myself'. A second letter a few months later continues the same theme:

> *We are just as you left us, much in the same cross humour. I cannot endure to go into the house since you left it. God send you safe hither and out of the hands of your enemies. Otherwise, God knows what will become of your family ... I have nothing to add but, what I am sure you will believe, that I am sincerely your faithful friend.*

Whether Nash's 'enemies' refers to political problems or to creditors is not clear.

The end of the Aglionby story is of a somewhat rapid decline into financial problems. This letter to Nash was dated 14 November 1729:

> *If ever you'll oblige me whilst you live, and I sincerely profess I would risk everything I have in the world to serve you, I beg you'll go sometime in the beginning of the next week to the northside and endeavour to raise £30 upon your and my bond ... If poor Quayle [Quayle Curphey of Kirk Christ Lezayre] can spare it, perhaps he may be so generous as to assist us ... I will sooner rot and be damned than let any suffer upon my account. Beside, if it come to the worst, I will give them bills [presumably on his son for the quarterly allowance] to receive it in March next and the quarter following so they may pay themselves, and then give me the remainder overplus ...*

What I aim at by this request is downright ease and peace of mind and thy favour will entirely ready me whilst I live. I have hitherto spent my time in tolerable reputation and now to lose it would confound me to the last degree. Good Nash, consider of this and keep everything absolutely secret from all mankind.

According to a message from Nicholas Fitzsimmons, Nash was indeed going to the northside within the next few days. However:

I thought to have spoke to you this night at my own chamber, if you had been so kind as to come, as I desired Clark to tell you. I begged some days ago you would try your interest in the northside to procure £30 for six or eight months ... but your not going, and never mentioning a word more to me that you intended me such a favour, makes me doubt that he [Nick] did not deliver your answer to me rightly. However, you may depend that I shall secure you so well that you or some other friend shall not run the least danger by their kindness in assisting of me at this critical juncture. I have enclosed a letter to Quayle about the affair and, if you continue your resolution to serve me, pray take it along with you. If not I am sorry to have given you all this trouble. Pray write me an answer for I am ashamed to ask favours of this nature. I am, without a compliment, your faithful friend JA.

Nash was in Wales and he did not return to the Island for several months. Aglionby died on 4 December 1729. The story did not end with Aglionby's death, however. Nash still owed some of the Whitehaven merchants for brandy and tobacco:

	£
Walter Lutwidge	61
James Gartside & Clement Nicholson	16
Lutwidge & Nicholson	200

Note: The mention of Clement Nicholson is of particular interest as he had been dealing with the Isle of Man in the tobacco trade since the end of the seventeenth century.[199]

On 8 April 1730 Nash and his wife, Elizabeth, mortgaged their houses and gardens in Douglas together with all their goods and effects 'of what nature or kind whatsoever' to Quayle Curphey against a debt of £126 owed to him. The mortgage was to take effect in five years' time. In the meantime, the Earl of Derby had awarded Walter Lutwidge and Clement Nicholson the houses and gardens against what was owed to them. Curphey took his claim to the Manx Courts and, finally, in February 1741 he agreed to pay Lutwidge and Nicholson £70 for the houses and they were to keep the rent due to the end of the following May.[200]

By this stage, Nash had absconded from the Island to avoid punishment because he had helped Thomas Kelly, who had been imprisoned for debt, to escape on board a ship. Nash chose a somewhat bizarre outfit for his departure: 'he had a blue coat on and red waistcoat and breeches'. Pat Audley 'borrowed' his brother-in-law's coat in an attempt to disguise Nash.[201]

Postscript

As Isaac Allgood had suffered from Mary Hendrick's behaviour, so Nicholas Fitzsimmons had problems with his landlady, Adam Christian's wife. He was charged in the Chancery Court with a debt of £20 for diet and lodging at the Christians's house between 1731 and 1733. Fitzsimmons did have his linen washed at the house, and slept there, but when Christian's wife sent for him to dine with her, 'he very often refused, cursing and damning the messengers, by reason he was reflected on by a great many that he was too familiar with her'. When Fitzsimmons moved out of the house completely, Christian's wife summoned John Clark into her parlour and Adam produced a small paper book, in which Clark was requested to write out what Fitzsimmons owed. On Adam's instigation, Clark wrote down 2s a week for the full time period. Then his wife asked Clark to produce a summary account on two separate papers. Their case was dismissed.[202]

John Bignall 1714-1736

In 1714 John Bignall moved from Douglas to Ramsey. There were several advantages attached to the northern port – he was away from Douglas and any loss of credit there occasioned by John Murray's case against him for the £72; the rents were lower; there was less competition with other merchants – at this stage the only other Ramsey merchants of any significance were Hugh Black and Edward Christian - and he was further from the view of the authorities. At a later stage Thomas Fenwick, the deputy searcher at Ramsey, became a personal friend.

Some aspects of Bignall's trade were described in his will, dated 1735. He requested that his housekeeper, Jane Curghey:

> *do continue in my house one year after my death and take into her care and possession all the brandies, wines, tobacco, whether roll or leaf, and all the merchant-goods whatsoever, and retail the same as formerly and make a fair account of what will be sold at the year's end to my executors (the grocery-goods of the shop and the cash in the white mug excepted, which is entirely her own). House rent and house keeping, with all other charges that will attend the selling of the goods, to be allowed her.*
>
> *In case the goods be not all sold in one whole year, then I do order that she shall continue six months longer to dispose of the same. And for her trouble and care I do leave her £15 Irish value, together with two silver spoons and one silver cup, containing about a pint.*

Over £64 worth of goods were sold by Jane Curghey. In addition, Bignall left her:

his two houses and one garden in Ramsey,
all the earthenware, pots and wooden vessels, kitchen furniture, all his books, 'the bed which I lie in as it now stands', half of his sheets and table linen.[203]

Bignall's customers ranged from Skye, along the north Solway shore and into Cumberland. He supplied these people with brandy, wine and tobacco, sometimes in partnership with other merchants, such as John Hunter and Isaac Turner, John Wattleworth junior of Ramsey or William Thwaites and Michael Sampson of Dublin but also as a sole trader.[204]

There is no detailed information about the customers for four wherry-loads of goods sent to Skye in 1721.[205] Bignall's customers in south-west Scotland did include the Jacobite Maxwells of Caerlaverock and Kirkconnell.

Inevitably, many of these people owed him money and there were several outstanding debts at his death. It was the task of his two Irish executors, John and Norris Thompson, to collect as many of these debts as possible.

John Malcolm of North Britain

Malcolm owed Bignall £50. He claimed that Thomas Copland, who was now dead, had paid £42 of the debt and that Bignall had given him a receipt for the money. As Bignall was also dead there were no witnesses to this payment. The receipt still existed, however, and evidence was taken to prove whether the signature was in Bignall's handwriting.

One of these witnesses was the Reverend Thomas Christian of Kirk Marown. He claimed that he had known Bignall very well and was 'acquainted with his handwriting, having received many letters from him'. Christian was convinced that it was Bignall's signature, 'by the similitude of the writing'. In 1746 Christian was accused of disaffection (see pp. 107-108).

Another witness was Lancelot Dawes, who had fought at the battle of Preston, on the government side and now lived in Ramsey (see p.99). It was agreed that Malcolm had made a partial payment of £42 and he paid the £8 balance to the executors.[206]

The Stewarts of Kirkcudbright

Captain John Stewart was as a merchant in Kirkcudbright, renting a warehouse there in 1737.[207] He lived south-east of the town on the road to Torrs. There is no evidence whether or not he was related to Stewart family of Stewartfield, also on the outskirts of Kirkcudbright.

Bignall supplied Stewart with brandy, visiting the house regularly. There he met Stewart's daughter, Sarah. They had a baby, who was known as Mary Bignall. At this stage Bignall was a widower, his wife Mary having died in 1724, so that he was free to marry Sarah. Whatever the reasons for remaining apart, Sarah continued to live with her father and Bignall stayed in Ramsey on the Isle of Man.

In the summer of 1732 the *John* of Ramsey, John Christian master, landed six casks of brandy at Manxsman's Lake, near Kirkcudbright. Henry Steward sold the brandy but, as all the casks were seized before they reached the customers, he only received £1 of the money owed. The seizures could be proved by Sarah Stewart, described as a gentleman's daughter, who was on the Island in January 1733, when Deemster Christian was authorised to take her statement:

> *In summer last past Henry Steward came to this deponent's father's house, desiring leave to lodge some casks of brandy thereabouts. The answer that Henry Steward got was that the collector's daughter was there ... and that it was not safe for him to carry any brandy to that place. But [she] advised him to lodge the same at the Torrs, thinking it the safest place. A few days after the deponent saw three casks of brandy go by her father's door on horseback, which was said to belong to Steward, and seized upon by a 'gaugier'. The rest of Steward's brandy, the deponent was then told, had been seized upon by custom house officers. All this was done some time in summer last, as abovesaid, about two miles from Kirkcudbright in North Britain.[208]*

Presumably Sarah was on the Island to see Bignall – their daughter was born about this time.

When Bignall died in 1735, his executors went to Scotland in the hope of collecting some of the debts. Their expenses included:

1736	to a boat for carrying us to Scotland to recover several debts due there	£1 4s 6d
	to our expenses during the time we stayed in Scotland: horse hire & guide etc	£7 17s 2d
	to a boat that carried us back to the Isle	£1 4s 6d
1747	to Mr Gourdon, our attorney in Scotland, for prosecuting and suing several persons for debts due to Mr Bignall before his death and since, being for many years	£30 6s 8d

When the Thompsons went to Kirkcudbright, Sarah Stewart applied to them

> *for a sum of money for the maintenance of her child by Mr Bignall, which child she produced to us. We told her she had no right to make a demand upon us for that Mr Bignall had made provision for the child in his will.* [Noase in Kirk Christ Lezayre, worth 10s Lord's rent].

James Curlett, master of the *Margaret* of Ramsey, was with the Thompsons at their lodgings in Kirkcudbright when

> *there came a certain person, whose wife had been nurse to the child of Sarah Stuart ... [who] told the gentlemen that Sarah Stuart had left the child at his house and gone out of town, telling them that Kirkcudbright should not see her again for a twelvemonth and a day. The person declared further that Sarah ordered him to bring the child to the executors of Mr Bignall, who were then in Scotland, and that for his part he would not keep it because he could not tell what to do with it.*

Curlett could confirm that the child was Mary Bignall, 'having often seen the child before whilst with the mother and nurse'. The Thompsons instantly employed him to take Mary to the Island, 'which he accordingly did'. The expenses involved were:

To Mrs Stuart for the maintenance and clothes for the deceased's daughter, Mary Bignall	£8 1s 8d
to a person that took care of Mary Bignall and carried her to the Island while we were in Scotland, she being left on our hands	12s 3d

When the executors finalised the accounts, Captain Stewart still owed Bignall's estate £20.[209]

Postscript

There was one condition in Bignall's will.

> In case **Jane Curghey** marries, then I leave and bequeath the £15, the two silver spoons and the cup, with all the household goods and the two houses and garden to my illegitimate daughter **Mary Bignall** in Scotland, and that **Jane Curghey** shall oblige herself to return the same to her in case she marries, and not otherwise.

In 1736 an inventory had been taken of all the goods which Jane would forfeit, if she married:

In the kitchen
a warming pan, 2 dozen of pewter plates, a fir table and frame, a small fir oval table,
a corner cupboard, a fir press, 8 pewter dishes, 3 small oak chairs, 4 ash chairs,
5 brass candlesticks, a Delft punch bowl, 2 smoothing irons with heater, 3 brass skillets,
a cheese toaster, 3 iron spits and a grid iron and a pair of racks, 3 pairs of tongs,
2 fire shovels and 2 pokers, a frying pan, a tea kettle, a copper fish pan,
a tin colander and dripping pan, a sauce pan, 14 pans and a tin dish cover,
8 Delft pans, an old copper guard, 3 tubs, 2 cans, 3 trays and a rush candlestick,
2 old ringers, a silver cup, 2 silver spoons, a pair of bellows, a dish, a toasting iron,
a Delft teapot, 2 dishes and a butter dish, 2 iron pots and an iron kettle   £10   2s 9d

In the room over the kitchen
a chest of drawers, an oval table, a finished bed with curtains, 8 oak chairs,
an old oak oval table, half the sheets and table linen   £6 16s 6d
                                                                                   £16 19s 3d
cash to be forfeited by Jane in case of her marriage   £15   0s 0d

Mary Bignall married John Cowle at Maughold on 24 October 1747 and, after he was drowned off the coast of Scotland, she married William Christian on 26 June 1756, also at Maughold. Jane Curghey remained a spinster until 3 August 1758, when she married Edmund Christian at Lezayre.

Mary Christian als Cowle als Bignall claimed the two houses and gardens in Ramsey, the goods listed in the inventory and £15 Irish, as stipulated in her father's will.

Jane Christian als Curghey claimed that Bignall's stipulation was 'unlawful, as repugnant to the Law of Nature and prejudice to the Commonwealth'. The case was heard at Lincoln's Inn on 12 March 1760, before Edmund Hoskins, the Duke of Atholl's commissioner. Although it appears that Jane won on this occasion, there is some evidence that Mary finally gained her full inheritance.[210]

A GOVERNMENT SOLDIER FROM THE BATTLE OF PRESTON

Lancelot Dawes, formerly a cornet in Brigadier Honeywood's Regiment of Dragoons
but then on the Isle of Man, gentleman.[211]

Lancelot Dawes came from Barton Kirk near Penrith. There is no information about when he joined the army or Brigadier Honeywood's regiment of dragoons. In November 1715 Honeywood's regiment was attached to General Wills at Chester. They were instructed to advance towards Wigan, where Wills marshalled all his troops into three brigades, the first under Honeywood.

The Brigadier led the first attack on the Churchgate barrier. Dawes was one of the survivors of the onslaught from the Highlanders and Borderers but the Brigadier was wounded. Despite this, on 13 November he was able to lead his men, preceded by trumpets and drums, into Preston from the Wigan/Manchester end of the town. They met up with the other government troops, now led by General Carpenter, in the Market Place and supervised the collection of arms from the rebels.[212] Dawes was on the Isle of Man by the 1730s, when he was living in Ramsey with his wife, Jane.

On Thursday, 1 August 1734 Dawes was walking past Edward Corlet's house, when he heard Philip Christian's voice. As Christian was his friend, Dawes went to the doorway of the house to speak to him.

Edmond Curghey, who was with Christian, asked Dawes if he would drink King George's health. Naturally Dawes replied, 'with all his spirit'.

Curghey then said, 'God damn him (meaning King George), who the devil cares for King George or who the devil cares for you?'

Dawes went further into the house and 'sharply' reproved Curghey for 'using His Majesty's name and abusing him in so disrespectful a manner'. He threatened Curghey with his stick, saying 'he owed him a beating and would pay it him'.

Curghey ran at Dawes and 'violently assaulted and very much abused him, in the presence of Christian and several others persons', including William Kissage. The argument continued in the street, where Dawes did hit Curghey with his stick.

The following week Dawes reported the incident to Charles Stanley, the water bailiff. Evidence was heard from the witnesses and Curghey was bound in £20, with Robert Shimmin of Ballasalley and John Norris of Castletown in £10 each, that he would keep the peace. On 8 May 1735 Curghey declared that he was 'very sorry and submissive for his offence'. As this appeared to have been 'the effect of liquor more than any design to abuse His Majesty', his bonds were cancelled.[213]

Postscript

Lancelot Dawes gave evidence to the Consistory Court held at Kirk Michael on 28 March 1737 about John Malcolm's debt to John Bignall. He claimed that during Bignall's last sickness he had 'sometimes frequented' Dawes's house. 'But that he never saw nor understood that Bignall received any money from Thomas Copland, deceased, nor to his knowledge ever saw the persons in company one with another'.[214] This suggests a certain level of intimacy between the two men, because Dawes was aware of Bignall's financial situation. He was not, however, one of the sixteen people bequeathed a ring in Bignall's will.[215]

Time had passed. Instead of keeping company with Jacobites Bignall now visited the house of a government trooper.

THE END OF AN ERA

William Murray and William Seddon died in 1756 and 1758, respectively.

All the other people, who had been involved one way or another in disaffection to the English government during the 'Fifteen, and who had remained on the Isle of Man, were dead before the 'Forty-five rebellion.

Name	Details	Date of Death	Location
John Aglionby	His house a meeting place for Jacobite sympathisers. He was accused of disaffection in 1716.	1729	Douglas
William Aldridge	Accused of disaffection in 1716.	1719	Ballaugh
John Bignall	Frequently in company with Jacobite sympathisers.	1735	Ramsey
John Hale	King's officer in Douglas. House a meeting place. Accused of disaffection in 1716.	1718	England
Thomas Harley	Included because of suggestion he was a Jacobite	1741	Castletown
William Henderson	King's officer in Ramsey. Not a Jacobite but accused Richard McGwire of being one.	1743	Ramsey
John Hendrick	Presumably shared Mary's 'whiggish' views	1726	At sea
Richard McGwire	In his defence to Henderson's remonstrance he did not deny that he was a Jacobite	1727	Dublin
Philip Moore	Frequently in company with Jacobite sympathisers. Refused to give evidence against John Hale.	1738	Douglas
John Murray	Frequently in company with Jacobite sympathisers. Refused to give evidence against John Hale	1741	Douglas
William Ross	Refused to accept *The independent Whig* at Castletown	1727	Maughold
John Rowe	With William Seddon collected evidence against those accused of disaffection.	1725	Castletown
William Rushton	Accused John Hale of disaffection.	1722	Douglas
Abraham Silk	Frequently in company with Jacobite sympathisers	1755	Presumed dead long ago
William Wybrants	Frequently in company with Jacobite sympathisers	1724	Ballahott

Table VIII: People who were dead before the Second Rebellion in 1745

THE JACOBITE REBELLION OF 1745

This desperate attempt to subvert our present constitution (which in the opinion of everyone who understands the nature of civil liberty, is surely the best that ever any nation or people were blessed with) will I hope now soon be defeated and serve to strengthen and confirm it. That such measures shall soon be taken ... as shall secure the people their civil rights and properties from all future illegal acts of violence from one who avows an unconditional dominion and the arbitrary exercise of lawlessness and power founded upon unalienable right, derived to him by birth, to our lives and properties, which he may dispose of as his proper goods and chattels. Such a claim so directly inconsistent with the natural and civil rights of mankind must have a frightful sound in the ears of free men, who have tasted the sweets of civil liberty. [Governor Lindesay to the Duke of Atholl, 30 October 1745][216]

Governor Lindesay's thoughts about the threat posed by the Pretender's claims on his 'people' are very similar to those expressed in the letters written by William Craik of Arbigland to his Jacobite friends the Earl of Nithsdale and James Maxwell of Kirkconnell (see Appendix IV).

1745

25 July	The Pretender's son, known as Bonnie Prince Charlie, landed in Scotland
19 August	He raised the Pretender's standard at Glenfinnan
17 September	The Jacobites entered Edinburgh
20 September	Battle of Prestonpans won by the Jacobites
30 October	**Governor Lindesay reported to the Duke that the Island was armed, as well as may be**
8 November	The Jacobite army crossed the river Esk
	They captured Carlisle castle
6 December	They reached Derby
18 December	**Fast held on the Isle of Man**
19 December	The Jacobites returned to Carlisle
	Bonnie Prince Charlie stayed at Drumlanrig castle (see Figure 5)
24 December	He was at Hamilton palace, near Glasgow
26 December	The Jacobite 'Court' was held at Shawfield

1746

3 January	The Jacobites arrived at Bannockburn house
17 January	Battle of Falkirk won by the Jacobites
16 April	Battle of Culloden won by the Hanoverians
7 May	**Governor described the celebrations on the Island to the Duke**
8 June	**Prayers, and thanksgiving, on the Isle of Man**
19 September	Bonnie Prince Charlie sailed from Scotland, never to return

1745 and 1746: on the **Isle of Man** and in Great Britain

In February 1744 Louis XV of France planned an invasion of Britain. 10,000 French troops collected at Dunkirk ready to embark for Maldon in Essex. Once more, the weather intervened and a storm wrecked the fleet. In July 1745 the Young Pretender, Bonnie Prince Charlie, organised his own invasion of Scotland with the help of the privateer captain, Antoine Walsh. The Prince boarded a small frigate with seven companions, including William Murray, Marquis of Tullibardine, and a small supply of arms and ammunition. The larger frigate, with the main military supplies and several French volunteer soldiers on board, was attacked by HMS *Lion* off Ireland and returned to Brest.

On 25 July 1745 Bonnie Prince Charlie landed near Arisaig. He stayed for one week at Glen Borrodale house, on the south coast of the Ardnamurchan peninsula, and a second week at Kinlochmoidart, meeting his supporters. The clan chiefs advised him to return to France. Instead, on 19 August 1745 he raised his father's standard at Glenfinnan. Despite their victory at Prestonpans, there were constant disagreements within the Jacobites. Lord George Murray represented the more pragmatic Scottish view but the Prince preferred advice from his Irish supporters.

In marked contrast to Governor Horne's problems over persuading the House of Keys to arm the Island in 1715, on 30 October 1745 Lindesay reported to the Duke of Atholl, 'as soon as I had certain notice of this insurrection we got some of our militia out and had the arms, which were purchased last summer, delivered to them, had a good many ball cast and cartridges made up'.

He continued, however, 'but we are so poorly armed and our men though loyal enough yet of such poor spirits that I am afraid if any force was to be landed upon us we should make but a bad figure … All our watches are doubled and strictly kept night and day'.[217]

Bonnie Prince Charlie decided to march south into England, hoping to find more support there. Some of the Highlanders returned home but the remainder of the Jacobite army crossed the river Esk on 8 November and succeeded in capturing Carlisle castle on the 15th November.

The previous day the collector at Whitehaven had put 'all the king's books and papers that I thought material into boxes and sent them on board a vessel to the Isleman'. There was considerable apprehension in the port. Several Whitehaven merchants, including Walter Lutwidge, wrote to the leaders of the government forces at Newcastle, begging them to free Carlisle from the rebels, because they feared that their town would be the next to succumb. The response was somewhat unhelpful. Marshall Wade was due to march the next day, 26 November 1745, so that he could not spare 'a sufficient body' of men. Instead, he thought 'the most effectual method of doing it would be to beat the rebels and then of course they must evacuate Carlisle'.[218]

In the meantime, Bonnie Prince Charlie and the remainder of the Jacobite army had set off towards London. They reached Derby on Friday, 6 December 1745. The Prince still wanted to advance on the capital but the majority of his followers, now clearly led by Lord George Murray, were anxious to return home. They reached Carlisle on 19 December and the next day re-crossed the Esk, which was in full flood. They stayed at Drumlanrig Castle, near Dumfries. While they were at the castle one of the Prince's supporters reputedly slashed with his sword the painting of William III in Figure 5.

Bishop Wilson & Fasts: 1745
Governor Horne had complained about Bishop Wilson not using the prayers which were sent to him in 1715. There appears to have been no similar hesitation on the part of the Bishop in 1745.

George II issued a proclamation for a general fast to be held in England on Wednesday, 18 December 1745, 'to implore a blessing on His Majesty's armies'. Governor Lindesay wrote to Bishop Wilson stating that the people on the Island should obey this instruction not only because of their loyalty to the crown but also for their own safety and preservation. As a result, all the clergy were instructed to say prayers for the prosperity of the King's armies, both by land and sea, against all his enemies and 'especially against the unnatural rebellion broke out in Great Britain'. Anyone who did not attend church that day would be presented for contempt and proceeded against 'in such manner as the law directs'.[219]

By 25 December the Whitehaven collector had retrieved his books and papers from the Isle of Man. From the English viewpoint the crisis appeared to be over.

William Craik

Adam Craik had been deeply involved in the running trade – his brother-in-law was John Aglionby and he had several other connections with merchants on the Isle of Man. His eldest son, William, understood 'Latin, Greek, Hebrew, French and Italian and had made some progress in Spanish. He was a tolerable architect and chemist, read much on learned subjects and generally rendered himself master of whatever he set his mind upon'.[220] William's interest in farming was encouraged by his father, who gave him the farm of Maxwelfield. Here he grazed cattle, studying the 'shapes of the best kinds'. When William inherited Arbigland in 1736 it was in a natural state, 'very much covered with whins and broom, and yielding little rent ... That young gentleman was among the first that undertook to improve the soil; and the practice of husbandry which he pursued, together with the care and trouble which he took in ameliorating his farm, was very great. Some of it he brought to such perfection, by clearing off all weeds and stones, and pulverized it so completely, that I, on walking over the surface, sunk as if I had trodden on newly fallen snow'. In 1776, Craik founded the Society for the Encouragement of Agriculture in Galloway and Dumfriesshire 'but that institution was soon enfeebled by the president's age, and the secretary's bad health'.[221] In 1755 Craik redesigned the house at Arbigland himself.[222]

Figure 27: William Craik (1703-1798)

Although he could have been fully employed with his hobbies, William needed a regular income. He was appointed as a surveyor general of customs at Dumfries.

William Craik, surveyor general, 62, married & 5 children, appointed from 30 June 1733

This post was unlike that held by Robert Douglas, as surveyor of the land carriage at Glasgow. Craik's main task was to supervise the king's boat stationed at Carsethorn and to keep the collector informed about any potential smuggles along his section of the coast, to the west of the Nith estuary. There is no evidence that Craik played an active part in attempting to halt the running trade, which was practiced even along the shoreline of his property.[224] The Maxwells were supplied with brandy by John Bignall and it is possible that Craik was also one of his customers.

His approach to his post appears to have been somewhat dilettante. On 23 July 1782 Craik's son Adam (aged 40), was drowned with his servant and four members of the king's boat, crossing the Solway to visit friends in Cumberland. His body was cast ashore near a small village called Mowbray between Allonby and Skinburness, together with that of his servant and two of the king's boatmen.[225]

Because the rebels were at Carlisle, no English ships were allowed to sail to the Solway ports. In February 1746 Craik wrote to the collector at Whitehaven, explaining that 'by the disturbances there on account of the rebels he was hindered of lying in his winter coals'. As he had no supplies of peat or turf, 'his family now is under great distress for want of fuel'. Craik wanted permission to send his gabbart, presumably not the king's boat, to Whitehaven for a few chalders of coal. He confirmed that the rebels were now at Inverness and the intervening country well protected by the government forces. The Board of Customs in London agreed that coal could now be shipped with safety to Dumfries, Kirkcudbright and Annan.[226]

The Jacobites had won the battle of Falkirk on 17 January 1746. Before the battle of Culloden in April, each man was issued with orders from the Old Pretender. 'Every person [must] attach himself to some corps of the army and remain with that corps night and day, until the Battle and pursuit be finally over … if any man turn his back to run away, the next behind such man is to shoot him … the Highlanders to be in their kilts, and no body to throw away their guns'. [227]

The Jacobites were crushed at this battle. Bonnie Prince Charlie lurked as a fugitive in the Highlands for many months before a French ship arrived to take him back to the continent, apparently not calling at the Island en route.

Thanksgivings on the Isle of Man in 1746
Both Governor Lindesay and Bishop Wilson rejoiced at the end of the Second Rebellion. The governor wrote to the Duke of Atholl on 7 May 1746:

> *When we had the first uncertain reports that the army under his Royal Highness had defeated the Rebels, we had volunteer rejoicings by bonfires and fiddles for three nights and days, almost without interruption. Last Sunday I had a letter from my son, dated Edinburgh 26 April, with the Scottish paper containing the account, sent from Inverness on the 19th by a king's messenger and further accounts from my son by letters he had from Inverness of the 20th.*
>
> *I ordered next day the flag to be displayed and in the afternoon went to the Cross [at Castletown] where we drank all the royal and several loyal healths under a discharge of all the cannon of the Castle, which were answered by the cannon of Derby fort, and the castle soldiers joined by the town company fired a volley of small arms at every toast. At night I gave a supper to the officers and the better sort of the inhabitants. And all the windows were illuminated and a great bonfire at the Cross. There were also great rejoicings at Douglas, Peeltown and Ramsey. All voluntary.*
>
> *The people in general have all along, since the first rise of this rebellion, expressed great marks of their affections to the present government. At Douglas they broke all the papists' windows, which they grumbled at a little but bore it with patience. We have no Catholics anywhere else in the Island.[228]*

This prayer was said in all the Manx churches after the general thanksgiving at the morning and evening services on Sunday, 8 June 1746: [229]

> *We, thy unworthy servants, most gracious Lord, do again humbly beg leave to prostrate ourselves before thee, adoring thy infinite goodness, as for our many former deliverances from the wicked abettors of popish superstition and lawless power so for the late signal victory vouchsafed to His Majesty's forces under the wise and valiant conduct of His Royal Highness, the Duke of Cumberland, over the same cruel and blood-thirsty enemies.*
>
> *Blessed be thou O Lord, that hast not for our manifold and great offences delivered us up as a prey to them. Let, we beseech thee, a just sense of thy suffering and mercy turn us from the evil of our ways, and may we live henceforward as becomes those who have been the peculiar care of thy providence.*
>
> *That it may please thee still to increase thy loving kindness to us, till all the world confess, that thou art our Saviour and mighty deliverer. Permit no design to prosper which shall be formed against thy true religion, thy anointed servant our most gracious sovereign King George, or the peace and welfare of us thy people.*
>
> *Crown with success His Majesty's armies and councils; and in thy own good time vouchsafe to us the blessings of a safe, honourable and lasting peace. That with devout and joyful hearts, we may from generation to generation utter forth thy praise.*

The Effect on the Running Trade

On 29 January 1746 the collector at Whitehaven forwarded an affidavit from Charles Lutwidge, supervisor of the preventive officers in Cumberland, about a seizure he had made in the Borders to the Board of Customs in London. The collector added:

> *We cannot but observe that since the rebels came first to Carlisle the smuggling trade from the Isleman to the Borders has been vastly increased by their encouragement and open protection. For whilst their garrison remained in that city they not only granted the smugglers passports for themselves and goods to travel at noon day but gave them broadswords and pistols in exchange for their brandy so that now the runners in each Border are well supplied with arms to the great terror of His Majesty's officers and subjects.[230]*

In theory, there should be two ways of confirming this increase in the trade: the customs outgates and subsequent court cases on the Island because of debt. The detailed information about the goods on board boats leaving the Island was not recorded after the early 1730s. The increase in the debt cases heard in the Chancery Court does not indicate a high proportion of customers in the north-east of England. In fact, this date marks the beginning of a boom period in the smuggling trade that had more factors involved in it than the temporary arming of the smugglers.[231]

An atypical legal market had developed for the Island's claret and brandy. On 14 May 1745 George Moore of Peel imported on the *Margaret* of Cherbourg, 'for and in behalf of the present or future owners or proprietors of the vessel, John Fevre master, from Bordeaux under passport from His Majesty of Great Britain bearing date 21 August 1744' 120 hogsheads containing 20 ton of wine and 37 pieces and a small cask of brandy, total duties payable to the Lord £28.[232] It is probable that this cargo was destined for the government troops in Scotland.

Governor Lindesay reported to the Duke of Atholl on 13 February 1746 that he had received a letter from Campbell, sheriff of Argyll, with an order to send Major General John Campbell four hogsheads of best claret. This had been purchased from Moore, who was charging £10 per hogshead. Lindesay had been to Peel and paid Moore himself. He added, 'of late we have had so great a demand from Clyde' where the troops were gathered to suppress the rebellion, 'that in a few weeks I believe we shall hardly have anything to sell'. By 3 March the wine stocks were 'so low that vessels coming for it could not be provided.[233]

The governor's comments are confirmed from the comparatively low customs duties collected on wine and claret during the crucial period. Brandy, however, was on the increase.

	1744 £ duty	1745 £ duty	1746 £ duty
Wine	51	43	66
Claret	2	-	1
Brandy	848	1307	1308
Geneva	11	-	4
Spirits	312	350	444
Total duties on these items	1224	1700	1823

Table IX: Duties collected on wine and spirits imported into the Isle of Man from 1744 to 1746[234]

Postscript

'Notes from a Manx clergyman's diary' were published by Glasgow University in 1840. They provide a moving story about Stewart of Appin and his daughter, Flora, who, using the name Ginest, were lurking in an isolated cottage on the Isle of Man after the battle of Culloden. The clergyman, referred to as 'Dr H', visited them regularly and recorded their conversations in his diary.

Is this diary authentic or not? The notes from it were found amongst the papers of Reverend Hugh Stowell (1768-1835) of Ballaugh. Yet none of the incumbents on the Isle of Man during the time when the Stewarts would have been at the cottage could be referred to as 'Dr H'. William Bridson who was the vicar at Ballaugh from 1729 until his death in 1751 has been described as 'rough, course and ignorant'.[235] He could not have written the diary.

In 1840 the editor of the Notes remarked that on his last visit to the Island he had searched among the tomb stones of 'Kirk B' and found 'a dilapidated tomb' without a date on it but 'at some time hieroglyphic characters' on the centre of it might have formed the named Flora Stewart. 'Manxmen call it grave of a stranger'. No reference has been found in the Manx records to the burial of a Flora Ginest or a Flora Stewart.

There are several comments in the Notes about current events, and in particular about the clan Stewart of Appin. It has not been possible to confirm these comments from primary source material. Because of these reservations, the story is not told here.[236]

It is possible, however, that numbers of fugitives from the troubles in Scotland did come to the Island. This is discussed in the section on the Scottish Connection.

ANOTHER DISAFFECTED CONVERSATION: THOMAS CHRISTIAN 1746

Figure 28: Parish Church of Marown

Thomas Christian of Ballakilley was the vicar of Marown from 1734 until his death in 1752. On Tuesday, 29 April 1746 Nicholas Kewley, a carpenter in Douglas, and his brother, John, were at Ballafreer, when Christian came into the house. They talked about the 'rebellion in Scotland'.

Christian stated that the Pretender was the heir to the crown. Nicholas replied that he was nothing but a bricklayer's son, brought into the house in a warming pan (see page 35).

When Christian countered, 'how can you tell that?' Nicholas repeated the warming pan story.

Christian said, 'how then would the emperor of Germany give him his niece for a wife?'

He added that the Pretender should have been the next king after James II, only his father had lost the crown for him. Nicholas said, 'I believe you are for the Pretender'. Christian swore that Kewley was a liar and that he was for the present government. Afterwards they talked of 'indifferent matters'.

The next morning Nicholas Kewley was in Hugh Cannon's smithy with Peter Sidebotham, the king's officer at Douglas. Kewley mentioned his 'great dispute' with Parson Tom, saying tempers had run so high that he was surprised they were not reduced to blows. Inevitably, Sidebotham asked what the dispute had been about and when Kewley explained, he said, 'I have information enough. Blacksmith, I take you as witness'. He then asked Kewley if there had been anyone else there the night before. Nicholas replied, 'there were none present, unless there were some women'.

Sidebotham reported the affair to Governor Lindesay on 2 May and four days later the evidence was taken before the governor, John Taubman, deemster, and John Quayle, comptroller. Christian was arrested and before he could be released he had to produce a recognisance of £30 with two further securities of £10 apiece – these were John Wattleworth senior, and John Kewley of Kirk Marown.

On 7 May Governor Lindesay sent the Duke information about this case. He added:

> *Had this indiscretion, I shall call it by no worse name, happened at any other time or had the information been made by anybody other than the king's officer, who is a mighty weak creature, it might have been overlooked. But as he is prompted by a mad fellow here, one John Gill, one of our attorneys, who is ready to misrepresent us in the worst light, I could do no less, and I submit it to your Grace whether it may not be proper to advise with your friends what ought further to be done. For I shall suspend all further proceedings against the parson until your Grace's pleasure shall be known. I have also sent a copy to the Bishop, that he may have his thoughts how far he ought to proceed against him, by way of ecclesiastical censure, which perhaps may be the most proper way ... But I hardly think the Bishop will do any thing in it.*[237]

On 14 May 1746 the Bishop suspended Christian 'ab officio', until the Consistory Court could consider, 'what reparation he ought to make for the injury done and the offence given by his licentious way of talking, and meddling with matters which no way appertain to his duty'. In his appeal to the Bishop, dated 28 June 1746, Christian stated:

> *I am heartily sorry for the offence given by my late indiscretion in talking to people on subjects, which they did not understand. Now, to satisfy all such as may have been prejudiced thereby, [I] do transmit to your Lordship the following declaration of my loyalty and principles ...*
>
> *I declare myself to be a loyal subject of His Majesty, King George, and that his Majesty has the sole and undoubted right to the imperial crown of these realms and do acquiesce in and am thoroughly satisfied with the succession in the illustrious house of Hanover, as by law established. I renounce a popish Pretender, as also the errors of the Church of Rome, as containing doctrines that are superstitious and idolatrous.*

As a result, he was 'restored to the exercise of his office'. Nevertheless, in order to satisfy 'such as have been offended by his indiscretion', the declaration of his loyalty and principles was published in the chapel at Douglas the following day, 29 June 1746.

Postscript
On 11 February 1745 Governor Lindesay wrote to the Duke of Atholl, exasperated by Sidebotham's attempts to interfere with the shipping at the Isle of Man. Lindesay referred to 'the foolishness of the man', adding 'I desired to see his commission or orders ... But to this he made answer, as he did formerly on the like occasion viz. that he had not them about him ... I wish the commissioners [of Customs in London] would direct this officer to show me his powers and instructions, to prevent any mistake and that I may give him proper assistance ... in the execution of his duty, consistent with your Grace's rights and prerogatives in this Isle. For I daresay the commissioners have given him no orders which are inconsistent with these'.[238]

When Sidebotham died in April 1751, the inventory of his belongings included:

a gold laced hat, 3 old hats, a campaign wig, a fox tail wig, 2 old wigs
a broad cloth coat, a red riding coat, another old coat, another coat & pair of breeches, another cloth pair of breeches, a pair of scarlet breeches, an old pair of breeches, a scarlet silver laced waistcoat,
a scarlet gold braided waistcoat, a blue tinselled waistcoat, a gold laced cloth waistcoat, an old waistcoat,
a pair of ruffled sleeves, 6 shirts,
a pair of old shoes, 4 pair old stockings, 2 pair thread stockings.
A silver watch, a pair of pistols and six old pamphlets.[239]

A NEW ERA? THOMAS FOLEY'S MEMORIAL: 1750

In early 1746 Thomas Foley spent four days on the Isle of Man, spying for the collector of customs at Whitehaven. This version of his report was dated 6 August 1750.

> *The town of Douglas contains many inhabitants, who are chiefly smugglers, and who have resorted thither from all parts, some of which are outlawed in England and Ireland, and who by smuggling have greatly enriched themselves. These smugglers are now come to such a height, by being protected and countenanced by the two deemsters or deputy governors of the Island, and others, that they often assemble themselves together, caballing and forming schemes against His Majesty and government, and drink his damnation and all his royal issue, and such like healths, and prosperity and success to the Pretender. This has been complained of by His Majesty's officer of customs, Mr Sidebotham, in the Island, to the two deemsters. But their answer is they have nothing to say to it, that the Duke of Atholl is their sovereign only ... they have no law in that Island to punish such offenders and that His Majesty was nothing to them. So that these smugglers glory in their treasons, and are suffered to do so, together with their illegal proceedings, with impunity.*[240]

This was refuted in a memorial from Bishop Wilson to George II, dated 19 March 1751. He claimed that Foley's misrepresentations were

> *very infamous and prejudicial to the character of the native people of this Isle, wherein they are represented as disaffected to your Majesty's person and government, favourers of the Pretender and his cause, with many other accusations wrongfully laid against them, that tend to make a whole nation of people obnoxious to your Majesty's person and government. Whereas they are in every respect the reverse of what is laid against them; as I, who have been resident in this diocese upwards of 50 years, can assure your Majesty; during which time I have made it my constant endeavours, with the assistance of my clergy, to instruct the people, by the providence of God committed to our care, in the true principles of the Christian religion and of loyalties to your Majesty and your predecessors.*
>
> *That the inhabitants of this Isle consist chiefly of natives and some strangers, who come hither from the neighbouring nations, on account of trade or some misfortunes. As for the natives, they are in general an orderly, civil and peaceable people, well instructed in the duties of Christianity, as professed in the church of England, more constant and regular in their attendance on the public worship of God and behaving with more seriousness and decency here than in many other places, where there are better opportunities of learning and instruction. And so far are they from being disaffected to your sacred Majesty and Royal Family that I can assure your Majesty (so far as consists within my own knowledge, or the best enquiry I could ever make) that I do verily believe, and solemnly declare, as in the presence of Almighty God, that <u>there are not three persons of the natives who are of disloyal or disaffected principles</u> or that were ever guilty of such unbecoming excesses and disrespects, as that memorial has laid against them.*
>
> *That during the time of my residence in this Isle there have been two rebellions in Great Britain, and yet on the strictest enquiry I can not find that any one man of the natives was ever concerned against your Majesty or your late Royal Father; but on the contrary many of them had served and lost their lives both in your Majesty's fleet and armies; so that in the Memorial the people of this Isle are exceedingly injured and abused by Foley, who as he was not above four days upon the Island could not possibly in that time have any knowledge of the genius, morals or disposition of the people, yet he most grievously accuses the whole body of the natives with such irregularities and enormities, as I never knew any of them, or even strangers, guilty of within this Isle, any individual of whom, if guilty, would most certainly have been punished either by the Ecclesiastical or Civil Government, as severely as in any of your sacred Majesty's dominions.*[241]

This was an example of Bishop Wilson defending his flock. In 1731 he had encouraged his clergy to preach against the sin of smuggling.[242] He did not name the two Manxmen who had been disaffected.

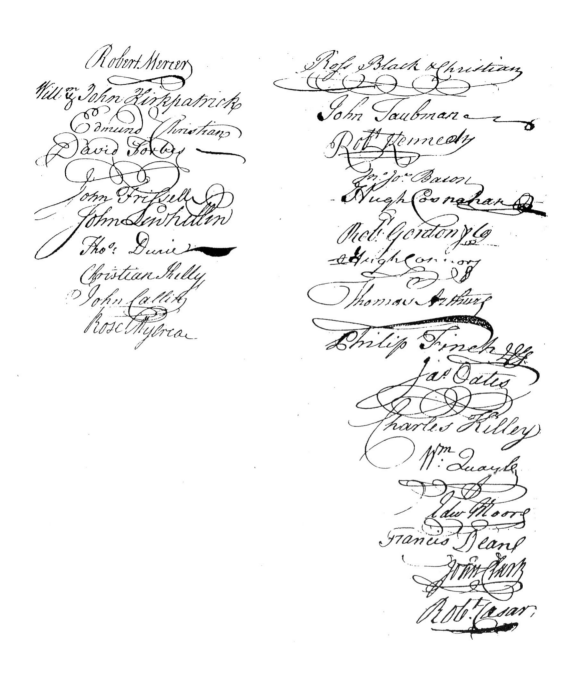

Figure 29: Signatures of the principal merchants and traders on the Isle of Man

THE SCOTTISH CONNECTION: POST 1745

I must give up business as it will not do for me ... I cannot give the attention that it deserves and to leave it to be transacted by other people is no satisfaction ... Many uneasy hours I have had at the [unfair] usage of those I employed. Those that [profess] gentilities makes no scruple in [cheating] whenever they have an opportunity. From this and many other instances too tedious to mention I have developed a dislike to business and I think you are happy that is out of trade, for there is nothing but trouble and vexation attending it. [Robert Kennedy at Liverpool to John Taubman, 8 October 1774][243]

It would be all too easy to conduct a 'witch-hunt', attributing Jacobite or non-Jacobite sympathies to every Scottish merchant who took up residence on the Isle of Man from the 1740s onwards. This would be unjustifiable. Not only were families split in their affiliations but particular individuals changed sides, at least once, during their lifetimes. This section looks at some of the Scottish merchants who are of particular interest, because their lives touched the Jacobite network, regardless of their personal feelings.

In the early 1760s the 'principal merchants and traders' on the Isle of Man (see Figure 29) sent a petition to the Duke and Duchess of Atholl, explaining their concern over the recent royal proclamation authorising revenue cruisers to patrol the Island and seize contraband and high duty goods on vessels within its harbours. This would discourage the merchants from 'pursuing their just and lawful business', which they had been able to practice peaceably 'without interruption or molestation, time immemorial'. The merchants hoped that the Atholls would protect them against this proclamation. Otherwise, they would be 'under an absolute necessity of declining all further connections in trade' and withdraw to another country, 'where business may be carried on with greater safety and protection'. There were twenty-nine signatures, including David Forbes and his nephew, Thomas Durie, the Scottish, Irish & Manx partnership of Ross, Black & Christian, Robert Kennedy and Robert Gordon & Co.

David Forbes and the Duries

There was a dispute amongst the merchants living on the Isle of Man because in debt cases the native Manx were paid first. As there was seldom sufficient money to cover these debts, the non-Manx merchants believed that they were discriminated against unfairly. Their complaint was referred to the Chancery Court, where the situation was affirmed. This had 'greatly alarmed those gentlemen, who are called foreigners', and as 'the greatest part of the trade of this Isle' was carried on by them, this was 'a cruel custom to the great discouragement of trade'. The attorney general suggested that the Manx laws should be changed but the governor preferred to refer the problem to the Duke of Atholl. One solution was for the non-Manx merchants to become naturalised.[244]

David Forbes had 'traded and dealt' on the Island for many years before he applied for naturalisation in November 1756. The Duke approved of his request, provided an oath was administered that, 'reserving his allegiance to His Majesty of Great Britain, he should true faith and fidelity bear to His Grace and noble successors, Lords of this Isle, and support and maintain the laws and prerogatives thereof'. David Ross, Robert Black and Robert Kennedy were naturalised at the same time. Governor Lindesay reported to the Duke that this had made 'these men very happy'.[245]

David was not the only Forbes on the Isle of Man. He was related to <u>Edward Forbes</u> of Douglas, mariner, and son of another David, who supposedly had been forced to spend a season on the Island because of his Jacobite sympathies.[246] He was also related to <u>James Forbes</u>, of Ramsey, who married Ann Christian, related in turn to John Christian of Ross, Black & Christian. Their daughter Jane, married the Kirkcudbright merchant John Kirkpatrick.

Forbes had two nephews 'of the full blood', Thomas and John Durie, presumably from Stonehaven, who had joined him on the Isle of Man. He also had several relations in the north-east of Scotland:

<u>Captain Charles Forbes</u> of His Majesty's 22nd Regiment of Foot.

<u>Baillie George Forbes</u>, a merchant in Aberdeen.

<u>Mary Forbes</u>, who married Lieutenant John Guise at St Nicholas church in Aberdeen on 28 August 1749. She was described by Thomas Durie as his '<u>aunt</u>' so confirming that she was David's sister.

<u>Phebe Forbes</u>, who married Thomas Brodie of Montrose, now a writer to the signet in Edinburgh.

<u>William Forbes</u>, minister of the gospel at Fordoun, who married Susannah Walker at St Nicholas church in 1748. When he died, his widow returned to Aberdeen.[247]

This suggests that at least three members of the family, Charles, George and Mary's husband John Guise were connected with the government. Why did David Forbes leave the Aberdeen area, and choose the Isle of Man as his home?

He was on the Isle of Man by 1744. Between then and his death in 1771 he became one of the Island's main merchants. His imports included rum from Barbados, St Croix, St Kitts and Boston; wine from Bordeaux and Saloe; Guinea goods for the slave trade from Liverpool and Rotterdam and tea from Gothenburg.[248]

Figure 30: Kirroughtree House – July 2001

Forbes married Margaret Heron of Kirroughtree house near Kirkcudbright on 18 January 1745. There are two versions of an event in September 1748, when the couple were on their way to visit the Herons at Kirroughtree. Governor Lindesay reported to the Duke of Atholl, 'we have just heard that a sloop in ballast from Ramsey to Kirkcudbright was taken by the *Wolfe* man of war, as she was entering that harbour … The sloop was carried to Whitehaven, where all aboard were made prisoners.

We have yet no more particulars but that the sloop had not ten ankers of brandy on board and that Mr Forbes knew nothing of it'.[249]

The collector at Whitehaven had been sent a copy of the petition from John Kirk, master of the *Neptune* sloop of Kirkcudbright, under seizure at his port, and the Board of Customs in London asked him for 'a true state of the case with our observations and opinion thereon'. This was his response:

> On the 5th July last the sloop sailed from hence with coals for Belfast and in her return home put into Derbyhaven in the Isle of Man on or about 13th August, where she continued for three or four days, and then set sail for Kirkcudbright. But on her way touched at Ramsey in the Island for some passengers bound thither. On the 19th in the Channel at the mouth of the river that runs up to Kirkcudbright she fell in with Captain Tarelton in the Sincerity sloop, who boarded her and finding Mr Forbes of Ramsey and several others from thence upon deck he made a strict rummage and found 17 casks, 3 stone bottles and 12 papers containing 11½ lbs. tea, 16 gallons brandy, 55 rum and 8 geneva. Upon which he seized the sloop and brought her hither. We have no doubt but all or most of the goods were taken in at the Isle of Man but are of opinion, in case of a claim, we shall not be able to prove it, having already used our endeavours to get evidence thereof to no purpose.[250]

The main discrepancy appears to be over the vessel that seized the *Neptune*. There is no information about how long David Forbes and his wife, and the other passengers, had to remain at Whitehaven.

It was through his connections with the Heron family that Forbes became involved with the Douglas Heron bank (see John Christian below). The investors in this bank included:

Larger investors	£	Each investing £500
Charles, Duke of Queensbury & Dover (Douglas)	2,000	William, Earl of March & Ruglen
Hon. Archibald Douglas of Douglas	2,000	James Wilson junior, merchant in Kilmarnock
William Douglas, younger of Kelhead	1,000	Hugh Parker, merchant in Kilmarnock
Henry, Duke of Buccleuch (Douglas)	1,000	David Ferguson, provost of Ayr
Patrick Heron of Heron	1,000	Patrick Douglas, surgeon in Ayr
David Maclure, merchant in Ayr	1,000	Robert Whiteside, merchant in Ayr
		Robert Kennedy of Pinmure
Total investments	150,000	

Table X: Investors in the Douglas Heron Bank[251]

David Maclure and Robert Whiteside had been deeply involved in the running trade with the Isle of Man. George Moore supplied Patrick Douglas with brandy and other goods. When Douglas failed to pay a large outstanding debt, Moore employed David Ferguson to take legal action against him.[252] There is no evidence that the Douglases of Morton and Fingland invested in this bank.

The only clue to David Forbes's possible investment is found in the list of his creditors.[253]

Major Patrick Gordon by Bond — £2000. 0. 0
Patrick Heron of Heron Esq. by d[o] — 3000. 0 —
Rob[t]. Maxwell Esq[r] — by d[o] — 1600. 0 —
6600. 0. 0

Figure 31: The Heron tomb at Monigaff parish church, Newton Stewart – July 2001

This monument is in memory of Patrick Heron of Heron and Patrick Heron of Heron Esquires.
The last died 26 September 1761 aged 60. The first died three weeks thereafter aged 83.
As they lived respected and esteemed so they died regretted by all who knew them.

David Forbes died at Edinburgh on 26 January 1771, intestate. Thomas Durie, as his next of kin, was appointed his sole administrator by the Manx Ecclesiastical Court. Forbes left a 'considerable estate', together with property in Ramsey and Douglas.

Thomas Durie first appeared on the Isle of Man in 1756 as master of the *Annandale* of Annan.[254] This was an 80 ton snow with a crew of nine men and two guns, built in Liverpool in 1751. She was owned by David Forbes and:

John Allan	a Scottish merchant living in Douglas
Thomas Arthur	an Irish merchant living in Douglas
John Callin	a Manx merchant living in Peel
John Johnson	the provost of Annan
David Ross	a Scottish merchant living in Douglas
Jacob Sandilands	Bartholomew and George Sandilands were merchants in Bordeaux Jacob ran the company's branch in Barcelona

These owners suggest the ship's intended use – to import wine and brandy to the Isle of Man and then run it on to the north Solway coast.

In May 1756 David Forbes, John Allan, Hugh Cosnahan, Martin Creagh, John Folie, Ross, Black & Christian and William Johnston, her former master, imported brandy at Ramsey, which the *Annandale* had brought from Saloe.[255]

At this stage the ship was re-registered and Durie became one of the owners. According to her crew's protection against impressment into the navy, the *Annandale* was now 'of the Isle of Man'. Her next voyage was not successful. She called at the Island in October 1756 before sailing to Dublin. She cleared out from there for Lisbon. Then she sailed to the Mediterranean. Her destination is unclear but in February 1757 she was taken by a privateer and carried into 'a small port near Naples'. There are no details about the ransom arrangements.

There is no further information about Durie's subsequent career as a shipmaster. He had left the sea and was living on the Isle of Man by May 1760, when he married Ann, a daughter of William Fine, a Catholic Irish merchant who had settled in Douglas. They did not have any children.

Durie appears frequently in the Douglas customs ingates between 1762 and 1763. He was importing goods from two main sources: Rotterdam and Gothenburg.[256] Although he had inherited David Forbes's estate in Ramsey, Thomas built a large house in Douglas, later known as Durie house in Drury Lane. He actually lived at the Nunnery, on the opposite side of Douglas River, which he rented from Peter John Heywood.

This letter written to John Taubman on 4 November 1778 suggests that his health was declining:

> We are now removing from the Nunnery to Douglas. Had I been well enough would have done myself the pleasure of waiting upon you on this occasion. But have not been able to travel so far for some time past ... I have been speaking to Mr Heywood about some few jobs that are necessary to be done in the gardens about this season, such as pruning the vines, covering the asparagus buds etc. Mr Heywood has my old garner employed for some time. I begged he would send him up as soon as possible to prune the vines, as he has done for some years past and understands it better than a stranger. It would be a great pity if they were neglected. My own servants shall assist in anything they can do that is wanted in the garden as soon as we get our effects moved to Douglas, which will be in a few days. We will be very much obliged to you for leave to sit in your seat in Douglas chapel, while it is convenient for your family.[257]

On 2 July 1771 Durie was in Dumfries. He made out an 'instrument' vesting his goods etc. in his wife Ann and John Christian (by this stage cashier of the Douglas Heron & Co Bank in Ayr) in trust for his nephew and nieces, the children of John Durie of Ramsey.[258] Back in Douglas on 28 January 1779 he made a codicil to the instrument. This complicated the probate of his will because the two documents had to be proved in different places – Edinburgh and on the Island. His nephew David Forbes Durie was dead and his nieces were suspicious that their aunt had embezzled their inheritance. They insisted that detailed accounts should be presented to the Ecclesiastical Court.[259]

Figure 32: Thomas Durie (-1779)

Durie was buried in Old Kirk Braddan churchyard on 3 February 1779. His epitaph read: [260]

Of all that knew him beloved and esteemed for his Probity, Piety and Hospitality.
A good neighbour.
A most affectionate husband.
A kind master.
Reader imitate his virtues.

The tomb, lettering etc. cost his widow nine guineas.

His debts totalled over £357. Twenty-four of these debts were defined as 'bad'. They included:

Debtor	Date debt contracted	Classified as	£
John Thomson	1760	Bad	118
David McLoy	1763	Dead	116
Robert Leany	1760	Bad	44
James Morrison	1761	Bad	17
John Gordon	1761	Dead	19

It became extremely difficult to claim smuggling debts after Revestment in 1765. The debtors had no reason to visit the Island, none of their belongings were 'in the hands' of merchants there and the British courts, following the lead of Ireland, refused to accept that these debts were legal.

Durie had attempted unsuccessfully to sue both Captain John Gordon and David McLoy in the Manx Chancery Court <u>before</u> they died.[261]

After the 'Forty-five a list of the rebels from every district in Scotland was produced by the Commissioners of Excise. The list from the Montrose district included John Durie, a merchant in Stonehaven. He had 'carried arms, bought up tartans and shoes and pressed horses for the service of the rebels. Read the Pretender's manifesto publicly upon a Sabbath day, frequently mounted guard and threatened to force others to follow his example'. He was currently 'lurking'.[262]

It is probable that this individual was David Forbes's nephew John Durie. He was on the Isle of Man by 31 August 1750, when he imported rum from Barbados on board the *Grand Turk*, Hugh Wilkie master, at Ramsey. He married Jane Lewhellin in November 1757 and they had three children.

John Durie died intestate on 6 September 1764. As usual, four men were instructed to make a complete inventory of all his goods, before they were sold to pay off any debts. One of these was John McCulloch, a merchant from Kirkcudbright who had also settled in Ramsey. McCulloch and his son, James, moved to Guernsey in 1765.[263] The goods listed included a wide range of articles suggesting that Durie was not only involved in the running trade but also sold merchandise in a shop. Goods that were probably purchased for the running trade included:

Rum, sugar and coffee beans from the West Indies, brandy from France and Spain, French white wine and claret, geneva (gin) from Holland, tea (common bohea, congo, hyson, soutchong and singlo) from Gothenburg and Barcelona handkerchiefs from Spain.

China would be shipped in the tea chests as ballast. Durie's china included plain gilded, ribbed gilded and blue cups & saucers, teapot, sugar basins, slop bowls & plates.

His probable shop goods were:

Cravats, silk handkerchiefs, table cloths, blue Manchester velvet, Irish printed cotton and linen checker
Thread and cotton stockings for men, women, youths and infants
Thread & cotton laces (probably from Ireland)
Shelled and coarse barley and candles.

The inventory continued with Durie's personal belongings. When cash found in the house was added to the goods, chattels and effects the total was £253. Only half of this belonged to the estate, the remainder was passed to Ann Durie.

There were three major creditors. Brother Thomas claimed debts on behalf of two merchant houses in Gothenburg: Robert, John and Benjamin Hall for £192 and George Carnegie for £46. John Lewhellin, another merchant in Ramsey and John's father-in-law, claimed £420. In other words John Durie's assets did not equal what he owed.

The Presbyterians

The merchants of the Presbyterian 'persuasion' on the Isle of Man applied to the Duke of Atholl on 26 August 1763 for a minister from Scotland, who would help them 'in the principles in which we were early educated'. The signatories included David Ross, Robert Kennedy and Robert Gordon.[264]

The Rosses

The first reference to David Ross 'of North Britain' is in 1726 when Robert Maddrell charged him with a debt of £55. From 1740 onwards, he appears regularly in the Island's ingates both as a shipmaster and importing goods in his own right. By 1746, he was sufficiently well-established to be appointed one of the harbour supervisors of Douglas, with Philip Finch. In 1747, his ship was on its way to Holland when 'by some unavoidable accident' it had to put into Milford Haven in Wales. There she was seized and confiscated because the casks of saltpetre in her cargo had been taken on board at the Isle of Man.[265]

On 16 February 1751 Ross, aged 'forty and upwards', sent 42 ankers of brandy, two casks of wine and a box of soap to Ramsey in a Manx boat with a coast permit. Captain George Dow of the *Sincerity* revenue cruiser of Whitehaven stopped the boat, actually in Ramsey bay. When he found a letter on board, suggesting that Ross was going to send these goods to Scotland, 'which intention might or might not take place', Dow seized the boat and cargo. Ross was recommended to claim the boat and goods before the Commissioners of Customs in London, within 24 days, and if this failed then he was to claim them in the Court of Exchequer. This could be a test case - it would be shown that the English Exchequer Court had no jurisdiction over seizures made in the Isle of Man and so make similar situations 'much easier for the future'. The boat and her cargo were released.[266]

Ross went into partnership with Robert Black of Douglas in 1748. Black was the second son of John Black of Belfast, who was the uncle of Walter Lutwidge's son-in-law, James Arbuckle, also of Belfast. They were in the Guinea trade but also dealt in brandy, wine, tobacco and tea and ran a brewery. In 1753 they landed a cargo of rotten tobacco from Holland and on application to the Duke of Atholl the duties were remitted.[267] Their cashier, John Christian of Ramsey, joined them formally in 1760 to become one of the Island's major companies: Ross, Black & Christian. Inevitably, their network of customers was extensive, involving people in Scotland, England, Wales and Ireland.

On 3 March 1767 Ross died, unmarried. According to his will, he left legacies to his housekeeper on the Island, Mrs Margaret Neilson, and to various relations in the Tain area of north-east Scotland.

Grandniece: Elizabeth Ross, only daughter of Alexander Ross, tacksman of Little Dun,
and her sons David & William
Niece: Christian Simson, married to Murdo Ross in Tain
Niece: Anna Simson
Niece: Jean Simson, married to John McKenzie, Dunsheathness
Brother German: Hugh Ross
Grandniece: Jean Ross, eldest daughter of David Ross, Priesthill
Godson: Ross Thompson, son of John Thompson
Children of: Hugh Simson, gunsmith in Tain
Children of: Alexander Simson of Loanding
Children of: Arthur Simson of Dornoch
Children of: David Simson, Hill of Tain

These bequests totalled over £2,165. The list of rebels in the Ross district included: Angus, Thomas and William Ross of Tain and Kenneth Simpson of Nairn.[268]

After Revestment, Robert Black returned to Belfast, where he became a linen merchant, exporting cloth to London. John Christian went to Ayr, as cashier to the Douglas Heron bank. This bank was set up on 6 November 1769, initially for 21 years. Within the next ten days branches had opened in Dumfries and Edinburgh. One of the stipulations was that the cashier, who was secretary at the meetings of the directors, was not to engage in any trade or business, 'which may interfere with his duty and attendance due to the company'. Christian was a partner in several ventures at Ayr, including the Oliphant & Co. wine business. On 25 June 1772 the bank collapsed. Their main mistake had been 'over-trading and endeavouring to force a circulation of the company's paper [notes] beyond natural limits'. The liabilities totalled over £1,000,000. Robert Arthur of Irvine was convinced that Christian had embezzled all the stock belonging to several Manx merchants, including George Moore and Christian Kelly, who owed Arthur money. Nothing could be proved.[269] Christian moved to Dunkirk.[270]

The Kennedys

George Moore's main outlet for goods was Ayrshire, where a string of agents was responsible for collecting debts on orders which Moore himself contracted during his annual two month visit to Scotland.[271]

Figure 33: Culzean Castle – November 2000

His only proven contact with the Jacobites in this area was with Archibald Kennedy, who as the factor for Sir Thomas Kennedy of Culzean. Orders sent to Moore were recorded in Kennedy's notebook:

24 June 1750
commissioned from Mr George Moore per Breckenrig
[James Breckenrig, the Scottish master of a Manx wherry]
1 ten, 2 fives Jamaica [one 10 gallon cask and two 5 gallon casks of Jamaica rum]
4 tens, 2 fives plain rum
1 ten 2 fives brandy
2 fives canary [wine]
and from Mr John Callin [another Peel merchant]
10 lbs. coffee and 10 lbs bohea tea.

6 October 1752
commissioned from Mr Moore per James Rodger [another wherrymaster]
7 quarter casks of white Lisbon [purchased by John Allan of Ballantrae from Moore and then sold to Kennedy]
1 hogshead of good claret and another smaller one
12 tens of very best rum
1 ten of common rum
2 fives of 'good old Nantes' [brandy]
25 lbs. best green and bohea teas (half and half) either by canisters or in the common way [in waterproof bags][272]

There was a problem with this order. Rodger would not take the hogsheads – they were too bulky for speedy unloading on the Scottish coast. As a result, Moore employed Archibald McClure, who was taking two orders of small casks to the Troon Point. The revenue cruisers were so active off the Ayrshire coast that the wherries doubled back and relanded their cargoes on the Island. A second attempt was made by John McClure, using a boat from Ireland, but this time the goods were actually seized at sea. The fate of the two hogsheads of wine is not recorded.

Robert Kennedy was related to the Kennedys of Culzean. He had come to the Island as part of the (Whig) Duke of Atholl's staff. He settled in Castletown, where he married Robert Maddrell's sister and became a merchant - he was one of those naturalised in 1756.

Between 1760 and 1774 Kennedy was involved in twenty-four slave trade voyages from Liverpool. After Revestment he moved to that port, where he also owned two ships in the Greenland fishery. On 15 August 1774 the *Dolphin* returned from Greenland with two large fish and 2,700 seals.[273]

Despite John Taubman's opinion that Kennedy would never give up trade, his son, John, wrote in April 1774 explaining that their two Guinea ships were only going out to Calabar to collect old debts and that they would be sold on their return. 'A convincing proof of which, is, that he is now in Scotland laying the foundation of a House intended for the residence of himself and family'. This was Greenan House near Culzean.[274] The *May* and *Cassillis* returned to Liverpool on 6 March and 31 August 1775 respectively. By this time Kennedy was living in Scotland.[275]

On 18 February 1780 John wrote to Taubman from Greenan House:

> *After paying the last mournful duties to the remains of a beloved and revered father, I would not omit acquainting you among his friends of the melancholy event of his death. I came into this country in September when I found your old friend very much reduced, since which, his health declined rapidly till the 10th inst. When nature quite exhausted with a long painful illness he expired with all the ease, composure and serenity of countenance that a Christian should die with and all of us must wish to make our departure with ... I have every reason to lament the death of a father who indulged me – beyond my wishes.[276]*

The Gordons
A Robert Gordon was in partnership with John Murray and John Cannon, all of Dumfries, when in 1711 they were charged in the Chancery Court on the Isle of Man with a debt of £30 owed to John Dickenson of Lancaster for tobacco.

On 27 February 1760 Governor Cochrane forwarded to the Duke of Atholl a petition from Robert Gordon, described as 'a relation of Kenmure', who had been executed in London in 1716, asking to be naturalised. Gordon had been in business at Liverpool for some time and 'comes hence with a very good character'. As there was 'much opposition' on the Island to Gordon's naturalisation, the Duke suggested to the governor that 'it had better be left a while'.[277]

This coincides with the opposition on the Island to naturalisation of papists. Although Gordon was not listed as one of these people in the petition from the Manx merchants, it suggests that he may have been a Catholic.

Robert Gordon & Co. (Gordon's partner was the Manx merchant John Stowell) were involved in the slave trade, importing Guinea goods from Holland to be collected by the Liverpool slavers on their way to the West African coast and then importing rum, one of the products of that trade, which was subsequently run to customers along the Irish Sea coasts.

When the William Gordon, Thomas and Richard Foster and Samuel Brooks partnership in Liverpool became bankrupt during 1764, John Crosbie and Benjamin Heywood attempted to recoup some of their debts by arresting rum in Robert Gordon's cellar. The case was dismissed.[278]

Even at this late stage in the Island's running trade the opportunities for making money were considerable. In his own right, Gordon also imported brandy from Bordeaux, wine from Lisbon and Saloe and tea from Gothenburg. There is no evidence about where Robert Gordon went after he left the Island post-Revestment.

Postscript

After 1715 William Gordon settled in Christiansand (see p. 70), which in the eighteenth century was part of Denmark and so operated under Danish law. The trade included importing tobacco, which was re-shipped to the Isle of Man, or sold directly to the Scottish smugglers. Local exports were timber and herrings. Salt for curing the herrings was imported from Portugal.

Robert Arthur was a merchant in Irvine who had strong trading links with the Island, having been in partnership with John Kelly and John Callin and, by default, George Moore. In 1764 Arthur and James Oates, his partner in the tobacco trade who was based in Douglas, sent 60 hogsheads of tobacco, purchased from Alexander Speirs in Glasgow, to Christiansand. Gordon sold 40 of these hogsheads and the remaining 20 were re-shipped to the Isle of Man.

In the meantime, Arthur had purchased nine hogsheads of tobacco from Hunter & Co. of Ayr, which were sent to Gordon on board the *Grizzie*, John Barbour master. Barbour returned with a draft for £130, which was protested for non-payment.

As Gordon provided convincing reasons for the delay in his payments, in 1769 Arthur purchased a further 20 hogsheads from Alexander Speirs & Co. These were sent on the *Cumberland*, Peter Urie master, to Christiansand.

Urie returned with a draft from Gordon on Edie & Laird of London for £200. They claimed that they had no money belonging to Gordon in their hands. He had depended on a cargo of herrings sent to Barcelona to pay for this but it had been seized by an Algerine pirate. The insurance money was not yet paid to Edie & Laird. Arthur continued to be sympathetic. He commented that Gordon had been 'ill-treated' by his London correspondents.

When William Gordon failed in business on 8 May 1772 he still owed Arthur £183. One recourse was to arrest the *Grizzie*, which Gordon held in partnership with Barbour. But his share was only one eighth. Gordon left Christiansand and went to live in Drogheda, Ireland. On 1 August 1772 Arthur wrote to William Wilson, a writer in Edinburgh:

> *I am not sure whether William Gordon is a native of Scotland. If he <u>was</u>, he went to Norway when young and has remained there ever since. I am told he has an estate in the east country. He is now well advanced in years.*[279]

This forms a somewhat sad epitaph for a Jacobite.

TAILPIECE
RAGWORT aka SENECIO JACOBEA aka CUSHAG

Figure 34: The Pressed Ragwort

This plant was found pressed on John Murray and Phil Moore's letter refusing to give evidence against John Hale. Ragwort was also known as St Jacob's Bloom. No claim can be made that it was named after the Jacobite cause, because this name was first used in 1532. The Jacobites may have adopted the plant as an emblem during the 'Forty-five. Research into the exact date when Cushag became associated with the Isle of Man is still ongoing.[280]

APPENDIX I: THE ENGLISH MONARCHS AND THE LORDS OF MAN 1405-1689

	Monarchs		Lords of Man
1399	Henry IV		Island owned by Scroop family
		1405	**Stanleys** Sir John Stanley I
1413	Henry V		
		1414	Sir John Stanley II
1422	Henry VI		
		1432	Lord Thomas Stanley I
		1460	Lord Thomas Stanley II
		1485	**Earls of Derby** Thomas Stanley, 1st Earl
1461	Edward IV		"
1470	Henry VI		"
1471	Edward IV		"
1483	Edward V		"
1483	Richard III		"
1485	Henry VII		"
		1504	Thomas Stanley, 2nd Earl
1509	Henry VIII		
		1521	Edward Stanley, 3rd Earl
1547	Edward VI		"
1553	Mary		"
1558	Elizabeth I		"
		1572	Henry Stanley, 4th Earl
		1593	Ferdinando Stanley, 5th Earl
			Queen Elizabeth's Governors
		1595	Sir Thomas Gerard
		1596	Peter Legh
		1599	Cuthbert Gerard
		1600	Cuthbert Molynieux
1603	James I & VI	1603	English Rule through
		1607	Henry, Earl of Northampton & Robert, Earl of Salisbury
		1610	**Stanleys Restored** William Stanley, 6th Earl of Derby & Countess Elizabeth
1625	Charles I	1627	James Stanley, 7th Earl of Derby
1649	**Commonwealth**	1651	**Commonwealth**
		1652	Lord Fairfax
1660	Charles II	1660	**Stanleys restored** Charles Stanley, 8th Earl of Derby
		1672	William Stanley, 9th Earl of Derby
1685	James II & VII		"
1689	William & Mary		"
1694	William III		"
1702	Queen Anne	1702	James Stanley 10th Earl of Derby
1714	George I		
1727	George II		
		1736	**The Atholls** James 2nd Duke
1760	George III		"
		1764	John 3rd Duke

Note: This is a simplified version of the situation. For greater details see A W Moore: *A History of the Isle of Man*

APPENDIX II: GOVERNORS AND BISHOPS

	Governor		**Deputy Governor**
1678	Robert Heywood		
1690	Roger Kenyon	1692	William Sacheverell
1693	William Sacheverell		
1696	Nicholas Sankey		
1701	James Cranstown		
1702	Charles Stanley*		
1703	Robert Mawdsley		
1713	Charles Z Stanley**	1713	Alexander Horne
1718	Alexander Horne***		
1723	John Lloyd		
1725	Thomas Horton		
1736	James Murray***		
1744	Patrick Lindesay***		
1751	Basil Cochrane***		
1761	John Wood***		

*   Chief governor and Commander-in-Chief
**   Chief governor
***   Governor and Commander in Chief

Bishop

1684	Baptista Levinz
1693-1698	Vacant
1698	Thomas Wilson
1755	Mark Hildesley

Note: This is a simplified version of the situation. For greater details see A W Moore: *A History of the Isle of Man*

APPENDIX III JACOBITE MANIFESTO AT KELSO: 1715

A manifesto at Kelso churchyard 24 October professing to contain the sentiments of the Scottish adherents of James VIII. It set out with the well-known Tory principles of the unalienable right by which they were bound to His family, and person. It then lamented the factions by which their fundamental constitution was destroyed; it lamented also the unhappy union of Scotland and England; it deplored the loss of national resources, consumed in ruinous wars; the infraction of the Hereditary rights of subjects; the suborned, or packed up character of the British parliament; the impeachments and attainders of patriots who had suffered for their endeavours to restore Trade, Plenty and Peace; the bringing in a foreign Prince unacquainted with British manners, customs and language; the support of his designs by foreign troops; and the contempt with which the military services of British troops were treated. It proposed the determination to resort to the last extremities, in order to remedy these grievances, and to have their laws, liberties and properties secured by the Parliaments of both Kingdoms, trusting, at the same time, that by good example and conversation with learned Divines, His Majesty would, in time, lose the prejudices attributable to his education in a Popish country, and be induced to give absolute security to the Protestant religion, against all efforts of arbitrary Power, Popery and all its other enemies. It, lastly, professed the hope that by a system of economy, such as the reduction of troops and garrisons, taxes would be removed, and the public credit sustained.

The reward of present military service in this expedition was next explained: it was declared that every officer should enjoy the post he then held, and should be advanced and preferred according to his rank and station, and the number of men he was enabled to bring; that each foot-soldier should have twenty shillings sterling, and each trooper, or dragoon, who might bring horse and accoutrements with him, twelve pounds sterling gratuity, besides pay. The manifesto concluded with the hope, that, undisturbed by 'a Pretender's' interests and council from abroad or by a restless faction at home, the blessing and aid of Almighty God would be continued to so good and just a cause, and would be extended to the succour of the Royal Family of Stuart and their country, from sinking under oppression ...

This manifesto which, in many respects, was more applicable to the Scottish than to the English views, and which, in its reference to the religion of James VIII of Scotland, could not fail to have been distasteful to the Roman Catholic party, is said to have been received with loud acclamations. The cry, however, which succeeded of 'No Union' – 'No malt-tax' – 'No salt-tax', shewed that the approbation which it obtained, had proceeded from the Scottish rather than the English Insurgents.

Source: Hibbert Ware pp. 53-54

APPENDIX IV: CORRESPNDENCE BETWEEN WILLIAM CRAIK
JAMES MAXWELL OF KIRKCONNELL AND WILLIAM MAXWELL OF NITHSDALE: 1745

James Maxwell of Kirkconnell was determined to join the Jacobites. He wrote to Craik:

> By accounts this day from Edinburgh, almost everybody is going along with the stream, so that a short delay would lose all the merit. This has determined me to do the thing so suddenly that I have not time to send for you, unless it were to see me go off, which is impossible ... Farewell, dear Willie; God bless you. Ever yours. James Maxwell

> Saturday - I set out before daylight tomorrow.

According to the List of Rebels, Maxwell served in 'the Pretender's son's life guards till the defeat at Culloden' and his whereabouts were not known after the '45. He had escaped to Europe and was living at St Germains.

William Craik of Arbigland corresponded with William Maxwell of Nithsdale about the pros and cons of the rebellion. This is the reply to a letter from Nithsdale, dated 13 October 1745.

> It must give me great pleasure that you have not determined to engage in the present enterprize, which, from several apparent symptoms, I had reason to apprehend; and if you stick by your promise of doing nothing rashly (fit only for desperados indeed!) in a matter of such moment, I shall be set at ease from the anxiety I felt on your account ...

> [Maxwell believed] if the scheme misgive, all Scotland becomes involved in the guilt, and may expect the outmost severities this Government and the people of England can afflict them with; but, on the other hand, should the undertaking be crowned with success, as Scotsmen have the merit of it, they must become the peculiar favourites of the family they have raised to the throne, and reap all the advantages they can promise themselves from a grateful and generous prince ...

> [Craik's view] The maxims by which our hereditary princes conducted themselves were sufficiently felt, to the sad experience of our forefathers. Thank God, we were reserved for happier times. Their history will inform you of their repeated and unwearied attempts to subvert the constitution and enslave a free people. Their sacrificing the interest of the nation to France; their violating their oaths and promises; their persecutions, and their schemes to establish a religion which in its nature is inconsistent with the toleration of any other, though reasons of State may make it wink at this on particular occasions ...

> The present family have now reigned over us these thirty years, and though during so long a time they may have fallen into errors, or may have committed faults, (as what Government is without,) yet I will defy the most sanguine zealot to find in history a period equal to this, in which Scotland possessed so uninterrupted a felicity; in which liberty, civil and religious, was so universally enjoyed by all people, of whatever denomination, nay, by the open and avowed enemies of the family and constitution; or a period in which all ranks of men have been so effectually secured in their property. Have not trade, manufacture, agriculture, and the spirit of industry in our country extended themselves further during this period, and under this family, than for ages before? Has any man suffered in his liberty, life, or fortune contrary to law? Stand forth and name him if you can! ...

> Look into the reigns of the James's and the Charles's and tell me whether these divine and hereditary princes were guided by the same spirit of mildness and forgiveness. I am sensible how often and how many destructive designs have been imputed to the prince upon the throne and his ministers; of the cry raised against standing armies; of the complaints of corruption; long Parliaments; and Hanoverian interest pursued in opposition to that of Britain; but I am also sensible there is not a true friend to liberty, a dispassionate and sober man, but who (now the mask is laid aside) perceives they were at bottom the artifices and popular pretences of men struggling to force themselves into power, or those who in the dark were aiming the destruction of our happy constitution ...

According to the List, William Maxwell, Lord Nithsdale, 'went to Edinburgh and waited some time upon the Pretender's son' but did not take an active part in the rebellion.

Source: The Book of Carlaverock. Memoirs of the Maxwells, Earls of Nithsdale Lords Maxwell & Herries by William Fraser Volume II Correspondence and Chargers 1873

WHO WAS WHO

<u>Note</u>: This does not include all the individuals mentioned in the book but a selection of some of the more significant ones.

AGLIONBY, JOHN (1663 - 1729)
In 1675 Aglionby married Dinah Stuthart of Crosthwaite and they had one son, Henry (1684 – 1759), who represented Carlisle in two different Parliaments during George I's reign and was an alderman and mayor of Carlisle. John and Dinah went to the Isle of Man in the early 1700s and the Aglionby house became a focal point for Jacobite sympathisers – Isaac Allgood, John Murray of Douglas and Philip Moore. In 1716 Aglionby was accused of drinking 'disaffected healths'. Despite this, he remained on the Island, where he was in a partnership with Edward Nash and Patrick Savage. One of their suppliers was Walter Lutwidge.

ALDRIDGE, WILLIAM
A miller of cloth first at Braddan and then Ramsey, Aldridge is the best example of someone who was probably 'set up' for the accusation of disaffection following problems with Paul Gelling and his son.

ALLEN, THOMAS
There are two possibilities. The less likely is Thomas Allen who was vicar of Maughold. In February 1717 the alternative Thomas Allen was at a house in Douglas, when he claimed that he had lost a silver buckle. During the ensuing argument, he pulled a crown piece out of his pocket and stated that was all the money he had until he returned to Liverpool. He was denied even £20 worth of credit on the Isle of Man. This was unfair because his master, who was worth £15,000, had lent the Earl of Derby £200. William Griffiths, who was in the house at the time, claimed that even the Earl's worst servant could lend him £200, without going to Allen's master. He then told Allen to sit down and stop being quarrelsome. There is no clue about the identity of his master.

ALGOOD, ISAAC
Probably from Brandon White House, Nunwick in Northumberland, the son of Reverend Major Allgood, rector of Simonburn, although Isaac was a common name in the Allgood family. He married Hannah Clark and their son, Lancelot (born in 1710), was High Sheriff of Northumberland under George II and MP of the county in 1748. He was knighted by George III in 1760. Isaac Allgood was lame and so instead of joining the Northumbrian Jacobites he went to the Isle of Man, to await a call to London to take up his post in the Stuart government. Having had an affair with his landlady, Mary Hendrick, Allgood, his wife and maid went to lodge with John Hale. Mary subsequently gave evidence to the governor about Allgood's disaffections. There is no information about him after 1717.

BIGNALL, JOHN (-1735)
Probably born in Belturbet, county Cavan, during the Williamite wars, he moved to Dublin, where he became a merchant, marrying Mary Rickersby there. They moved to the Isle of Man in 1708, living first at Douglas and then in Ramsey. Bignall was in several partnerships – with Jacob Turner and John Hunter; Michael Sampson (John Murray of Douglas's brother-in-law) and William Thwaites, both of Dublin and with John Wattleworth junior of Ramsey. Deeply involved in the running trade, Bignall sent goods to customers on Skye and in Dumfries and Galloway and Cumberland. Jane Stewart, daughter of Captain John Stewart of Kirkcudbright was the mother of his only child, Mary, who finally inherited his house in Ramsey.

BLACK, JAMES (-1713)
A merchant from Alison Bank in Annandale, importing tobacco from Virginia and Maryland, Black was involved in the running trade from the Isle of Man. When he died suddenly in 1713 he left all his affairs unsettled, including tobacco unsold in the hands of John Murray of Douglas. His

widow, Barbara, appointed John Wattleworth junior of Ramsey as her surety, responsible for ensuring that Black's effects remained on the Island until the court had received all the claims against his estate. She asked John Murray of Dumfries to act as her attorney there and this resulted in a long battle over the ownership of 8 hogsheads of tobacco.

BLACK, ROBERT

Second son of John Black of Belfast. This family included European merchants and the captain of a Guinea ship, sailing from Liverpool. Black was one of the more successful merchants on the Island. When his father visited Douglas, he was very impressed by his son's new house there. Black went into partnership first with David Ross and then John Christian. There were ongoing problems with Walter Lutwidge over family debts.

BREW, RICHARD

A soldier, loyal to Queen Anne. In December 1713 he challenged John Murray of Dumfries to a duel on Douglas Green and then reported him to the deputy governors for drinking disaffected healths.

BUTLER, HENRY

Probably a Jacobite sympathiser from Rawcliffe in Lancashire, whose son Richard fought at the battle of Preston and whose estate was seized and sold in 1718. He was on the Isle of Man at Easter 1715, when he was accused of disaffection.

CORBET, JAMES

A Glasgow merchant, Corbet married his daughter, Margaret, to Robert Douglas, who was then surveyor of the landcarriage at Glasgow. Corbet became involved in business with his son-in-law. There may have been some resulting family friction because when her husband went to fight with the Jacobites Margaret was living with her father-in-law at Gate Slack.

CRAIK FAMILY

Adam and his son William lived at Arbigland, which was well placed near the Solway shore. Adam's contacts on the Isle of Man included his brother-in-law, John Aglionby. William was an expert agriculturalist. He was employed as a surveyor of customs for the port of Dumfries but appears to have been inactive in terms of catching smugglers.

CROSS, WILLIAM CAPTAIN

A naval captain who went to live on the Isle of Man.

DALRYMPLE, CHARLES

Probably from Ayrshire – he was married at Kilmarnock in 1700. By 1708 Dalrymple was described as a merchant in Glasgow. He had 'good credit' on the Isle of Man and was involved in partnerships with John Hunter and Robert Douglas. He was one of the people who broke down Mary Hendrick's inn the *Royal George*, which she had put up after the battle of Preston.

DAVIES, ROBERT

When Davenport Davies was christened at St John the Baptist, Chester, on 15 November 1715, his parents were listed as Robert and <u>Mrs.</u> Robert Davies. Nearly forty years earlier, on 23 March 1676, Robert Davies married Elizabeth Davenport, daughter of Samuel Davenport, at Manley in Cheshire. There are three possible dates for the birth of their son Robert, of Manley Hall. – about 1687, 1690 or 1694. He married Salisbury Lee, daughter of Nathaniel Lee of Darnhall on 16 January 1714 at St John the Baptist in Chester. Samuel Davenport is listed as a relative. Davies joined Dalrymple and others in pulling down Mary Hendrick's sign, abusing both Mary and her husband, when he was charged with this. Believing that he had the protection of the Act of Grace, he drank a health to the Duke of Ormonde in 1717. He also criticised the governor, claiming that he would sell his estate of Manley Hall to get him out of his position.

DEALE, WILLIAM

Deale was an Irish merchant lurking on the Island to avoid his debts in Ireland. In 1717 he was accused of drinking the Duke of Ormonde's health.

DYMOND, JAMES

Formerly a merchant in Dublin, Dymond came to the Isle of Man in early 1715. He frequented Mrs Margaret Thompson's house in Castletown until he died intestate in October 1717, leaving considerable debts.

DOUGLAS, ROBERT of Auchenshinnoch

2nd son of Archibald Douglas of Morton Castle and Fingland, Robert was surveyor of customs for Glasgow. He was also involved in the running trade, and an expert horse thief. Douglas appears to have had the ability to persuade people to follow his lead – two men were prepared to perjure themselves for him in a court case on the Isle of Man over ownership of a cargo of brandy and he supplied a troop of men to the Northumbrian Jacobites. He married Margaret, daughter of James Corbet, a tobacco merchant in Glasgow. He was captured at the battle of Preston, was imprisoned but escaped and nothing further is known about him. His sister Grizel married the merchant John Murray of Dumfries and his sister Sara married William Johnson, collector of customs for Dumfries.

DOYLE, ALEXANDER

Doyle was master of various Dublin vessels, which landed on the Isle of Man goods from France and Spain between 1717 and 1728. He was intimately connected with both Jacobite sympathisers and Hanoverians.

DUCKENFIELD, SIR CHARLES

Great grandson of Robert Duckenfield, who occupied the Isle of Man on behalf of Parliament in 1651. Charles fled to the Island in the 1740s, to avoid his debts. He was followed by his niece, Jane Done, who had entrusted him with her inheritance from her father. She married John Livingston in Castletown and following Duckenfield's death in 1742 they spent several years in the Manx courts attempting to obtain recompense. [Not mentioned elsewhere in the book]

DURIE, JOHN

Probably a known Jacobite from Stonehaven in Scotland and nephew of David Forbes, he first appeared on the Island as a ship captain but he soon settled in Ramsey to become a major merchant. He married Jane Christian of Ramsey and their daughter, Jane, married the son of Thomas Kirkpatrick, a Jacobite and merchant in Kirkcudbright.

DURIE, THOMAS

Elder brother of John Durie. He settled as a merchant in Douglas, subsequently renting the Nunnery from Thomas Heywood. One of the major merchants pre Revestment, he remained on the Island and continued to trade. As the heir to David Forbes, he inherited considerable wealth. After his death in 1773, his nieces and nephew challenged his widow, whom they accused of embezzling the Forbes money and estates.

FORBES, DAVID

From the Aberdeen area and presumably a Jacobite as he was related to David Forbes of Douglas. There is no apparent explanation why he appeared on the Island in the 1740s. He developed a major trade with the Dumfries area and in 1745 married Margaret, heiress to the Heron family of Kirroughtree near Kirkcudbright. Through this connection Forbes became one of the investors in the ill-fated Douglas Heron Bank (aka the Ayr Bank). John Christian of Ramsey and a partner in the firm of Ross, Black & Christian was nephew John Durie's brother-in-law. After Revestment he became the cashier at the Ayr branch of the Douglas Heron bank and when the bank crashed in 1772 he went to Dunkirk and became a merchant there.

GORDON, THE FAMILY

The Gordon name comes originally from Gordon in Berwickshire. There were three branches in the family: Haddo, Strathbogie and Lochinvar. When Sir Adam of Gordon was granted Strathbogie castle, he renamed it Huntly. 'Young' Lochinvar was William de Gordon of Kenmure castle near New Galloway. The Gordons fought on both sides in 1715 and 1745. The 2nd Duke of Gordon fought with James III at Sheriffmuir whilst the 3rd Duke was with the Hanoverians against Bonnie Prince Charlie at Culloden. The Duke's brother, Lord Louis Gordon, had raised two battalions of troops to fight for the Jacobite cause – he died in France during 1754. Robert Gordon, son of the 6th Viscount Kenmure, who was attainted and beheaded, died in 1741, aged 28. He was succeeded by his brother, John (1713-1769).

HALE, JOHN

One of the king's officers on the Island and yet accused of drinking 'disaffected healths', Hale died intestate, in England at the beginning of March 1718, leaving a widow, Anne, and nine children. The inventory of his effects, which totalled over £46, provides a detailed description of the contents of his house in Douglas, where he took in lodgers and which included a parlour, five rooms and garrets with beds in them, a kitchen, pantry and cellar. He also owned a cow, a pig and a sow. These goods were in the hands of Robert Davies and Ambrose Wall.

HARLEY, NICHOLAS

Son of Captain Thomas Harley, who fought in Ireland under Charles I. He arrived on the Island in the 1670s and attempted to survive through legal trade. He applied, unsuccessfully, to the Lord Chancellor (Robert, Earl of Oxford and another Harley) for the post of tidesurveyor so that he could stop the Manx smuggling trade. When he died, his estate was insufficient to cover his debts.

HARLEY, THOMAS

Son of William Harley of Castletown. Spent several years off the Island, returning in the 1720s as factor to Poole & McGwire, farmers of the customs. Purchased Big Tree house in Malew Street, Castletown. His only child was Jane, by Alice Tiffin, wife of Jonathan Tiffin, a shipmaster of Workington.

HENDERSON, WILLIAM

The king's officer in Ramsey, Henderson successfully applied for a Manx boat and crew so that he could pass messages to the collectors of customs at Dumfries and Whitehaven. A deeply religious man, he charged Richard McGwire, one of the farmers of customs on the Island, with disaffection.

HENDRICK, JOHN

Possibly, originally from the south-west of England, Hendrick was the master of a herring boat sailing from Douglas. (see Mary)

HENDRICK, MARY

One of the more significant figures in the story of the 'Fifteen, Mary was the wife of John Hendrick (see above). She kept a drinking and lodging house in Douglas – at one stage called the *Royal George*. She was presented for having had an affair with Isaac Allgood and, in revenge, she repeated several of their conversations, about the Jacobites. After John's death, she married Dr George Smith of Liverpool.

HENRY, JOHN

Born at Londonderry in 1700, Henry married Anne, daughter of the Belfast tobacco merchant, James Hamilton. He was one of Walter Lutwidge's main contacts in Ireland. For over seven years Henry was a merchant in Castletown, dealing mainly in brandy and tobacco – his main suppliers were Thomas Coates of Whitehaven and William Whittaker of Workington. His banker was Sir Alexander Cairnes. When Henry he failed in business, he returned to Ireland, leaving considerable debts. [Not mentioned elsewhere]

HORNE, ALEXANDER

Deputy governor on the Island from 1713 to 1718, Horne became then governor in his own right from 1718 to 1723. A staunch supporter of the Earl of Derby and the crown, he never fully understood the Manx ethos, remaining not only a 'stranger' but also an 'outsider'.

HUNTER, JOHN

From Shillah Hill in North Tyneside, Hunter was a Borderer and a smuggler, involved in partnerships with Charles Dalrymple of Glasgow and John Bignall and Jacob Turner. Having served under Queen Anne, he led a troop of horse at the battle of Preston under the Earl of Derwentwater. As there were three John Hunters on the Jacobite side at that battle, there is some uncertainty about what happened to him subsequently.

JACKSON, WILLIAM

Jackson was on the Isle of Man during 1716 & 1717 – he dealt mainly in brandy and claret, which was exported to Ireland.

JOHNSON, WILLIAM

Collector of customs at Dumfries and strongly criticised for his inaction by the burghers of the town. This inactivity may be explained by the fact that in 1703 he married Sara, sister of Robert Douglas of Auchenshinnoch. Douglas was removed from his post at Glasgow in late 1710 and at about the same time Johnson stopped being collector at Dumfries.

KEMP, NICHOLAS

Agent on the Isle of Man for Sir Thomas Johnstone of Liverpool, who was a major tobacco merchant and staunch Hanoverian – in 1716 he was paid £25 per head to ship prisoners from Chester castle to the Plantations.

KENNEDY, ROBERT

Kennedy came to the Isle of Man originally as part of the Duke of Atholl's staff. He married in Castletown and established himself as a merchant. Even before Revestment he had transferred most of his interest to Liverpool, where he was involved in over 20 slave trade voyages. Driven by ill health to give up is business in the early 1770s, Kennedy built a house on the Culzean estate and moved to live there with his wife.

LUTWIDGE, THOMAS & WALTER

Thomas Lutwidge (1660 – 1745) had served as an officer in William III's army in Ireland. Afterwards he moved to Whitehaven, where he became a major tobacco importer and invited his nephew, Walter, to join him in business there. Expert smugglers, they developed an intricate system of delivering their cargoes either at their home port or at Kirkcudbright, Dumfries and Annan. According to the collector of customs at Dumfries, they were responsible for much of the illegal traffic in tobacco through the border country to Newcastle. Although they were in close contact with several Jacobite sympathisers, in 1745 Walter begged the government to defend Whitehaven against the rebels – and so protect his trade.

MCCARTNEY, GEORGE

Colonel in Queen Anne's army, who murdered the Duke of Hamilton after he had killed Lord Mohun in a duel. John Murray of Dumfries believed that he recognised him on the Isle of Man in 1713 – at this stage McCartney was in Holland.

McCULLOCH, JOHN

Merchant in Kirkcudbright who forwarded all the correspondence between the Island and the Duke of Atholl. He moved to Ramsey in the 1750s and was naturalised in 1756. After Revestment both he and his son moved first to Guernsey and then to Dunkirk, where they continued to supply the Scottish coast with smuggled goods.

MADDRELL, ROBERT

Steward of the garrison in Castletown and attorney on the Island for William Park of Beith. According to his will, he disinherited half his children, for no apparent reason.

MOORE, GEORGE

Son of Philip Moore, George set up as a merchant in Peel. He was involved in the running trade with an intricate network of agents and customers stretching from Tarbert in Argyll to Stranraer in the south. He supplied the Jacobite Kennedys of Culzean with wine and brandy.

MOORE, PHILIP

Son of a London merchant, Philip became one of the major merchants in Douglas at the beginning of the eighteenth century. He was also a member of the House of Keys. With John Murray of Douglas he frequented John Aglionby's house during the 'Fifteen. His sons Philip and George also became important merchants on the Island.

MURRAY, JOHN OF DOUGLAS

One of the major Manx merchants during the first half of the 18th century. He dealt with a wide range of other merchants, regardless of their political persuasion. In private he held Jacobite sympathies.

MURRAY, JOHN OF DUMFRIES

Also known as John Murray of Barnhorrey, an estate on the coast between Dumfries and Kirkcudbright, and cousin of John Murray of Douglas. A tobacco merchant, with close trading links to the Island, in 1712 he married Grizel, sister of Robert Douglas of Auchenshinnoch. Murray's visit to the Island in December 1713, as attorney to Barbara Black of Annandale, was somewhat significant – he thought that he recognised Colonel George McCartney and he became the first person to be charged with drinking disaffected healths on the Island. There is no information about him after the estate of Barnhorrey was sold in 1721.

MURRAY, JOHN OF HYDWOOD

Also referred to as Murray of Townhead, Bankend, near Dumfries. Apparently not related to John Murray of Douglas, he was another Scottish tobacco merchant with contacts on the Island, including John Wattleworth junior of Ramsey. When the collector at Dumfries became too interested in his smuggling activities, Murray applied for a job in the customs service. He abandoned his post to fight in the battle of Preston. Having evaded capture, he returned to the Borders where he preyed on other smugglers, charging them a toll for passing along 'his' roads.

NASH, EDWARD

Although Nash claimed that he was an Irishman from Kilkenny, all the evidence point to the fact that he was from Wales. He was in partnership with Patrick Savage and John Aglionby using Aglionby's 'intimacy' with the Whitehaven merchants to expand his trade. Eventually debts and helping a prisoner to escape drove him from the Island.

O'BRYAN, DENNIS

Described as 'of North Britain', O'Bryan was deeply involved in the running trade. By 1713, he was based in Douglas and was entrusted by John Murray of Dumfries to report to the governor his suspicions about the presence of George McCartney on the Island.

PARK, WILLIAM

An apothecary or chirurgeon from Beith in Ayrshire, he married Beautrix, the 29-year-old daughter of Robert Houston on 5 March 1700. Margaret's younger brother, Robert (born 1678), was a tobacco merchant in Glasgow. Park was involved with James Corbet, Robert Douglas's father-in-law, in a cargo of wine, which was seized against Douglas's debt of over £500 to John Murray of Douglas. Park attempted to reserve some of the goods to cover Douglas's £400 debt to Houston.

POOLE, JAMES

With Richard Dutoral and Henry Toren he replaced John Sanforth as collector of customs under Poole & McGwire.

READ, JAMES

Formerly a soldier on Jersey, where he married the daughter of a wealthy merchant, Read deserted his home and set up on the Isle of Man as a shipmaster, deeply involved with the main merchants running goods into Dumfries and Galloway and Cumberland, and a small time merchant. He married Elizabeth Corrin and they had a large family. When his Jersey son arrived on the Island he was accused of bigamy.

ROSS, DAVID

Probably connected with Jacobite sympathisers in the north-east of Scotland, Ross came first to the Island as a shipmaster. He soon transferred to become a merchant, in partnership with Robert Black and then John Christian.

ROSS, WILLIAM

First of all water bailiff and then a cleric and schoolmaster, Ross refused to accept a copy of The Independent Whig for the library in Castletown.

RUSHTON, WILLIAM

A watchmaker from Liverpool, now living on the Island, in 1716 Rushton accused John Hale of drinking a 'disaffected health'.

SABBARTON, JOHN

Originally from Hertfordshire, Sabbarton was a purser on board several warships in the Royal Navy. He had two sons, Joseph who lived on the Island with his father, and Benjamin, who was at school in Cheshire. Misidentified by John Murray of Dumfries as George McCartney, Sabbarton was often present in company when disaffected healths were drunk. He stood surety for the good behaviour of Henry Butler and John Aglionby. He married the widow Dulcibella Parr, who married William Seddon on Sabbarton's death.

SANFORTH, JOHN

Collector of customs under Poole & McGwire, who lodged in his house at Douglas. In December 1726 Sanforth was replaced by James Poole, Richard Dutoral and Henry Towers, who continued to act as factors for him in his private business. In 1727 Sanforth claimed that the farmers still owed him £1,000.

SEDDON, WILLIAM

Sometime member of the House of Keys, comptroller and one of the deputy governors on the Island, who heard evidence against people accused of drinking disaffected healths. Displaced by Poole & McGwire, the farmers of customs, he was accused by the Earl of Derby of not paying all the customs duties – Seddon claimed that the bags of money stolen from his office had been those earmarked for the Lord. On his death, aged 81, Governor Cochrane commented 'he died as he lived, an evil man'.

SILK, ABRAHAM

Often in company with Aglionby and Allgood, Silk warned Mary Hendrick that by putting up the *Royal George* sign she had effectively finished her business in Douglas. He owned land on the Island, sold to defray its taxes in 1755 – by which time it was supposed that Silk had died.

THOMPSON, WILLIAM

Originally from Kilbrondick in county Cavan, Captain William Thompson settled in Castletown. He acted as attorney on the Island for Charles Dalrymple of Glasgow. Having married the widow,

Margaret Halsall, he was Anthony Halsall's stepfather. On his death in June 1712, Margaret continued to live in Castletown, where her house became a meeting place for visiting merchants. Although William's brothers, John and Thomas, were to be John Bignall's executors, there is no evidence that he was in contact with Bignall on the Island.

TOREN (TOWERS), HENRY
Originally a clerk in John Sanforth's office, he was promoted by McGwire and became more and more powerful. He was used by Michael Sampson and William Thwaites in their attempt to sort out their business accounts with John Bignall. His son Barendt was a merchant in Rotterdam and his son-in-law was James Geyhin of Douglas.

TURNER, JACOB
A Quaker merchant from Lurgan in county Armagh, Turner was in partnership with John Bignall and John Hunter in a cargo of brandy and wine in 1710.

VANCE, THOMAS
Lived in Peel and was master of the *Joseph* of Sligo, owned by Charles Dalrymple and John Hunter.

WATTLEWORTH, JOHN
There were four John Wattleworths on the Island during this period, two of whom were members of the House of Keys and two of whom were referred to as 'junior'. Captain John Wattleworth was deputy searcher of Ramsey. His son John was deeply involved in the running trade, his partners including John Bignall. Both aggressive and violent, he died in 1728, shortly after having his ears cut off for verbal abuse of the water bailiff John Sanforth. The other member of the Keys lived at Knock Rushen. His son was charged with attacking the Earl's eagle with a stick, after it had pecked at him from its perch as he walked along the street.

FURTHER READING

Adams, Percy W C *A History of the Douglas Family of Morton in Nithsdale (Dumfriesshire) and Fingland (Kirkcudbrightshire) and their descendants* Bedford The Sidney Press 1921

Bennett, J H E Cheshire and 'The Fifteen' *Journal of the Chester Archaeological Society* New Series Vol 21 1915 pp 30-46

Bromley, J S The Jacobite Privateers in the Nine Years War in *Statesmen, Scholars and Merchants. Essays in Eighteenth Century History presented to Dame Lucy Sutherland* Oxford Clarendon Press 1973 pp. 17-43

Craig, Maggie *Damn' Rebel Bitches The Women of the '45* Edinburgh Mainstream Publishing 1997

Cruickshanks, Eveline & Corp, Edward eds. *The Stuart Court in Exile and the Jacobites* London Hambledon Press 1995

Devine, T M *The Tobacco Lords A Study of the Tobacco Merchants of Glasgow and their Trading Activities c. 1740-90* Edinburgh John Donald Ltd 1975

Devine, T M *The Scottish Nation 1700-2000* London Allen Lane The Penguin Press 1999

Dickinson, J R *The Lordship of Man under the Stanleys: Government and Economy in the Isle of Man* Preston Carnegie Publishing for the Chetham Society, Manchester 1996

Dickson, William Kirk *The Jacobite Attempt of 1719 Letters of James Butler, 2nd Duke of Ormonde, relating to Cardinal Alberoni's Project for the Invasion of Great Britain on behalf of the Stuarts, and to the landing of a Spanish Expedition in Scotland* Edinburgh The Scottish History Society 1895

Dobson, David *Jacobites of the '15* Scottish Association of Family History Societies 1993

Doherty, Richard *The Williamite War in Ireland 1688-1691* Dublin Four Courts 1988

Donaldson, William *Jacobite Song; Political Myth and National Identity* Aberdeen University Press 1988

Douglas, Hugh *Jacobite Spy Wars Moles, Rogues and Treachery* Stroud Sutton Publishing 1999

Fielding, Henry ed. W B Coley *The Jacobite's Journal and Related Writings* Oxford University Press 1975

Fraser, George MacDonald *The Steel Bonnets: The Story of the Anglo Scottish Border Reivers* First published by Barrie & Jenkins 1971 Harper Collins Publishers 1995

Fritz, Paul *The English Ministers and Jacobitism between the Rebellions of 1715 and 1745* Toronto & Buffalo University of Toronto Press 1975

Gibson, John S *Playing the Scottish Card: the Franco-Jacobite invasion of 1708* Edinburgh University Press 1988

Gibson, John Sibbald *Lochiel of the '45* Edinburgh University Press 1994

Gillow, Joseph *A Literary and Biographical History or Biographical History of the English Catholics from the break with Rome in 1534 to the present times.* 6 volumes New York & London Burnes & Oates 1885

Gooch, Leo *The Desperate Faction? The Jacobites of North East England 1688-1745* The University of Hull Press

Gregg, Edward *Jacobitism* London The Historical Association 1988 (New appreciation in History 11)

Grove, Doreen *Fortress Scotland and the Jacobites* Batsford 1995

Hughes, Edward *North Country Life in the Eighteenth Century The North-East, 1700-1750* London Oxford University Press 1952

Jarvis, Rupert C *Collected papers on the Jacobite risings* 2 volumes Manchester University Press 1971 - 1972

Jarvis, Rupert Charles The Jacobite Risings and the Public Monies *Transactions of the Lancashire and Cheshire Antiquarian Society* Vol. 59 1948 pp. 131-154 (1715)

Jarvis, R C The Rebellion of 1745: The Passage through Lancashire from contemporary News-Sheets *Transactions of the Lancashire and Cheshire Antiquarian Society* Vol 46 pp. 123-151

Jarvis, Rupert Charles The Rebellion of 1745: The Turmoil in Cheshire from contemporary News-Sheets *Transactions of the Lancashire and Cheshire Antiquarian Society* Vol. 57 pp. 43-70

Jarvis, Rupert C The Forty-five and the Local Records *Transactions of the Lancashire and Cheshire Antiquarian Society* Vol. 65 pp. 70-90

Jarvis, Rupert C The Mersey Bridges: 1745 *Transactions of the Lancashire and Cheshire Antiquarian Society* Vol. 68 1959 pp. 69-84

Jarvis, Rupert C The Lieutenancy and the Militia in Lancashire and Cheshire in 1745 *Transactions of the Lancashire and Cheshire Antiquarian Society* Vol. 62 1953 pp. 111-132

Jarvis, Rupert C The Port of Liverpool in the '45 *Transactions of the Historic Society of Lancashire and Cheshire* Vol 98 1948 pp 53-74

Jarvis , Rupert C Whitehaven Port Records and the Forty-Five *Transactions of the Cumberland & Westmorland Antiquarian & Archaeological Society* Vol XLV New Series 1946

Kinross, John *The Battlefields of Britain* Newton Abbot David & Charles 1979

Lenman, Bruce *Jacobite Risings in Britain 1689-1746* Scottish Cultural Press 1995

Macrory, Patrick *The Siege of Derry* Oxford 1988

McDonnell, Frances *Jacobites of 1715 North East Scotland* F McDonnell 1995

McDonnell, Frances *Jacobites of 1745 North East Scotland* F McDonnell 1996

Millar, A H *A Selection of Scottish Forfeited Estates Papers 1715; 1745* Edinburgh The Scottish History Society 1909

Monod, Paul Kléber *Jacobitism and the English people 1688-1788* Cambridge University Press 1989

Moss, Michael *The 'Magnificent Castle' of Culzean and the Kennedy family* Edinburgh University Press 2002

Nicholson, Albert Lancashire and the Rebellion of 1715 *Transactions of the Lancashire & Cheshire Antiquarian Society* 3 1885 pp 66-88

Ó Ciardha, Éamonn *Ireland and the Jacobite cause, 1685-1766 A fatal attachment* Dublin Four Courts Press 2002

Patten, Robert *The History of the Late Rebellion: with original papers, and the characters of principal noblemen and gentlemen concerned in it* 2nd ed. London T Warne 1717

Payne, J O *Records of English Catholics of 1715* 1889

Pittock, Murray G H *Poetry and Jacobite politics in eighteenth century Britain and Ireland* Cambridge University Press 1994

Pittock, Murray G H *Jacobitism* Basingstoke Macmillan 1998

Porteus, T C New Light on the Lancashire Jacobite Plot, 1692-1694. An account of the Plot Papers Found at Standish Hall 1757 now preserved in the Wigan Public Library *Transactions of the Lancashire & Cheshire Antiquarian Society* 50 (1934-35) pp 1-64

Reid, Stuart *Killiecrankie, 1689; First Jacobite Rising* Leigh-on-Sea Partizan Press 1989

The Jacobite Attempt of 1719 The Scottish History Society 19. 1894-95

Memorials of John Murray of Broughton 1740-1747 The Scottish History Society 27. 1896-1897

Highland Papers Volumes 1 & 2 The Scottish History Society 5. 1910-1911 & 12. 1914-1915

Seton, Sir Bruce Gordon & Arnot, Jean Gordon *The Prisoners of the '45 edited from the estate papers* Volumes 1-III The Scottish History Society 1928 & 1929

Sharpe E France ed. The Registers of Estates of Lancashire Papists 1717-1788 *Record Society of Lancashire & Cheshire*, 98, 108 (2 volumes) 1945, 1960

Simms, John Gerald *The Williamite confiscation in Ireland 1690-1703* London Faber 1956

Simms, J G *Jacobite Ireland* Dublin Four Courts Press 2000

Sinclair-Stevenson, Christopher *Inglorious rebellion: the Jacobite risings of 1708, 1715 and 1719* London Hamish Hamilton 1971

Sinclair, Charles *A Wee Guide to The Jacobites* Goblinshead 1998

Szechi, Daniel *The Jacobites; Britain and Europe, 1688-1788* Manchester University Press 1994

Szechi, Daniel *Jacobitism and Tory Politics 1710-1714* Edinburgh John Donald 1984

Watson, Godfrey *The Border Reivers* First published by Robert Hale & Co 1974. Reprinted by Sandhill Press Ltd, Warkworth, Northumberland 1998

Whatley, Christopher Allan *Scottish Society, 1707 – 1830: beyond Jacobitism, towards industrialisation* Manchester University Press 2000

Woolf, Neville *Jacobite Medals: medallic record of the Jacobite movement* Spink & Son 1990

Youngson, A J *The Prince and the Pretender Two Views of the '45* Edinburgh Mercat Press 1996

www.localie/general/history/williamite: This site includes several sections on the Williamite War in Ireland, including an introduction and background material and a detailed chronology, biographies of the main protagonists on both sides and excellent descriptions of various battles, with maps.

NOTES

Key:
BL   British Library
CRO   Cumbria Record Office
DAC   Dumfries Archive Centre
LRO   Lancashire Record Office
MNHL   Manx National Heritage library
NAS   National Archives of Scotland
PRO   Public Record Office, Kew
PRONI   Public Record Office of Northern Ireland

Du Bois   David Eltis *Trans-Atlantic Slave Trade* a Database on CD-ROM Cambridge University Press 2000

Hibbert Ware, Samuel Lancashire Memorials of the Rebellion, 1715, *Chetham Society*, 5 1845. This book is treated as essentially a primary source

---

[1] Hibbert Ware p. 58

[2] Encyclopaedia Britannica 1st edition 1771

[3] Hibbert Ware p.172, quoting *Patten's History etc.* 2nd Ed p.100

[4] MNHL: MS 10071 Liber Canc 1707-1718. 1709, 1710, 1711 f13; MS 10071 Petition File 1716 ff51, 52

[5] MNHL: MS 10071 Liber Canc 1730-1733. 1730 f107; MS 10071 Liber Scac 1730-1735 5 September 1730

[6] NAS: CE51 1/2 Dumfries collector to the Board of Customs in Edinburgh, 18 May 1724;
PRO: CUST 82/6 Whitehaven collector to the Board of Customs in London, 27 July 1750

[7] MNHL: MS 09707 APX73-12

[8] Henry Atton & Henry Hurst Holland *The King's Customs Vol. 1 An Account of Maritime Revenue and contraband traffic in England, Scotland, and Ireland, from the earliest times to the year 1800* 1908

[9] NAS: CE51 1/2 Dumfries Letters from the collector, John Crawford, to the Board of Customs in Edinburgh: 1 November 1721, 19 & 26 February, 9 & 23 September, 16 October, 25 November & 2, 3, 4, 5, 11, 18, & 23 December 1723, 1, 22 & 27 January, 9 & 17 February, 4 & 30 March, 4 & 29 April, 4, 5, 6 & 20 May, 10 (two letters) & 17 June, 7 September, 29 October & 16 November 1724. Letters from the collector, George Maxwell, to the Board 2 & 20 November 1726 & 7 October 1728.

[10] NAS: CE51 1/2 Dumfries collector to the Board, 4 March 1724

[11] NAS: CE51 1/2 Dumfries collector to the Board, 17 February 1724

[12] NAS: CE51 1/2 Dumfries collector to the Board, 16 November 1724.

[13] NAS: CE51 2/3 Dumfries Board to the collector, 19 March 1783 with extract of letter from Armstrong

[14] MNHL: MS 09707 AP60 (2nd) – 10

[15] NAS: CE51 1/2 Dumfries collector to the Board, 1 December 1724

[16] MNHL: MS 10071 Liber Canc 1697-1706. part of 1702, 1703, 1704 after f12

[17] MNHL: MS 10071 Petition File 1693 f16

[18] MNHL: MS 10071 Liber Scac 1700-1710. 1704, 1705, 1706 & part 1707 f37

[19] University of Nottingham Library: Portland Collection Harley Family papers Pw2Hy 948 & Pw2Hy 949

[20] MNHL: MS 10071 Liber Scac 1711-1722 f39

[21] MNHL: MS 10071 Liber Scac 1711-1722 f53

[22] MNHL: MS 10194 Nicholas Harley's will

[23] Memorial to Robert, Earl of Oxford in Brampton Bryan church

[24] PRONI: T/2529/6 Letters from the agent William Westgarth to the Barrett Lennard family

[25] Charles Sinclair *A Wee Guide to The Jacobites* pp. 20-23. Also the National Trust Guide to *Killiechrankie*

[26] MNHL: MS 10071 Petition File 1711-1713. 1713 f8

[27] MNHL: MS 10071 Liber Canc 1723-1726. 1726 f24; MS 10071 Petition File 1726 ff19, 20, 31; MS 10071 Liber Scac 1723-1729 6 December 1725, 3 March & 27 November 1727; MS 10194 John Wattleworth's will

[28] Hibbert Ware pp. 47 & 48; R Edgar *Introduction to the History of Dumfries* p. 257

[29] Hibbert Ware p. 47

[30] MNHL: MS 10058 Customs Ingates and Outgates. Ingates 1708

[31] NAS: CE51 1/1 Dumfries Collector William Johnson to the Board, 6 December 1708

[32] NAS: CE51 1/1 Dumfries Collector John McDowell to the Board, 15 October 1711

[33] MNHL: MS 10071 Liber Canc 1707-1718. 1709, 1710, 1711 ff31 & 32

[34] MNHL: MS 10071 Liber Canc 1707-1718. 1709, 1710, 1711 ff13, 38 & 46;
MS 10071 Chancery File 1710 ff17 & 32.

[35] MNHL: MS 10071 Liber Canc 1707-1718. 1707, 1708 ff95 & 73, 1707-1718. 1709, 1710, 1711 f25

[36] MNHL: MS 10071 Petition File 1711-1713. 1712 f59

[37] MNHL: MS 10071 Liber Canc 1707-1718. 1709, 1710, 1711 f53;
MS 10071 Petition File 1711-1713. 1711 ff11, 12

[38] MNHL: MS 10071 Liber Canc 1707-1718. 1709, 1710, 1711 ff29, 57 & 75; Petition File 1711-1713. 1711 ff9 & 40

[39] MNHL: MS 10071 Liber Canc 1707-1718. 1709, 1710, 1711 f53.

[40] MNHL: MS 10071 Petition File 1711-1713. 1711 f63

[41] Hibbert Ware p. 47

[42] John Gifford *The Buildings of Scotland. Dumfries & Galloway* 1996 p. 450

[43] Edgar's *Dumfries* p. 268

[44] MNHL: MS 10071 Petition File 1711-1713. 1711 f55

[45] Robert Edgar *The Records of the Western Marches Volume I An Introduction to the History of Dumfries* 1915 Appendix A (pp. 253-54) The petition of the merchant traffickers within the town of Dumfries

[46] NAS: E508/1/1/1, 2/1/12, 3/1/11, 4/1/13, 5/1/20/1

[47] MNHL: MS 10071 Petition File 1711-1713. 1711 f58

[48] MNHL: MS 10071 Petition File 1711-1713. 7111 f59

[49] MNHL: MS 10071 Liber Canc 1707-1718. 1709, 1710 & 1711 ff69-71; MS 10071 Petition File 1711-713. 1711 ff7, 53-73

[50] MNHL: MS 10071 Liber Canc 1707-1718. 1712, 1713, 1714 f10

[51] MNHL: MS 10071 Liber Canc 1730-1733. 1731 f22

[52] MNHL: MS 10071 Liber Canc 1707-1718. 1712, 1713, 1714 f7; MS 10071 Petition File 1711-1713. 1712 f15;
NAS: CC9/7/5 John Peadie Younger 5 June 1717

[53] MNHL: MS 10071 Liber Canc 1707-1718. 1712,1713,1714 f7

[54] NAS: CE51 1/1 Dumfries statement from Robert Stewart to the collector, dated 11 January 1711 and letter from collector John McDowell to the Board, 14 January 1711

[55] MNHL: MS 10071 Petition File 1714 f21

[56] MNHL: MS 10058 Customs Ingates and Outgates. Ingates 1711 Douglas, 30 October 1710; NAS: CE51 1/1 Dumfries collector, William Johnson, to the Board, 23 October 1710

[57] NAS: CE51 1/1 Dumfries collector to the Board, 26 November 1711

[58] MNHL: MS 10216 James Black's will

[59] MNHL: MS 10071 Liber Canc 1707-1718. 1712, 1713, 1714 f58

[60] Jonathan Swift *Collected Works* xvii

[61] Herbert Maxwell *A History of the House of Douglas from the earliest times down to the Legislative Union of England and Scotland* 1902 pp. 213-214

[62] Jonathan Swift *Letters to Stella* Letter LV 15 November 1712

[63] *Letters to Stella* Letter LV 16 November 1712 & 18 November 1712, LVII 26 December 1712 & LVIII 4 January 1713

[64] MNHL: MS 10071 Petition File 1714 ff1-6 & 8

[65] University of Nottingham Library: Portland Collection Harley Family papers Pw2 Hy 1008

[66] MNHL: MS 10071 Petition File 1714 f10

[67] Herbert Maxwell *A History of the House of Douglas from the earliest times down to the Legislative Union of England and Scotland* 1902 p. 214

[68] MNHL: MS 10071 Petition File 1714 f21

[69] MNHL: MS 10071 Petition File 1714 f11-22

[70] MNHL: MS 10071 Liber Canc 1707-1718. 1709, 1710, 1711 ff77, 78 & 81; *History of the Lands and their Owners in Galloway Vol 3* p. 325

[71] NAS: CE51 1/2 Dumfries collector to the Board, 3 June 1724 & 18 August 1725

[72] MNHL: MS 10071 Petition File 1715 f49

[73] For details of this period in Manx History see both A W Moore *A History of the Isle of Man* 1900 and *Here is the News An Illustrated Manx History*

[74] MNHL: MS 10058 Customs Ingates and Outgates. Outgates 1713 & 1714

[75] MNHL: MS 10071 Liber Scac 1700-1710. 1708 f59

[76] For further details of the clash between the governor and the Keys see MNHL: 10071 Petition File 1715 ff26 & 27

[77] MNHL: MS 10071 Petition File 1720 f39

[78] MNHL: MS 0907 APX3-8

[79] Information provided by Tynwald library

[80] MNHL: MS 10071 Petition File 1715 f36

[81] MNHL: MS 10071 Petition File 1715 f49

[82] MNHL: MS 10071 Petition File 1715 f50

[83] MNHL: MS 10071 Petition File 1715 f52

[84] MNHL: MS 10071 Liber Scac 1711-1722. 1722 f34

[85] MNHL: MS 06523 MD 401 DP 1721/18

[86] MNHL: MS 10071 Liber Canc 1740-1743. 1740 f84

[87] MNHL: MS 10071 Liber Plitor 1708-1717

[88] Hibbert Ware p. 91 quoting *Baines's Lancashire, Vol. iii* p. 450

[89] MNHL: MS 10071 Petition File 1717 ff19 & 20.

[90] MNHL: MS 10071 Petition File 1715 ff20-25; MS 10071 Liber Scac 1711-1722 30 & 31 May, 10 August & 22 October 1715

[91] MNHL: MS 10194 Liber Causarum 1714-1715 26 September 1715

[92] MNHL: MS 10071 Petition File 1715 f57

[93] NAS: AC9 Admiralty Court

[94] Hibbert Ware p. 53

[95] Hibbert Ware p 51

[96] MNHL: MS 10071 Petition File 1716 ff25, 29

[97] For more information about John Hendrick see *2,000 Manx Mariners*

[98] CRO (Carlisle) Gilpin correspondence

[99] MNHL: MS 10071 Petition File 1716 f25

[100] Charles Sinclair *A Wee Guide to The Jacobites* p. 40

[101] MNHL: MS 10058 Customs Ingates and Outgates. Outgates 1721; William MacKay *The Letter-Book of Bailie John Steuart of Inverness 1715-1752* Scottish History Society 1915

[102] MNHL: 10071 Petition File 1716 f25

[103] Hibbert Ware pp. 44-107

[104] Hibbert Ware p. 47

[105] Hibbert Ware pp. 47-48, quoting *Patten's History* p. 60 et seq

[106] Hibbert Ware p. 65

[107] Hibbert Ware p.107 quoting Peter Clarke

[108] Hibbert Ware p.121

[109] Hibbert Ware pp. 124-138

[110] J H E Bennett Cheshire and 'The Fifteen' *Journal of the Chester Archaeological Society* New Series Vol. 21 1915 p. 32

[111] Miss Dorothy Fitzherbery-Brockholes (Mrs Longueville) A Narrative of the "Fifteen" *Transactions of the Historic Society of Lancashire and Cheshire* 1913 p. 254. This article (pp. 249-254) provides yet another viewpoint of the battle of Preston. Hibbert Ware p. 166

[112] Graeme Douglas, personal communication, July 2001

[113] MNHL: MS 10194 Liber Causarum 1750 Book 3

[114] MNHL: MS 10071 Petition File 1716 f29

[115] Charles Sinclair *A Wee Guide to The Jacobites* p. 41

[116] MNHL: MS 10071 Petition File 1716 f25

[117] MNHL: MS 10071 Petition File 1716 f25; MS 10071 Liber Scac 1711-1722 24 October 716

[118] MNHL: MS 10071 Petition File 1716 f25

[119] MNHL: MS 10058 Customs Ingates and Outgates. Ingates 1717

[120] MNHL: MS 10071 Petition File 1716 f38

[121] NAS: CE51 1/1 Dumfries collector to the Board, 2 July 1711.

[122] MNHL: 10071 Liber Canc 1707-1718.1712, 1713, 1714 f33, 34 & 36

[123] MNHL: 10071 Liber Canc 1701-1718. 1712, 1713, 1714 nfn 25 February 1714 & f84

[124] NAS: CE51 1/2 Dumfries collector to the Board, 14 June 1727; DAC: 19/36 18 March 1723

[125] Hibbert Ware pp. 37, 124, 129, 130, 131, 175,176

[126] MNHL: MS 10194 Presentments 1716

[127] see above

[128] MNHL: MS 10058 Customs Ingates and Outgates 1716

[129] MNHL: MS 10071 Petition File 1716 ff1, 2 & 4

[130] MNHL: MS 10071 Petition File 1716 f8
[131] MNHL: MS 10058 Customs Ingates and Outgates. Outgates 1716
[132] MNHL: MS 10071 Liber Scac 1711-1722. 1716, 1717, 1718, 1719 4 July 1716
[133] MNHL: MS 10071 Liber Canc 1707-1718. 1716 & part 1717 f6; MS 10071 Petition File 1716 f24
[134] MNHL: MS 10071 Petition File 1716 f25
[135] MNHL: MS 10071 Petition File 1716 ff26-30
[136] MNHL: MS 10071 Liber Scac 1711-1722 21 October 1716
[137] MNHL: MS 10071 Liber Scac 1711-1722 24 October 1716
[138] MNHL: MS 10071 Liber Scac 1711-1722 2 November 1716
[139] MNHL: MS 10071 Liber Scac 1711-1722 9 November 1716
[140] MNHL: MS 10071 Liber Scac 1711-1722 19 November 1716
[141] MNHL: MS 10194 Liber Causarum 1716 22 December 1716 bound with MS 10071 Liber Scac 1711-1722
[142] MNHL: MS 10071 Liber Scac 1711-1722 20 December 1716
[143] MNHL: MS 10071 Liber Scac 1711-1722 5 January 1717
[144] MNHL: MS 10071 Liber Scac 1711-1722 18 January 1717
[145] MNHL: MS 10194 Presentments 1716
[146] MNHL: MS 10071 Liber Scac 1711-1722 30 July 1717
[147] MNHL: MS 10071 Liber Scac 1711-1722 16 August 1718
[148] All this information appears in MNHL: 10071 Liber Scac 1711-1722.
[149] MNHL: MS 10194 Presentments 1716
[150] MNHL: MS 10071 Liber Canc 1727-1729. 1728 ff31, 36 & 37. Information about Mary's marriage at Liverpool provided by Priscilla Lewthwaite, personal communication, March 2001. No will has been located at the Lancashire Record Office, Preston for either Mary Hendrick/Smith or George Smith.
[151] Hibbert Ware p. 169, quoting *Patten's History etc.* pp. 133-135.
[152] MNHL: MS 10194 Presentments 1716
[153] MNHL: MS 10071 Petition File 1716 f48
[154] MNHL: MS 10071 Petition File 1716 f7
[155] MNHL: MS 10071 Petition File 1716 ff1-7; MS 10071 Liber Scac 1711-1722 19 April 1716
[156] MNHL: MS 10216 William Rushton's will
[157] MNHL: MS 10216 John Hale's will
[158] Encyclopaedia Britannica 13th edition.
[159] MNHL: MS 10058 Customs Ingates and Outgates. Ingates 1713
[160] MNHL: MS 10071 Petition File 1716 f48; MS 10071 Liber Scac 1711-1722. 1716 30 October 1716 & 8 November 1716
[161] MNHL: MS 10216 William Aldridge's will
[162] PRO. 3 George I An Act of the King's most Gracious, General, and Free Pardon Statutes pp 499 511
[163] J H E Bennett Cheshire and 'The Fifteen' *Journal of the Chester Archaeological Society* New Series Vol 21 1915 p 30. Further details about the Cheshire Gentlemen are included in *Tatton Park The Mansion* Cheshire County Council
[164] MNHL: MS 10071 Liber Scac 24 October 1716; MS 10216 John Hale's will
[165] MNHL: MS 10071 Petition File 1717 ff43-46
[166] MNHL: MS 10071 Liber Scac 1711-1722. 1711 f7
[167] MNHL: MS 10071 Petition File 1717 f42
[168] MNHL: MS 10071 Liber Canc 1707-1718. 1718 f56; MS 10071 Liber Scac 1711-1722 25 February 1718
[169] MNHL: MS 10194 Liber Causarum 1737 21 June 1737
[170] MNHL: MS 10071 Petition File 1716 ff51, 52
[171] MNHL: MS 10058 Customs Ingates and Outgates 1717
[172] MNHL: MS 10071 Liber Scac 1711-1722. 1711 f7
[173] MNHL: MS 10071 Petition File 1714 f18
[174] MNHL: MS 10071 Petition File 1720 ff34-40
[175] Leo Gooch *The Desperate Faction? The Jacobites of North East England 1688 – 1745* pp. 111 & 113
[176] MNHL: MS 10071 Liber Canc 1719-1722. 1720 f71
[177] Gooch pp. 171-172
[178] MNHL: MS 10071 Liber Scac 1711-1722 1722 ff33-36; MS 10194 Liber Causarum 1721-1722 27 January 1722
[179] MNHL: MS MD 436 Fol. 20/6
[180] NAS: CE51 1/2 Dumfries collector to the Board, 11 November 1720
[181] MNHL: MS 10071 Liber Scac 1723-1729. 1725 5 November 1724

[182] MNHL: MS 10071 Liber Scac 1723-1729. 1726 15 June 1726

[183] BL: Add Ms 38462 Liverpool Papers ff38, 92

[184] MNHL: MS 10071 Liber Scac 1723-1729. 1726 22 September 1726

[185] MNHL: MS 10071 Liber Canc 1719-1722. 1719 f36

[186] MNHL: MS 10071 Liber Canc 1719-1722. 1719 ff1-4, 6-8, 10, 15-16, 22, nfn 13 April 1719, ff32-39. This story will be told in detail in *The Running Trade* (2004).

[187] MNHL: MS 10071 Liber Scac 1723-1729. 1726 f6

[188] MNHL: MS 10194 Liber Causarum 1738 Consistory Court Kirk Michael 17 July 1739

[189] MNHL: MS 10071 Liber Scac 1723-1729 Chancery Court 15 June 1726. There are no details of Doran's presence in Douglas harbour because the Ingates and Outgates do not exist for the time when Poole & McGwire were farmers of the customs

[190] MNHL: MS 10071 Liber Canc 1727-1729. 1727 f102

[191] The information about Thomas Harley and Big Tree house was obtained from an article by George Callister in Manx Notebook. He commented 'these notes by Sir J. D. Qualtrough were kindly loaned to me by his son Ian. They were obviously used for a talk which he gave to a church audience ...'

[192] MNHL: MS 10071 Liber Scac 1723-1729. 1727 3 March 1722

[193] Unless otherwise indicated, all the information in the section comes from MNHL: MS 10216 John Aglionby's will.

[194] See *2,000 Manx Mariners* p. 36

[195] MNHL: MS 10216 John Aglionby's will

[196] Captain Blackett, Arbigland House, personal communication, April 2000

[197] MNHL: MS 10071 Liber Canc 1744-1745. 1745 f74

[198] MNHL: MS 10071 Chancery File 1731 nfn 18 July 1730 claim from Clement Nicholson and accounts between Nash and Patrick Savage

[199] PRO: C 107/161 *Consigned Tobacco 1697 & Exportation of tobacco imported in the year 1697.*

[200] MNHL: MS 10071 Liber Canc 1734-1739. 1739 f41; MS 10071: Petition & Enquest Files Index 1732 f45

[201] MNHL: MS 10071 Liber Scac 1730-1735 1732 nfn 2 May 1732

[202] MNHL: MS 10071 Liber Canc 1734-1739. 1734 f4; MS 10071 Chancery File 1733-1734. 1734 nfn before f3

[203] MNHL: MS 10216 John Bignall's will

[204] There will be more details of John Bignall's smuggling partnerships in *The Running Trade* (2004)

[205] See *2,000 Manx Mariners* p. 40

[206] MNHL: MS 10071 Liber Canc 1734-1739. 1736 f34 & 1737 ff49 & 56; MS 10071 Chancery File 1736 nfn 4 November 1736 & f29 & 1737 f32; MS 10071 Liber Scac 1736-1742 nfn 3 June 1737 & MS 10194 Liber Causarum 1737 13 May 1736 & 1 March 1737

[207] Stewartry Museum, Kirkcudbright: Minutes of the Rating Committee 1737-1765. Roll of June 1737

[208] MNHL: MS 10071 Chancery File 1733, 1734. 1733 f14

[209] MNHL: MS 10216 John Bignall's will

[210] MNHL: MS 10071 Liber Scac 1754-1758 various papers relating to this case, including papers from Liber Causarum. MS 10216 John Bignall's will

[211] Mortgage agreement between the Dawes family of Barton Kirk and Edward Hasell of Dalemain 1736.

[212] Hibbert Ware pp. 104, 115, 123, 125, 126, 131 &146

[213] MNHL: MS 10071 Liber Scac 1730-1735 10 & 12 August 1734 & 8 May 1735,

[214] MNHL: MS 10194 Liber Causarum 1737 Consistory Court 28 March 1737

[215] MNHL: MS 10216 John Bignall's will

[216] MNHL: MS 09707 APX11-38

[217] MNHL: MS 09707 APX11-38

[218] CRO (Carlisle): D/Lons/73

[219] MNHL: MS 10194 Liber Causarum 1745 Book 2

[220] CRO (Carlisle): D/AY/5.9; D/AY/6.29 & 6.30

[221] *The Statistical Account of Scotland.* 1796 The Parish of Buittle

[222] John Gifford *The Buildings of Scotland Dumfries & Galloway* pp. 104-105

[223] NAS: CE51 1/3 Dumfries collector to the Board, 5 July 1764. For further information about Craik's career see the chapter on the King's Boat at Carsethorn in *Family Histories in Scottish Customs Records*

[224] See *Dumfries & Galloway's Smuggling Story* pp. 106-108

[225] NAS: CE51 1/4 Dumfries collector to the Board, 30 July 1782

[226] PRO: CUST82/5 Whitehaven collector to the Board, 26 February 1746

[227] The National Trust for Scotland Guide to *Culloden*

[228] MNHL: MS 09707 APX3-8

[229] MNHL: MS 10194 Liber Causarum 1746

[230] PRO: CUST82/5 Whitehaven collector to the Board, 29 January 1746

[231] This will be discussed in *The Running Trade* [2004]

[232] MNHL: MS 10058 Customs Ingates and Outgates. Ingates 1745

[233] MNHL: MS 09707 APX3-3 & APX3-4

[234] MNHL: MS 10058 Customs ingates and Outgates. Ingates 1744, 1745, 1746 & 1747

[235] Canon John Gelling *A History of the Manx Church* 1698-1911 p. 223

[236] *Notes from the Diary of a Manks Clergyman*. Glasgow University Album 1840 pp. 79-95.

[237] MNHL: MS 09707 APX3-8; MS 01171 Liber Scac 1746 6 May 1746 filed with MS 10194 Liber Causarum 1746. In addition from Liber Causarum 10 May, 14 May and 28 June 1746

[238] MNHL: MS 09707 APX11-12

[239] MNHL: MS 10216 Peter Sidebotham's will

[240] MNHL: MS GR/1/69

[241] MNHL: MS 10194 Liber Causarum 1750 Book 3

[242] MNHL: MD436 2/10 Letter from Bishop Wilson to Mr Curghy rector of Bride, Mr Allen vicar of Maughold and Mr Curghy vicar of Lezayre, 23 December 1731. See also *2,000 Manx Mariners*

[243] MNHL: MS 09591 Taubman correspondence Robert Kennedy to John Taubman 8 October 1774

[244] MNHL: MS 09707 APX28-20

[245] MNHL: MS 09707 APX28-20, 21, 32; MS 10071: Liber Scac 1754-1758. 1756 3 November 1756

[246] Several sources, including *Manx Note Book* Vol iii No. 11 and the *National Dictionary of Biography* in their entry for Professor Edward Forbes remark that his great grandfather, David, was one of the Forbes's of Watertown. He was born in 1707 and 'being implicated in the Jacobite troubles of 1745, settled in the Isle of Man for a time'. This was not the David Forbes referred to in this book.

[247] MNHL: MS 10216 Thomas Durie's will

[248] MNHL: 10058 Customs Ingates and Outgates. Ingates 1743-1745, 1747, 1749, 1750, 1752-1754, 1756-1758, 1762, 1763.

[249] MNHL: MS 09707 APX25-36

[250] PRO: CUST 82/5 Whitehaven collector to the Board, 16 September 1748

[251] William Robertson *Old Ayrshire Days* 1905 pp. 269-270

[252] See *George Moore & Friends* pp. 207-210.

[253] MNHL: MS10216 Thomas Durie's will

[254] D Richardson, K. Beedham, M. M. Schofield, *Liverpool Trade & Shipping, 1744-1786* [computer file]. Colchester, Essex: The Data Archive [distributor], 27 July 1992. 51/45 & 55/57: *Annandale*

[255] MNHL: MS 10058 Customs Ingates and Outgates. Ingates 1756

[256] MNHL: 10058 Customs Ingates and Outages. Ingates 1762 & 1762.

[257] MNHL: MS 09591 Taubman correspondence. Thomas Durie to John Taubman, 4 November 1778

[258] MNHL: 10216 Thomas Durie's will

[259] as above

[260] A. M. Cubbon *Thomas and Ann Durie An Eighteenth Century Douglas Merchant and His Wife* Journal of the Manx Volume VI pp. 41-42

[261] MNHL: MS 10216 Thomas Durie's will

[262] List of Persons concerned in the Rebellion (1745). Montrose District. The Scottish History Society 8 1889-1890

[263] MNHL: 10216 John Durie's will

[264] MNHL: MS 09707 APX17-15

[265] MNHL: MS 09707 APX58-2

[266] MNHL: MS 09707 AP54-27

[267] MNHL: MS 09707 APX30-19

[268] MNHL: MS 10216 David Ross's will; List of Persons concerned in the Rebellion (1745. Ross District.

[269] *The Precipitation and Fall of Messrs Douglas Heron & Co late Bankers in Ayr with the causes of their disasters and ruin investigated and considered by a Committee of Enquiry appointed by the Proprietors.* Edinburgh 1778; Frank Brady *So Fast to Ruin. The Personal Element in the collapse of Douglas Heron & Co* Ayrshire Collections Volume 11 No.2 *Ayrshire Antiquarian & Natural History Society* 1973 pp. 27-44; Henry Hamilton The Failure of the Ayr Bank *The Economic History Review* pp. 405-417; in preparation Frances Wilkins *A New Look at the Failure of the Ayr Bank in 1772*

[270] MNHL: MS 09591 Taubman correspondence John Christian to John Taubman 1783

[271] See Frances Wilkins *George Moore & Friends. Letters of a Manx Merchant 1750-1760*

[272] NAS: GD25/9/1 Archibald Kennedy's Business Affairs Notebook 1749-1754

[273] MNHL: MS 09591 Taubman correspondence Robert Kennedy to John Taubman, 15 August 1774

[274] MNHL: MS 09591 Taubman correspondence. John Kennedy to John Taubman, 11 April 1774

[275] Du Bois 91865 & 92543

[276] MNHL: MS 9591 Taubman correspondence. John Kennedy to John Taubman, 18 February 1780

[277] MNHL: MS 09707 APX10-5 & APX10-12

[278] MNHL: MS 10071 Liber Canc 1764-1765. 1764 f218

[279] Carnegie Library, Ayr: Robert Arthur letterbooks William Gordon 2 November 1768, 9 & 22 March, 4 June, 17 July, 14 August & 30 November 1770, 9 & 15 April 1771 & 12 February 1773; William Wilson 1 August 1772; Alexander Speirs 19 January, 1 February, 8, 22 & 27 March, 5 June & 27 November 1770; Alexander Borthwick 29 April, 23 December 1771, 23 December 1772; Captain Joseph Hunter 22 March 1770

[280] MNHL: MS 10071 Petition File 1716 f7